D0242315

Teaching for quality learning at university

SRHE and Open University Press Imprint
General Editor: Heather Eggins

Current titles include:

Catherine Bargh et al.: University Leadership
Ronald Barnett: The Idea of Higher Education
Ronald Barnett: The Limits of Competence
Ronald Barnett: Higher Education
Ronald Barnett: Realizing the University in an age of supercomplexity
Tony Becher and Paul R. Trowler: Academic Tribes and Territories (second edition)
Neville Bennett et al.: Skills Development in Higher Education and Employment
John Biggs: Teaching for Quality Learning at University
David Boud et al. (eds): Using Experience for Learning
David Boud and Nicky Solomon (eds): Work-based Learning
Tom Bourner et al. (eds): New Directions in Professional Higher Education
John Brennan et al. (eds): What Kind of University?
Anne Brockbank and Ian McGill: Facilitating Reflective Learning in Higher Education
Stephen Brookfield and Stephen Preskill: Discussion as a Way of Teaching
Ann Brooks and Alison Mackinnon (eds): Gender and the Restructured University
Sally Brown and Angela Glasner (eds): Assessment Matters in Higher Education
John Cowan: On Becoming an Innovative University Teacher
Gerard Delanty: Challenging Knowledge
Chris Duke: Managing the Learning University
G. R. Evans: Academics and the Real World
Andrew Hannan and Harold Silver: Innovating in Higher Education
Norman Jackson and Helen Lund (eds): Benchmarking for Higher Education
Merle Jacob and Tomas Hellström (eds): The Future of Knowledge Production in the
    Academy
Peter Knight and Paul Trowler: Departmental Leadership in Higher Education
Mary Lea and Barry Stierer (eds): Student Writing in Higher Education
Ian McNay (ed.): Higher Education and its Communities
Elaine Martin: Changing Academic Work
Moira Peelo and Terry Wareham (eds): Failing Students in Higher Education
Craig Prichard: Making Managers in Universities and Colleges
Michael Prosser and Keith Trigwell: Understanding Learning and Teaching
John Richardson: Researching Student Learning
Stephen Rowland: The Enquiring University Teacher
Maggi Savin-Baden: Problem-based Learning in Higher Education
Peter Scott (ed.): The Globalization of Higher Education
Peter Scott: The Meanings of Mass Higher Education
Anthony Smith and Frank Webster (eds): The Postmodern University?
Colin Symes and John McIntyre (eds): Working Knowledge
Peter G. Taylor: Making Sense of Academic Life
Susan Toohey: Designing Courses for Higher Education
Paul R. Trowler: Higher Education Policy and Institutional Change
Melanie Walker (ed.): Reconsructing Professionalism in University Teaching
David Warner and David Palfreyman (eds): The State of UK Higher Education
Diana Woodward and Karen Ross: Managing Equal Opportunities in Higher Education

Teaching for quality learning at university

What the student does

John Biggs

Society for Research into Higher Education
& Open University Press

Published by SRHE and
Open University Press
Celtic Court
22 Ballmoor
Buckingham
MK18 1XW

email: enquiries@openup.co.uk
world wide web: www.openup.co.uk

and
325 Chestnut Street
Philadelphia, PA19106, USA

First published 1999
Reprinted 1999, 2000, 2001, 2002

Copyright © John Biggs 1999

All rights reserved. Except for the quotation of short passages for the purposes of
criticism and review, no part of this publication may be reproduced, stored in a
retrieval system, or transmitted, in any form or by any means, electronic,
mechanical, photocopying, recording or otherwise, without prior permission of the
publisher or a licence from the Copyright Licensing Agency Limited. Details of such
licences (for reprographic reproduction) may be obtained from the Copyright
Licensing Agency Ltd of 90 Tottenham Court Road, London W1P 0LP.

A catalogue record of this book is available from the British Library

ISBN 0 335 20172 5 (hb)   ISBN 0 335 20171 7 (pb)

Library of Congress Cataloging-in-Publication Data
Biggs, John B. (John Burville)
    Teaching for quality learning at university / John Biggs.
        p.   cm.
    Includes bibliographical references and index.
    ISBN 0-335-20172-5.   ISBN 0-335-20171-7 (pbk)
    1. College teaching.   2. Learning.   3. Effective teaching.   4. Assessing for
learning quality.   I. Title.
LB2331.8526   1999
378.1'25 – dc21   98-44938
                                                                        CIP

Typeset by Type Study, Scarborough
Printed in Great Britain by St Edmundsbury Press, Bury St Edmunds, Suffolk

If students are to learn desired outcomes in a reasonably effective manner, then the teacher's fundamental task is to get students to engage in learning activities that are likely to result in their achieving those outcomes . . . It is helpful to remember that what the student does is actually more important in determining what is learned than what the teacher does.

(Thomas J. Shuell 1986)

Contents

Foreword

This book is an exceptional introduction to some difficult ideas. It is full of downright good advice for every academic who wants to do something practical to improve his or her students' learning. So much of what we read on this subject is either a recycling of sensible advice topped by a thin layer of second-hand theory, or a dense treatise suitable for graduate students with a taste for the tougher courses. Not many writers are able to take the reader along the middle road, where theory applied with a delicate touch enables us to transform our practice. What is unique about Biggs is his way with words, his outspoken fluency, his precision, his depth of knowledge, his inventiveness – or rather, how he blends these things together. Like all good teachers, he engages us from the start, and he never talks down to us. He achieves unity between his objectives, his teaching methods and his assessment; and thus, to adapt his own phrase, he entraps the reader in a web of consistency that optimizes his or her learning.

Perhaps not everyone will agree with Biggs's treatment of the academic differences between phenomenography and constructivism. I'm not sure I do myself. But does it matter? The author himself takes a pragmatic approach. In the daunting task that faces lecturers in responding to the pressures of mass higher education, reduced public funding and students who are paying more for their education, the bottom line of engineering better learning outcomes matters more than nice theoretical distinctions.

Readers of the present book will especially enjoy its marvellous treatment of issues of student assessment (particularly Chapters 3, 8 and 9). Biggs's most outstanding single contribution to education has been the creation of the Structure of Observed Learning Outcome (SOLO) taxonomy. Rather than read about the extraordinary practical utility of this device in secondary sources, get it from the original here. From assessing clinical decision-making by medical students to classifying the outcomes of essays in history, SOLO remains the assessment apparatus of choice.

There are very few writers on the subject of university teaching who can engage a reader so personally, express things so clearly, relate research findings so eloquently to personal experience and open our eyes to the wonder around us. John Biggs is a rare thing: an author who has the humility born of generosity and intelligence to show us how he is still learning himself.

Paul Ramsden
Brisbane

Preface

This book is intended to help university teachers reflect on and improve the quality of their teaching, despite the conditions of class size and student diversity that seem to make good teaching more difficult than ever.

There is no magic bullet, but there is by now quite a large knowledge base on teaching and learning, and effective use of that can certainly make life easier and more fulfilling for teachers. However, using that knowledge is not simply a matter of taking on board the latest technique for managing large classes, or the best technology for stimulating student interest. Teaching is a personal matter. New ideas need to be used reflectively, driven by conviction and tuned to one's own context. I will be talking about that knowledge base, and how it may be used and individually applied, throughout this book.

Allow me to talk briefly about myself, as a case study for what is to follow. I taught throughout the length of a tertiary teaching epoch, starting at a rural Australian university in the 1960s, through Canada and Newcastle (New South Wales) in the 1970s and 1980s, ending my official teaching days at the University of Hong Kong in the 1990s. During this time span, conceptions of teaching, and of the role of the tertiary sector generally, changed unrecognizably. At the University of New England, I transmitted certainties from the lecturing podium to students uniformed in their green gowns and brass lapel seniority bars. They pretended to take notes, but actually they were checking my spoken words against the illegally obtained written notes to the external students.

There could not have been a greater contrast between that experience and the heady, laid-back days of counter-culture Canada, with small classes and lavish resourcing. That changed at Newcastle, where neo-Thatcherite thinking and local politics gave us a foretaste of the cost-cutting and managerial meddling that academics everywhere were to suffer in the 1990s.

But before that was to happen, I was to relive the whole epoch on fast-forward in Hong Kong. When I arrived in 1987, I felt that in terms of educational philosophy and practice I was in a time warp back to the 1950s. Yet within ten years the former British colony was to show the rest of the world what implementing innovative teaching, and supporting staff development, were all about. All eight on-campus tertiary institutions, and the vocational sector, now have staff development units dedicated to improving teaching and learning, and millions of dollars annually are provided for research and development on tertiary teaching.

It was possibly the ethos of rapid change in Hong Kong, and very likely the initial challenges of coping with a different system, but I found myself reflecting about theory and practice in a way I had not done before. It was there that the words of the action researcher, Kurt Lewin, came to life: 'There is nothing so practical as a good theory.'

The key to the whole thing is what I quoted Tom Shuell as saying at the front of this book: 'what the learner does is actually more important than what the teacher does.' The full implications of that transform the process of teaching, whether in a small group of half a dozen students or a large class of 400. There is more to it than that, of course. What learners do depends on what you want them to do, and on what help you give them to do it. But that shift in focus, from what the teacher does to what the learner does, is nothing short of liberating. It all makes sense at last.

This book fills in the details. The major theme is that teaching is enhanced by aligning objectives, teaching methods and assessment tasks, which is done by focusing on the learning-related activities that are common across all stages of instruction. Students are allowed more freedom to construct and display their learning in ways comfortable to them. This caters very well for diversity in the classroom, and in particular for teaching international students. Banal stereotypes of 'passive rote learners' melt away. Class size imposes its own constraints, but as Davis and McLeod (1997) remind us, large classes provide a different teaching experience, not necessarily a worse one.

Constructive alignment has thus grown out of a large body of published research, including some of my own, but for me it all came to a head in the last few years of teaching in Hong Kong.

I hope you find it as liberating as I did.

Acknowledgements

There are many ideas in this book that came about through interacting with friends and colleagues over the years. It started in the 1970s, when the biennial 'Lancaster Conferences' provided the opportunity for those of us researching on student approaches to learning to interact, and to massage the emerging 'student learning' paradigm of research. I have to thank in particular Noel Entwistle, Ference Marton, Paul Ramsden and Elaine Martin for the stimulation they provided for my own thinking, and still do. Not that we agreed then, or would agree now, on some significant aspects of that paradigm, but I am sure we would all agree with Shuell. It *is* what the student does that counts.

I am grateful also to Lennart Svennson, who invited me to Gothenburg in 1977, where Ference and his team convinced me that student performances my colleague Kevin Collis and I had been trying to relate to stages in development were actually displaying levels of learning. So, with the unlikely coupling of Piaget with phenomenography, SOLO came to be born, to mature into an important part of the thinking underlying this book (see Chapter 3).

As mentioned in the Preface, Hong Kong played a crucial role in my development. In addition, it attracted a string of visitors who would have helped to shape this book in some way or another, so to Ference, Paul and Elaine again, and then to Gillian Boulton-Lewis, Denise Chalmers, Kevin Collis, Barry Dart, John Hattie, Chris Knapper, Mike Prosser and Keith Trigwell, and to David Watkins and David Kember who were already there, thank you.

I am very grateful to many Hong Kong students who by learning so well helped me to learn something special about teaching. I must mention in particular the 82 BEd students of the 1994–5 academic year, and my teaching assistant Mabel Sieh (see Chapter 10). My greatest debt, though, is to Catherine Tang, now Head of the Centre for Learning, Teaching and Supervision at the Hong Kong Institute of Education, whose original research into the backwash effects of assessment crystallized much of my work on alignment. She has been an enduring influence in my thinking ever since.

On returning to Australia, I conducted dozens of workshops for tertiary teachers, where I learned of many examples of good practice. I apologize that I can't attach names where credit is due. Finally, I must thank Denise Chalmers, Director of TEDI, University of Queensland, who was an extraordinarily helpful and surgically precise critic of the first draft of this book; Noel Entwistle, Centre for Research on Learning and Instruction, the University of Edinburgh, for his very valuable and insightful suggestions on a later draft; Paul Ramsden again for writing the Foreword; and Phil Moore, colleague from Newcastle days and co-author with me of another book on teaching, who was a valuable sounding board and constructive critic during many formative bush-walks in Hong Kong and on the New South Wales Central Coast.

John Biggs
Tumbi Umbi

1

Changing university teaching

In the days when university classes contained highly selected students, enrolled in their faculty of choice, the traditional lecture and tutorial seemed to work well enough. However, the expansion, restructuring and refinancing of the tertiary sector in the 1990s has meant that classes are not only larger but quite diversified in terms of student ability, motivation and cultural background. Teachers see major difficulties in maintaining standards. However, if we regard good teaching as encouraging students to use the higher-order learning processes that 'academic' students use spontaneously, standards need not decline. This is not a matter of acquiring new teaching techniques, as much as tapping the large, research-derived, knowledge base on teaching and learning that already exists. Through reflective practice, teachers can then create an improved teaching environment suited to their own context.

The nature of the change

The past ten years have seen an extraordinary and worldwide change in the structure, function and financing of the university system. Teaching and decision-making generally are more centrally controlled, and are much more subject to economic and managerial considerations than used to be the case. Undergraduate teaching, of international students in particular, is seen as a more lucrative source of funds than research and higher degree work. Academic staff tend to be older, now working in a different *kind* of institution from the one they have been used to. As far as teaching itself is concerned, the following changes are particularly salient:

1 A greater proportion of school leavers are now in higher education. Ten years ago the proportion was around 15 per cent; now it is over 40 per cent in many areas. The brightest and most committed students will still be there, as they have been in the past, but they will sit alongside students of rather different academic bent. The *range* of ability within classes is now considerable.

2 Most students will be paying increasingly more for their education. They will be demanding value for money.
3 Students are more diverse in other ways: in age and experience, in socio-economic status and in cultural background.
4 Classes have increased in size as well as in diversity. Fewer staff are teaching more students.
5 More courses are vocationally oriented than used to be the case.

The effect of each of these factors is greater in some institutions than in others, but academic staff generally are facing a new and very demanding situation, with attendant adjustment problems. Many of the factors mentioned – class size, increased student intake, fewer staff, new courses, reskilling of teachers – demand more in terms of teaching skill. Additional pressures come from the student-as-paying-client on the one hand, and from department heads to maintain research funding and publications on the other. All factors seem inexorably to suggest lower standards of teaching, and therefore of learning. This book has been written to suggest how teaching standards can be maintained.

When university classes contained highly selected students, the traditional methods of teaching, lecture followed by a tutorial, gave the appearance of working well enough. Today, with a much more diversified student population, these methods no longer seem to be working. To some, this suggests that many students should not be at university at all. But they are, and in numbers that seem to preclude any but the same methods of teaching and assessing that aren't working. With several hundred in a class, what can you reasonably do but teach by mass lecture, and assess by multiple choice and machine-marking?

The answer given here is to take a fresh look at what we mean by teaching. It is not just a matter of finding better techniques than lecturing. There is no single, all-purpose best method of teaching. Teaching is individual. We have to adjust our teaching decisions to suit our subject matter, available resourcing, our students and our own individual strengths and weaknesses as a teacher. It depends on how we *conceive* the process of teaching, and through reflection come to some conclusion about how we may do our particular job better.

This book invites you to begin this process of reflection, and provides the tools for doing so. The remainder of this chapter suggests a strategy for looking at teaching reflectively. The following chapter develops a framework for reflection, and each subsequent chapter develops an aspect of this framework. By the end of this book, you will, I hope, be in a position to nominate your main problems, and to design teaching and assessment procedures that will engage students in the activities most likely to lead to quality learning, consistent with your resourcing.

Student ability and teaching method: the pay-off

Let us look at two students attending a lecture. Susan is academically committed; she is bright and interested in her studies, and wants to do well. She has clear academic or career plans, and what she learns is important to her. So when she learns she goes about it in an 'academic' way. She comes to the lecture with sound, relevant background knowledge, and possibly some questions she wants answering. In the lecture, she finds an answer to her preformed question; it forms the keystone for a particular arch of knowledge she is constructing. Or it may not be the answer she is looking for, and she speculates, wondering why it isn't. In either event, she reflects on the personal significance of what she is learning. Students like Susan (see Figure 1.1) virtually teach themselves, with little help from us.

Now take Robert. He is at university not out of a driving curiosity about a particular subject or a burning ambition to excel in a particular profession, but to obtain a qualification for a job. He is not even studying in the area of his first choice. He is less committed than Susan, possibly not as bright, academically speaking, and has a less developed background of relevant knowledge; he comes to the lecture with few questions. He wants only to put in sufficient effort to pass. Robert hears the lecturer say the same words as Susan heard, but he doesn't see a keystone, just another brick to be recorded in his lecture notes. He believes that if he can record enough of these bricks, and can remember them on cue, he'll keep out of trouble come exam time.

Students like Robert (see Figure 1.1) are in higher proportions in today's classes than was the case twenty, even ten, years ago. They will need help if they are to achieve the same levels of understanding that their more committed colleagues achieve spontaneously. To say that Robert is 'un-motivated' may be true, but it is unhelpful. What that really means is that he is not responding to the methods that work for Susan, the likes of whom were sufficiently visible in most classes in the good old days to satisfy us that our teaching *did* work. But of course it was the students who were doing the work and getting the results, not our teaching.

The challenge we face as teachers is to teach so that Robert learns more in the manner of Susan. Figure 1.1 suggests that the present differences between Robert and Susan (point A) may be lessened by appropriate teaching (point B). There are three factors interacting here: the students' levels of engagement, the degree of learning-related activity that a teaching method is likely to stimulate and the academic orientation of the students (see Figure 1.1). Point A is towards the 'passive' end of the teaching method continuum, where there is a large gap between Susan's and Robert's levels of engagement. A lecture would be an example of such passive teaching, and we get the picture just described. If we look at the

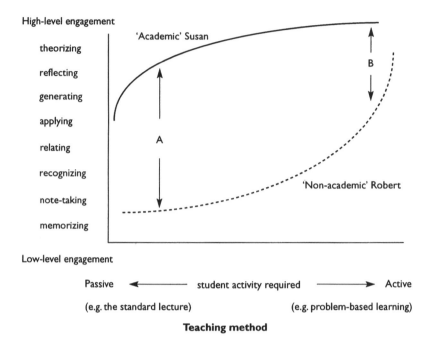

High-level engagement

theorizing

reflecting

generating

applying

relating

recognizing

note-taking

memorizing

Low-level engagement

Passive ◄——————— student activity required ———————► Active

(e.g. the standard lecture) (e.g. problem-based learning)

Teaching method

Figure 1.1: Student orientation, teaching method and level of engagement

ordinate of Figure 1.1, the student's level of engagement, we see that Susan is relating, applying, possibly theorizing, while Robert is taking notes and memorizing.

At point B, towards the 'active' end of the teaching method continuum, the gap between Susan and Robert is not so wide. Problem-based learning would be an example of an active method, because it *requires* students to question, to speculate, to generate solutions, so that Robert is now using the higher-order cognitive activities that Susan would be using spontaneously. The teaching has narrowed the gap between them, at least in terms of the kind of cognitive activity engaged.

Of course, there are limits to what students can do that are beyond the teacher's control – a student's ability is one – but there are other things that *are* within our control, and capitalizing on them is what good teaching is all about. Although Figure 1.1 is a hypothetical graph, it helps us to define good teaching, as follows:

Good teaching is getting most students to use the higher cognitive level processes that the more academic students use spontaneously.

Good teaching narrows the gap.

Teaching as a reflective activity

In order to improve teaching on this scale – so that the Roberts who enter our classes emerge more like Susan – a great deal of staff development will be required. It is therefore particularly important that staff development units, and units of teaching and learning, are not 'downsized' or even eliminated in a short-sighted attempt to save costs. To do so is rather like lightening an aircraft by throwing the doctors overboard when the pilot is having a heart attack. To 'save' on staff development in the present teaching crisis is just as short-sighted.

This book is addressed both to teachers and to staff developers. Individual teachers experience the problems, and will need, with help, to generate the solutions. Those solutions will not be found in learning a whole new bag of teaching tricks, any one of which may or may not be useful for your particular circumstances, but in reflecting on your teaching problems, and deriving your own ways of handling them within your departmental context.

Staff developers, for their part, have two roles: to consult with individuals, but, perhaps even more importantly, to consult on a departmental basis, to get the whole teaching context and departmental policies and procedures right. My main focus here is to address individual teachers, but there are strong implications for departmental and institutional policy and decision-making, as addressed in the last chapter. Other books (Ramsden 1998a; Toohey 1999) focus on the institutional aspects.

Academics have always been teachers, but the first priority of the great majority is to keep up with developments in their content discipline and it is hoped, to contribute to them through research. Developing teaching expertise usually takes second place: a set of priorities dictated as much by institutional structures and reward systems as by individual choice. But there is another body of knowledge apart from their content areas that academics also have a responsibility to address: the body of knowledge that underwrites good teaching:

> The professional authority of the academic-as-scholar rests on a body of knowledge; the professional authority of the academic-as-teacher should rest on a body of didactic knowledge. This comprises knowledge of how the subjects he or she professes is best learned and taught.
>
> (Ramsden 1992: 9)

There are two aspects to this 'didactic' knowledge. The first arises from formally conducted research. There is a large research-based literature on teaching and learning, much of it addressed in this book, forming the accepted theories of teaching. The second arises from your own personal experience as a teacher, out of which you have formed your personal implicit theory of teaching. The point is that by combining these two domains of knowledge, the public and the personal, you as a teacher become able to derive useful ways of improving your own teaching by using the thinking and the concepts of accepted theories. This is where the untapped potential for improvement in teaching lies: each of you can tap that knowledge of learning and teaching to improve your own personal practice.

Improving teaching through reflection

Wise and effective teaching is not, however, simply a matter of applying general principles of teaching according to rule; they need adapting to your own personal strengths and to your teaching context. A characteristic of award winning university teachers is their willingness to collect student feedback on their teaching, in order to see where their teaching might be improved (Dunkin and Precians 1992). Expert teachers continually reflect on how they might teach even better.

Such reflective practice is the basis of effective professionalism in whatever area (Schön 1983), including university teaching (Brockbank and McGill 1998; Cowan 1998). Reflective practice can be formally encouraged and directed as 'action learning' (Elliott 1991; Kember and Kelly 1993). Essentially, action learning is being systematic about changing your teaching, and making sure the changes are in the right direction, specifically that your students are now learning better than they used to. The target of action learning is the teaching of the individual herself or himself. The 'learning' in action learning refers not only to student learning, or even to learning about teaching, but to learning about *oneself as a teacher*, and learning how to use reflection to become a better teacher. Learning new techniques for teaching is like the fish that provides a meal today; reflective practice is the net that provides meals for the rest of one's life.

The driving conceptual process is reflection, using a theory of learning and teaching to reflect with. 'Reflection' as a term is actually slightly misleading. A reflection in a mirror is an exact replica of what is in front of it. Reflection in professional practice, however, gives back not what is, but what *might be*, an improvement on the original.

To transform what is to what might be is the role of theory. The theory makes you aware that there is a problem, and it helps to generate a solution to it. This is where many tertiary teachers are lacking: not in theories relating to their content discipline, but in well structured theories relating to *teaching* their discipline. Reflecting on your teaching, and seeing what is wrong and how it may be improved, requires you to have an explicit theory of teaching.

Task 1.1: What are the major problems in your own teaching that you would like to solve?

Take a semester or year-length unit that you are currently teaching, and that presents you with particular difficulties or problems that you want to solve (e.g. teaching large classes, motivating students, lecturing successfully, dissatisfied with current assessment methods, covering the syllabus, getting students to understand . . .). What are the *three most worrying*, problems in teaching that unit, and that you would realistically hope to minimize by reading this book?

1 _____

_____

_____

2 _____

_____

_____

3 _____

_____

_____

Comment _____

_____

In the following chapters, bear this unit in mind, even if the material being addressed is not particularly problematic. At the end, you have the chance to revisit these problems.

Every teacher has some kind of implicit theory of teaching (Marland 1997), but we need something more up-front, a consciously worked out theory that generates answers to teaching problems. The initial jolt that says 'There's a problem here' has to be defined in such a way that it becomes soluble. 'The stuff isn't getting across' doesn't define a soluble problem. 'The students are only giving me back what is in my lectures' does. The last statement is based on a theory: that when students only give back what is in the lectures, something is wrong. A good theory would suggest that the something resides in the teaching, rather than as some defect inherent in the students. It might be that the assessment procedures are letting students get away with repeating the lectures. So we need to present them with assessment tasks where this will not work.

To recognize and then to solve problems in teaching involves reflecting on what is happening, using a framework that gives you an angle on what is going on in your teaching. In the next chapter we develop such a framework, based on what we know about student learning, which you can use to reflect on your teaching.

Finally, complete Task 1.1. The idea is to formulate problems that are currently in your teaching, and would like to solve. Task 1.1 is the first of several reflective tasks; I have included one or two such tasks in each chapter. They are intended to help with your self-questioning, reflecting, and in your decisions about alternative ways to go. Staff developers might find these tasks useful, in conjunction with their own, in conducting workshops or consultations with individual teachers or with departments.

Summary and conclusions

The nature of the change

With the expansion and restructuring of the tertiary sector in the 1990s, university teachers face unprecedented problems of adjustment: to larger classes containing a greater spread of student ability and motivation, to under-resourcing and to market-driven courses. This seems like a recipe for declining standards, but not necessarily, if we take a fresh look at the *teaching* problem this poses. Good teaching is getting all students to use the higher cognitive level processes that academic students use spontaneously. The challenge is to achieve this in the face of the conditions now imposed on the tertiary sector.

Student ability and teaching method: the pay-off

Teaching 'works' by getting students to engage in learning-related activities that help them attain the particular objectives set for the unit or course, such as theorizing, generating new ideas, reflecting, applying, problem-solving, memorizing and so on. Academically oriented students spontaneously carry out the higher levels of these activities more or less independently of the teaching; for them, lecturing can 'work'. The majority of students, however, need more support in order to carry out these higher-level activities; teaching is precisely to provide that support. If we do so appropriately, we shall be getting ordinary students doing the sorts of things that only 'better' students used to do under 'thin' methods such as lecturing.

Teaching as a reflective activity

Improving teaching under these conditions is not a matter of simply learning a swag of teaching competencies. Teaching is personal, and the context in which each teacher works is different. What is effective for this teacher, for that subject, at this level, for those students, may not apply to other teachers, working under their own conditions. Individuals have to work out their own solutions. This requires *reflection*, a theory of teaching to reflect with and a context of experiences as the object of reflection. This process may be structured in the action learning paradigm, in which possible solutions are carefully monitored to gauge their success.

Further reading

On trends in higher education

Bourner, T. and Flowers, S. (1997) Teaching and learning methods in higher education: a glimpse of the future, *Reflections on Higher Education*, 9, 77–102.
Dearing, R. (1997) *National Committee of Inquiry into Higher Education (Dearing Report)*, Higher Education in the Learning Society, Report of the National Committee. Norwich: HMSO.
Ramsden, P. (1998) *Learning to Lead in Higher Education*, London: Routledge.
West, R. (1998) *Learning for Life*, Canberra: Australian Government Publishing Service.

Dearing and West, of course, are the official blueprints for the futures of higher education in England and Australia, respectively. What they spell out, under the rhetoric, is very much what has been outlined in the introduction to this chapter: larger classes, an increasingly diverse student population, market-force provision and big challenges to teachers.

Bourner and Flowers give their estimation of the seriousness of the situation, and their strategic solution, which is a highly diversified largely off-campus environment, action learning for students and lots of high tech. The present book nods in their direction (see Chapter 6) but takes a more conservative line, which is to assume that on-campus teaching will continue as the major mode of delivery, so that should remain the main target for improving teaching. We shall see who is right.

Ramsden addresses academic managers and heads of departments, suggesting how appropriate leadership can increase all of research productivity, teaching and staff morale.

2

Constructing learning by aligning teaching: constructive alignment

The key to reflecting on the way we teach is to base our thinking on what we know about how students learn. Learning is the result of the constructive activity of the student. Teaching is effective when it supports those activities appropriate to achieving the curriculum objectives, thereby encouraging students to adopt a deep approach to learning. Poor teaching and assessment result in a surface approach, where students use inappropriate and low-order learning activities. A good teaching system aligns teaching method and assessment to the learning activities stated in the objectives, so that all aspects of this system are in accord in supporting appropriate student learning. This system is called *constructive alignment*, based as it is on the twin principles of constructivism in learning and alignment in teaching.

Research into student learning

Learning has been the subject of research by psychologists for the whole of the twentieth century, but remarkably little has directly resulted in improved teaching. The reason is that until recently psychologists were more concerned with developing the One Grand Theory of Learning than in studying the contexts in which people learned, such as schools and universities (Biggs 1993a). This focus has been rectified in the past twenty years or so, and there is now a great deal of research into the ways that students go about their learning. Appropriately, the field of study is now designated as 'student learning' research.

Student learning research originated in Sweden, with Marton and Säljö's (1976a,b) study of surface and deep approaches to learning. They gave students a text to read, and told them they would be asked questions afterwards. Students responded in two different ways. The first group learned in anticipation of the questions, concentrating anxiously on the facts and details that might be asked. They 'skated along the surface of the text', as Marton and Säljö put it, using a *surface* approach to learning. What these students remembered was a list of disjointed facts; they did not comprehend the point the author was making. The second group, on the other hand, set out to understand the meaning of what the author was trying to say. They went below the surface of the text to interpret that meaning, using a *deep* approach. They saw the big picture and how the facts and details made the author's case.

Note that the terms 'deep' and 'surface' as used here describe ways of learning a particular task, *not*, as many subsequently used the terms, characteristics of students.

This series of studies struck a chord with ongoing work in other countries; in particular with that of Entwistle in the United Kingdom (e.g. Entwistle and Ramsden 1983), and that of Biggs in Australia (e.g. 1979, 1987a). The conceptual frameworks of these workers were originally quite different from that of the Swedish group, deriving in the first case largely from individual difference psychology, and in the second from cognitive psychology, but there was a common focus on the learning context, and some strong implications for teaching could be drawn.

How do we learn?

Theories of teaching and learning focusing on student activity are based on two main theories: phenomenography and constructivism. 'Phenomenography' was a term coined by Marton (1981) to describe the theory that grew out of his original studies with Säljö, and has developed considerably since then (Marton and Booth 1997). Constructivism has a long history in cognitive psychology, Jean Piaget being a crucial figure (e.g. Ginsburg and Opper 1987), and today it takes on several forms: individual, social, cognitive, postmodern (Steffe and Gale 1995).

One can get excited about whether phenomenography or constructivism is the way to go, but I take a pragmatic view on this. While there are differences in flavour between constructivist-driven and phenomenologically driven teaching (Prosser and Trigwell 1998; Trigwell and Prosser 1997), I assume that most teachers, including readers of this book, are not interested in theories of learning as much as in improving their teaching. For that we need a framework to aid reflection: a theory of learning that is broad-based and empirically sound, and that easily translates into practice. For my money that means constructivism, although there is a lot in common between the constructivist and phenomenological positions.

The most basic commonality is that meaning is not imposed or transmitted by direct instruction, but is created by the students' *learning activities*, their 'approaches to learning' (see below). The low cognitive level of engagement deriving from the surface approach yields fragmented outcomes that do not convey the meaning intended by the encounter, whereas the deep approach is more likely to help the student construe the meaning. The surface approach is therefore to be discouraged, the deep approach encouraged – and that is the working definition of good teaching used in this book.

What people construct from a learning encounter depends on their motives and intentions, on what they know already and on how they use their prior knowledge. Meaning is therefore personal; it must be, when you think about it. The alternative is that meaning is 'transmitted' from teacher to student, like dubbing an audio-tape, which as we see later is an untenable but not uncommon view.

Learning is thus a way of interacting with the world. As we learn, our conceptions of phenomena change, and we see the world differently. The acquisition of information in itself does not bring about such a change, but the way we structure that information and think with it does. Thus, education is about *conceptual change*, not just the acquisition of information.

Such educative conceptual change takes place when:

1 It is clear to students (and teachers) what is 'appropriate', what the objectives are, where all can see where they are supposed to be going.
2 Students experience the felt need to get there. The art of good teaching is to communicate that need where it is initially lacking. 'Motivation' is a product of good teaching, not its prerequisite.
3 Students feel free to focus on the task, not on watching their backs. Often, attempts to create a felt need to learn, particularly through ill-conceived and urgent assessments, are counter-productive. The game then becomes a matter of dealing with the test, not with engaging the task deeply.
4 Students can work collaboratively and in dialogue with others, both peers and teachers. Good dialogue elicits those activities that shape, elaborate, and deepen understanding.

These four points contain a wealth of implication for the design of teaching, and for personal reflection about what one is really trying to do. But first, let us elaborate the fundamental concept of approach to learning.

Surface and deep approaches to learning

The concepts of surface and deep approaches to learning are very helpful in conceiving ways of improving teaching. Sometimes it is useful to refer to an 'achieving' approach (Biggs 1987a), but this is less relevant for present purposes. The surface and deep approaches usefully describe how Robert and Susan typically go about their learning and studying – up to now. Remember that our aim is to teach so that Robert behaves more like Susan.

The surface approach

The surface approach arises from an intention to get the task out of the way with minimum trouble, while appearing to meet requirements. Low cognitive level activities are used, when higher-level activities are required to do the task properly. The concept may be applied to any area, not only to learning: to teaching, to doing business, to gardening. The common terms 'cutting corners' and 'sweeping under the carpet' convey its flavour; it is made to appear that the job has been done properly when it hasn't.

As applied to academic learning, examples include rote learning selected content instead of understanding it, padding an essay, listing points instead of addressing an argument, quoting secondary references as if they were primary ones; the list is endless. A common misconception is that memorization indicates a surface approach (e.g. Webb 1997). However, sometimes verbatim recall is wholly appropriate, such as learning lines for a play, acquiring vocabulary, learning formulae. Memorization becomes a surface approach when it is used *instead* of understanding, to give the impression of understanding. When Robert takes notes, and selectively quotes them back, he is under-engaging in terms of what is properly required. That is a surface approach, and the problem is that it often works:

> I hate to say it, but what you have got to do is to have a list of 'facts'; you write down ten important points and memorize those, then you'll do all right in the test . . . If you can give a bit of factual information – so and so did that, and concluded that – for two sides of writing, then you'll get a good mark.
>
> (A psychology undergraduate, quoted in Ramsden 1984: 144)

Now if the teacher of this student thought that an adequate understanding of psychology could be manifested by selectively memorizing, there would be no problem. But I don't think the teacher did think that. I see this as a case where an inappropriate assessment task *allowed* the students to get a good mark on the basis of memorizing facts. As it happened, this particular student wrote essays in a highly appropriate way – he later graduated with first class honours! The problem is therefore not with the student, but with the assessment task. This is an instance of unreflective practice by the teacher, highly reflective by the student.

Thus, do not think that Robert is irredeemably cursed with a surface approach. What we know is that *under current conditions of teaching* he chooses to use a surface approach. Teaching and assessment methods often encourage a surface approach, because they are not aligned to the aims of teaching the subject, as in the case of the above psychology teacher. The presence of a surface approach is thus a signal that something is out of kilter in our teaching or in our assessment methods, and therefore is something we can hope to address. The conclusion that in Robert we have an incurably surface student on our hands might in the end prove to be correct, but that conclusion is way down the track yet.

In using the surface approach, students focus on what Marton calls the 'signs' of learning: the words used, isolated facts, items treated independently of each other. This prevents them from seeing what the signs signify, the meaning and structure of what is taught. They cannot see the wood for the trees. Emotionally, learning becomes a drag, a task to be got out of the way. Hence the presence of negative feelings about the learning task: anxiety, cynicism, boredom. Exhilaration or enjoyment of the task is not part of the surface approach.

Factors that encourage students to adopt such an approach include:

From the student's side
- an intention only to achieve a minimal pass; such may arise from a 'meal ticket' view of university, or from a requirement to take a subject irrelevant to the student's programme;
- non-academic priorities exceeding academic ones;
- insufficient time, too high a workload;
- misunderstanding requirements, such as thinking that factual recall is adequate;
- a cynical view of education;
- high anxiety;
- a genuine inability to understand particular content at a deep level.

From the teacher's side
- teaching in a piecemeal fashion: providing 'lists', not bringing out the intrinsic structure of the topic or subject;
- assessing for independent facts, as is frequently done when using short answer and multiple-choice tests;
- teaching, and especially assessing, in a way that encourages cynicism: for example, 'I hate teaching this section, and you're going to hate learning it, but we've got to cover it';
- providing insufficient time to engage the tasks, emphasizing coverage at the expense of depth;
- creating undue anxiety or low expectations of success: 'Anyone who can't understand this isn't fit to be at university.'

The student's and teacher's sides should not be seen as entirely separate. Most of the student-based factors are affected by teaching. Is insufficient time to engage properly a matter of poor student planning or poor teacher judgement? Much student cynicism is a reaction to the manner of teaching and assessment. Even the last student factor, inability to understand at a deep level, refers to the task at hand, and that may be a matter of poor teacher judgement concerning curriculum content as much as the student's abilities. But there are limits. Even under the best teaching some students will still maintain a surface approach.

It is probably less likely that under poor teaching students will maintain a deep approach. Even Susan. Unfortunately, it is usually much easier to create a surface approach than it is to support a deep approach (Trigwell and Prosser 1991).

The first step in improving teaching, then, is to avoid those factors that encourage a surface approach.

The deep approach

The deep approach arises from a felt need to engage the task appropriately and meaningfully, so the student tries to use the most appropriate cognitive activities for handling it. Susan is interested in mathematics, is intrigued by mathematical structures and wants to get to the bottom of the subject; for her, cutting corners is pointless.

When students feel this need-to-know, they try to focus on underlying meaning: on main ideas, themes, principles or successful applications. This requires a sound foundation of relevant prior knowledge, so students needing to know will naturally try to learn the details, as well as making sure they understand. When using the deep approach in handling a task, students have positive feelings: interest, a sense of importance, challenge, even of exhilaration. Learning is a pleasure. Students come with questions they want answered, and when the answers are unexpected, that is even better.

Factors that encourage students to adopt such an approach include:

From the student's side
- an intention to engage the task meaningfully and appropriately; such an intention may arise from an intrinsic curiosity or from a determination to do well;
- appropriate background knowledge; the ability to focus at a high conceptual level, working from first principles, requires a well structured knowledge base;
- a genuine preference, and ability, for working conceptually rather than with unrelated detail.

In the teaching environment
- teaching in such a way as to bring out the structure of the topic or subject explicitly;

- teaching to *elicit* a positive response from students, e.g. by questioning or presenting problems, rather than teaching to *expound* information;
- teaching by building on what students already know;
- confronting and eradicating students' misconceptions;
- assessing for structure rather than for independent facts;
- teaching and assessing in a way that encourages a positive working atmosphere, so students can make mistakes and learn from them;
- emphasizing depth of learning, rather than breadth of coverage;
- in general, and most importantly, using teaching and assessment methods that support the explicit aims and objectives of the course; this is known as 'practising what you preach'.

Again, the student-based factors are not independent of teaching. Encouraging the need-to-know, instilling curiosity, building on students' prior knowledge are all things that teachers can attempt to do; and conversely, they are things that poor teaching can discourage. There are many things the teacher can do to encourage deep learning. Just what will be a lot clearer by the end of this book.

To summarize, then, deep and surface approaches to learning describe the way students relate to a teaching/learning environment; they are not fixed characteristics of students, their 'academic personalities' so to speak. Some people speak of students' approaches to learning as if they were learning *styles* that apply whatever the task or the teaching (Schmeck 1988). At the other extreme, Marton and Säljö (1976a, b) speak of approaches as entirely determined by context, as if students walk into a learning situation without any preference for their way of going about learning.

The truth lies in the middle. Students do have predilections or preferences for this or that approach, but those predilections may or may not be realized in practice, depending on the teaching context. We are dealing with an *interaction* between the personal and the contextual, not unlike the interaction between heredity and environment. Both factors apply, but which predominates depends on particular situations. Turn back to Figure 1.1. At point A, under passive teaching, student factors make the difference, but at point B, active teaching predominates, lessening the differences between students.

If you want to assess predilections for different approaches to learning, this can be done using questionnaires such as the *Approaches to Study Inventory* (ASI) (Entwistle and Ramsden 1983), or the *Study Process Questionnaire* (SPQ) (Biggs 1987a). Responses to these questionnaires also tell us something about the quality of the teaching environment, because students' predilections tend to change when they are faced with a particular kind of teaching environment; they adapt to the expected requirements. This means that questionnaires can be useful for evaluating teaching environments (Biggs 1993a; Kember *et al.* 1998). For example,

Eley (1992) found that students adapted their approaches to learning to their perception of what different units demanded; Meyer (1991) refers to this as 'study orchestration'.

The 3P model of learning and teaching

Figure 2.1 puts all this together in the '3P' model of teaching and learning, elaborating Dunkin and Biddle's (1974) linear model of teaching to include approaches to learning to create an interactive system. The 3P model describes three points in time at which learning-related factors are placed: presage, before learning takes place; process, during learning; and product, the outcome of learning (hence the 3P model).

Presage factors are of two kinds:

1 *Student based*: the relevant prior knowledge the student has about the topic, interest in the topic, student ability, commitment to university and so on.
2 *Teaching context based*: what is intended to be taught, how it will be taught and assessed, the expertise of the teacher, the 'climate' or ethos of the classroom and of the institution itself and so on.

These factors interact at the process level to determine the student's

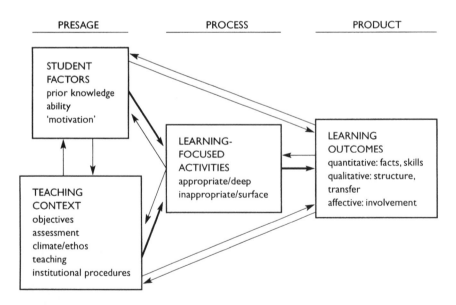

Figure 2.1: The 3P model of teaching and learning

immediate learning-related activities, as approaches to learning. Possible interactions here are manifold. A student with little prior knowledge of the topic will be unlikely to use a deep approach, even where the teaching is expert. Another student who already knows a great deal, and is very interested in the topic, is pre-set for a deep approach, but will be unlikely to use it if under severe time pressures. Yet another, who typically picks out likely items for assessment and rote learns them, finds that won't work under portfolio assessment, so goes deep. You can see why it is inappropriate to write particular students off as 'surface learners'.

The learning outcome is determined by many factors, acting in interaction with each other. The general direction of effects is marked by the heavy arrows: student and teaching presage factors jointly determine the approach a student uses for a given task, and that in turn determines the outcome. The light arrows connect everything to everything else, because all components form a *system* (Biggs 1993b).

A system is a set of components that interact to produce a common outcome in service to a common goal (Romizowski 1981). Here the common goal is learning, and the immediate system is the tertiary classroom. The components in this system derive from the students, and from the teaching context. Collectively they determine the cognitive processes the students are likely to use, which in turn determine the detail and structure inherent in the learning outcomes, and how the students feel about the outcome.

This systems feature explains why no two classes you teach are ever the same. You may be the same, but the students are not; you as it were strike a different deal with each group of students each time, so in a functional sense it is not even true that you are the same. Likewise, you and a colleague teaching the same class create a different system, because one of the components is different, the teacher, and accordingly each achieves different results. Then there is the larger institutional system of which the classroom is one component; that too strikes its own balance.

But to return to the classroom system, all components as they affect each other have to be considered, not individual ones separately or additively. The 3P model contains within it various theories of teaching that we examine in the next section. Before we go any further, however, let us see where individually we currently stand by completing Task 2.1.

Task 2.1: What are your theories of teaching and learning?

Learning is _____

_____

_____

_____

Teaching is _____

_____

_____

_____

When you have finished this chapter, come back to these statements and see how they check out against the transmission and student learning models, and the theories of teaching outlined in the chapter. Where do your own views lie? Now that you have seen these other views, have you changed your theory of teaching?

_____

_____

Comments _____

_____

_____

Levels of thinking about teaching

The 3P model depicts three sources that might affect the learning out-come: a direct effect from the student-based factors, another direct effect from the teaching-based factors and an interactive effect from the system as a whole. Each of these ways of determining learning forms a theory of how teaching works:

1 Learning is a function of individual differences between students.
2 Learning is a function of teaching.
3 Learning is the result of students' learning-focused activities, which are engaged by students as a result both of their own perceptions and inputs, and of the total teaching context.

These different 'theories' of teaching are in order of complexity and sophistication, and so we refer to them as 'levels'. They include what others call intentions or conceptions (Trigwell and Prosser 1996).

Teachers tend to hold these theories at different points in their teaching career, some progressing to level 3, others staying at levels 1 or 2 (Biggs 1996c). They describe a sequence in the development of teaching skill: a route map towards reflective teaching, if you like, where the level you are at depends on what you focus on as most important.

Level 1. Focus: what the student is

Teachers at level 1 are struck by student differences, as most beginning teachers are. They focus on the fact that there are good students, like Susan, and poor students, like Robert. As teachers, their responsibility is to know the content well, and to expound it clearly. Thereafter, it's up to the student to attend lectures, to listen carefully, to take notes, to read the recommended readings and to make sure it's taken on board and un-loaded on cue.

At level 1, teaching is as it were held constant – it is transmitting information, usually by lecturing – so differences in learning are due to differences between students in ability, motivation, what sort of school they went to, A level results and, yes, their 'innate' approaches to learning. Ability is usually seen as the most important factor, an interesting conse-quence of which is that teaching becomes not so much an educative activity as a *selective* one, assessment the instrument of sorting the good students from the bad after teaching is over. Many common practices spring from this belief, which are addressed in Chapters 8 and 9, on assessment theory and practice.

The view of university teaching as transmitting information is so widely accepted that delivery and assessment systems the world over are based on it. Teaching rooms and media are specifically designed for one-way deliv-ery. A teacher is the knowledgeable expert, the sage-on-the-stage, who expounds the information the students are to absorb and report back accurately, according to their ability, their motivation, even their ethnicity (see Chapter 7). The curriculum is a list of items of content that, once expounded from the podium, have been 'covered'. How the students receive that content, and what their depth of understanding of it might be, are not specifically addressed. The language is about what the teacher does, not what the student does. Level 1 is founded on a *quantitative* way of thinking about learning and teaching (Cole 1990; Marton *et al.* 1993), which manifests itself most obviously in assessment practices. Learning outcomes are quantified into units of knowledge of equivalent value: a word, an idea, a point. These are either correct or incorrect, and converted by a common currency, usually a percentage, to make them interchangeable. The number of units accrued becomes an index of learning ability.

Explaining the variability in student learning by students' characteristics makes this a *blame-the-student* theory of teaching, based on student deficit. When students don't learn (that is, when teaching breaks down), it is due to something the students are lacking:

> How can I be expected to teach that lot with their A levels? They wouldn't have been admitted ten years ago.

> They lack any motivation at all.

> These students lack suitable study skills. But that's not my problem, they'll have go to the Counselling Service.

In themselves, these statements may well be true: A level or HSC results might be poor, students nowadays may be less academically oriented; which is exactly the challenge outlined in Chapter 1.

Blame-the-student is a comfortable theory of teaching. If students don't learn, it's not that there is anything wrong with the teaching, but that they are incapable, unmotivated or otherwise not doing what they are supposed to be doing. The presumed deficit is not the teacher's responsibility to correct. Blaming-the-student is very common in teaching international students, as we see in Chapter 7.

The level 1 theory of teaching is totally unreflective. It doesn't occur to the teacher to ask the key generative question: 'What else could I be doing?' And until teachers do ask that, their teaching is unlikely to change.

Level 2. Focus: what the teacher does

The view of teaching at the next level is still based on transmission, but of concepts and understandings, not just of information (Prosser and Trigwell 1998). The responsibility for 'getting it across' now rests to a significant extent on good teaching. The possibility is entertained that there may be more effective ways of teaching than what one is currently doing, which is a major advance. Learning is seen as more a function of what the teacher is doing than of what sort of student one has to deal with.

The teacher who operates at level 2 works at obtaining an armoury of teaching skills. The material to be 'got across' includes complex understandings, which requires much more than chalk-and-talk:

I'll settle them down with some music, then an introductory spiel: where we were last week, what we're going to do today. Then a video clip followed by a buzz session. The questions they're to address will be on the OH. I'll then fire six questions at them to be answered individually. Yes, four at the back row, finger pointing, that'll stir that lot up. Then I speak to the answers for about seven minutes, working in those two jokes I looked up. Wrap up, warning them there's an exam question hidden in today's session (screams of 'Now he tells us!' Yuk, yuk). Mention what's coming up for next week; meantime read Chapter 10 of Bronowski.

There is plenty of variation in technique here, probably a good student response, but the focus of this description is entirely teacher-centred: on what *I* am doing as the teacher, not what *they* are learning as students.

Traditional approaches to staff development often worked on what the teacher does, as do 'how to' courses and books that provide prescriptive advice on getting it across more effectively:

- establish clear procedural rules at the outset, such as signals for silence;
- ensure clarity, project the voice, clear visual aids;
- eye-contact students while talking;
- don't interrupt a large lecture with handouts, as chaos is likely.

This may be useful advice, as we endorse in Chapter 6, but it is concerned with *management*, not with facilitating learning. Good management is important, but as a means of setting the stage so that good learning may occur, not as an end in itself.

Level 2 is also a deficit model, the 'blame' this time being on the teacher. It also carries strong quantitative overtones. It is a view of teaching often held by university administrators, because it provides a rationale for making personnel decisions. Good teachers are those who have more teaching competencies. Does Dr Jones 'have' the appropriate competencies for tertiary level teaching? If not, he had better show evidence that he has by the time his contract comes up for renewal. However, competencies may have little to do with teaching effectiveness. A competency, such as setting a reliable multiple-choice test, is useful only if it is appropriate to one's teaching purposes to *use* a multiple-choice test. Likewise, managing educational technology, or questioning skills, or any of the other competencies tertiary teachers should 'have', should not be isolated from the context in which they are being used. Knowing what to do is important only if you know when and how you should do it. The focus should not be on the skill itself, but whether its deployment has the desired effect on student learning.

Which brings us to the third level of teaching.

Level 3. Focus: what the student does

Level 3 sees teaching as supporting learning. No longer is it possible to say: 'I taught them, but they didn't learn.' Expert teaching includes mastery over a variety of teaching techniques, but unless learning takes place, they are irrelevant; the focus is on what the student does, on what learning is or is not going on.

This implies a view of teaching that is not just about facts, concepts and principles to be covered and understood, but also clear about:

1 What it means to 'understand' in the way we want them to be understood.
2 What kind of teaching–learning activities are required to reach those kinds of understandings.

The first two levels did not address these questions. The first question requires that we specify what levels of understanding we want when we teach a topic; the second what learning activities might best be appropriate for achieving those levels. Then follow the key questions:

• how do you define those levels of understanding?
• what do students have to do to reach the level specified?
• what do you have to do to find out if they have been reached or not?

Defining levels of understanding is basic to clarifying our curriculum objectives, the subject of the next chapter. Getting students to understand at the level required is a matter of getting them to undertake the appropriate learning activities. This is where a level 3 student-centred theory of teaching departs from the other models. It's not what *we* do, it's what *students* do that is the important thing.

Level 3 teaching is systemic. Good student learning depends both on student-based factors – ability, appropriate prior knowledge, clearly accessible new knowledge – and on the teaching context, which includes teacher responsibility, informed decision-making and good management. But the bottom line is that teachers have to work with what material they have. Whereas lectures and tutorials might have worked in the good old days when highly selected students tended to bring their deep approaches with them, they may not work so well today. We need to create a teaching context where the Roberts of this world can go deep too.

A note on thinking and doing

There is quite a large literature on views or conceptions of what teaching and learning are, of what is learned, of what to teach and how to go about teaching and assessing (Samuelowicz and Bain 1992; Trigwell and Prosser 1997). Do the conceptions we hold affect the way we teach? Gow and Kember (1993) showed that teachers who saw teaching as knowledge transmission created classrooms where students scored very low on the deep approach, while teachers who saw teaching as facilitating student learning created classrooms where students scored very low on a surface approach. Teachers' beliefs had created teaching environments to which the students reacted, by tuning their approaches to learning to suit the environment to which they were exposed.

Does enduring change in a teacher's effectiveness come about by *thinking* differently, by moving from levels 1 and 2 to level 3? Or by *acting* differently, by using more effective techniques, say, than lecturing and multiple-choice testing? This raises issues about helping teachers to improve their teaching that are discussed at greater length in Chapter 11.

Constructive alignment

Let me again quote in part Shuell's statement that is the theme of this book: 'If students are to learn *desired outcomes* in a *reasonably effective manner*, then the teacher's fundamental task is to get students to *engage in learning activities* that are likely to result in their achieving those outcomes' (Shuell 1986: 429; emphases added). Herein lies a blueprint for the design of teaching. In saying what the 'desired outcomes' are we are clarifying our objectives. In deciding if the outcomes are learned in a 'reasonably effective manner' we need to reference our assessment to those objectives and to define what 'reasonably effective' might mean in terms of our grading system. And in getting students to 'engage in (appropriate) learning activities' we are teaching them effectively. Most importantly, we are saying that all these aspects of teaching are mutually supportive; each is an integral part of the total system, not an add-on.

The principle of alignment

The 3P model describes teaching as a balanced system in which all components support each other, as they do in any ecosystem. To work properly, all components are aligned to each other. Imbalance in the system will lead to a breakdown, in this case to poor teaching and surface learning. Non-alignment is signified by inconsistencies, unmet expectations and practices that contradict what we preach.

The context that we set up is at the core of teaching. Apart from the students and ourselves, the critical components include:

1 The curriculum that we teach.
2 The teaching methods that we use.
3 The assessment procedures that we use, and methods of reporting results.
4 The climate that we create in our interactions with the students.
5 The institutional climate, the rules and procedures we have to follow.

Each of these needs to work towards the common end, deep learning. The institutional climate (5) is a given. We have to work within or around institutional requirements as best we may. As to the classroom climate (4), that is more under our control. The kind of atmosphere we create – authoritarian, friendly, cold, warm – can markedly affect the effectiveness of a teaching approach; for example, problem-solving in small groups won't work with a group leader who insists on telling students the answers. We cannot teach in a manner that is inappropriate for the mode of teaching we are using, or that is false to ourselves. Forcing teachers into an untenable role will destroy alignment.

As to the curriculum (1), the teaching methods (2) and the assessment procedures (3), we have to be specially careful to seek compatibility. When there is alignment between what we want, how we teach and how we assess, teaching is likely to be much more effective than when there is not. Cohen (1987) calls alignment between objectives and assessment (criterion-referenced assessment) 'the magic bullet', so effective is it in improving learning. I am going further and suggesting that teaching methods should be included in the alignment. You wouldn't lecture education students on how to run small groups, and then give them a written test. You would get them to participate in small groups, and to run their own.

Alignment itself, however, says nothing about the nature of what is being aligned. This is where constructivism as a theory of learning comes in. If we specify our objectives in terms of 'understanding', we need a theory of understanding in order to define what we mean; in deciding on teaching methods that address the objectives we need a theory of learning and teaching. Hence, 'constructive alignment', a marriage between a constructivist understanding of the nature of learning, and an aligned design for teaching (Biggs 1996a).

It is easy to see why alignment should work. In aligned teaching, there is maximum consistency throughout the system. The curriculum is stated in the form of clear objectives, which state the level of understanding required rather than simply a list of topics to be covered. Teaching methods are chosen that are likely to realize those objectives; you get students to do the things that the objectives nominate. Finally, the assessment tasks address the objectives, so that you can test to see if the students have learned what the objectives state they should be learning. All components in the system address the same agenda and support each other. The students are 'entrapped' in this web of consistency, optimizing the likelihood that they will engage the appropriate learning activities, but which paradoxically frees students to conceal their own learning. Cowan (1998: 112) makes a very similar point when he defines teaching as: 'The purposeful creation of situations from which motivated learners should not be able to escape without learning or developing.' This is deep learning by definition.

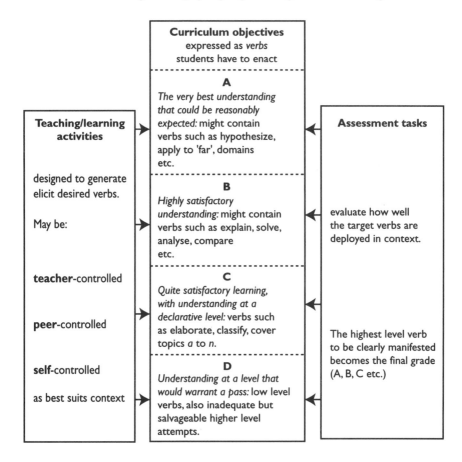

Figure 2.2: Aligning curriculum objectives, teaching and learning activities and assessment tasks

At this point we should say what constructive alignment is not. It is not 'spoon feeding'. Spoon feeding, like the other level 1 metaphors that refer to the more basic aspects of metabolism – 'regurgitating', 'chewing it over', 'ramming down their throats', 'getting your teeth into' – puts a stranglehold on the student's cognitive processes. Spoon feeding does the work for the students, so that they have little left to do but obediently swallow. Constructive alignment makes the students themselves do the real work; the teacher simply arranges things so that it is more likely that they will.

The design of aligned teaching

Figure 2.2 depicts the constructive alignment model. The curriculum objectives lie in the middle, which asserts their centrality. Get them right, and the decisions as to how they are to be taught, and how they may be assessed, follow. We express the objectives in terms of what constructive activities are most likely to achieve the desired outcomes for the topic or unit in question. Activities are *verbs*, so practically speaking we specify the verbs we want students to enact in the context of the content discipline being taught.

Turn back to Figure 1.1, which uses verbs in this way. We see that Susan tended spontaneously to use high level verbs such as theorize, reflect, generate, apply, whereas Robert used lower level verbs such as recognize, memorize and so on. Their level of engagement is expressed in the cognitive level of the verbs used: reflection is high level, memorizing low level. Precisely what is meant by 'level', and how to determine it, is a key issue addressed in Chapter 3.

Those verbs take objects, the content being taught. We can now explicitly go beyond the one-dimensional notion of 'covering' the topics in the curriculum, and specify the *levels* of understanding we want. Different levels will be differentially acceptable. The level of understanding in a bare pass is obviously less than that you would require in a high distinction. In the constructive alignment model, the first step is to arrange these levels of understanding in a hierarchy that corresponds to the grading system you use.

Exactly how this may be done is dealt with in the next chapter. For the moment, we simply express the objectives as a four-tier hierarchy corresponding to grade levels. Let us use the neutral A to D letter grades. A denotes a quality of learning and understanding that is the best one can reasonably expect for the unit and level of students in question. Obviously, that level will become increasingly higher from first year to higher years. B is highly satisfactory, but lacks the flair that distinguishes A. C is quite satisfactory, while D denotes a quality and complexity of understanding that is passable only, and anything less is fail. You will notice that in Figure 2.2 I have used sample verbs, which are quite general. You would of course use families of verbs to suit each level, and each content area. This practical matter is also addressed in the next chapter.

The categories are defined by a particular *quality* of learning and understanding, not by the accumulation of marks or percentages. That quality is determined from the assessment tasks. Finer discriminations within categories may be useful for reporting and other administrative purposes, but that is functionally quite a separate issue. The first priority is to state the objectives qualitatively, and to assess them accordingly. For example, the term 'first class honours' describes the way a student thinks, which is qualitatively different from the 'upper second' description, in a way that is not captured by saying that a 'first' has to obtain *x* more marks than an 'upper second'.

Once we have sorted out the objectives, we design teaching/learning activities, or TLAs, that are likely to encourage students to engage the optimal verbs. (TLA is a better term than 'teaching method' because it captures the reciprocal relationship between learning and teaching.) Finally, we select assessment tasks that will tell us whether and how well each student can meet the criteria expressed in the objectives. Objectives, teaching and assessment are now aligned, using the verbs in the objectives as markers for alignment.

To sum up, in an aligned system of instruction, the teacher's task is to see that the appropriate verbs are:

1 Nominated in the objectives.
2 Likely to be elicited in the chosen teaching/learning activities.
3 Embedded in the assessment tasks so that judgements can be made about how well a given student's level of performance meets the objectives.

Because the teaching methods and the assessment tasks now access the same verbs as are in the objectives, the chances are increased that most students will in fact engage with the appropriate verbs: by definition, a deep approach. Had our friend, Ramsden's psychology teacher, included in the objectives such terms as 'theorize', 'generalize' or 'comprehend the profundities of the founders of modern psychology', an assessment task that required only paraphrasing 'a bit of factual information for two pages of writing' would immediately be seen to be inadequate.

Constructive alignment is common sense, yet most university teaching is not aligned. There are several reasons for this.

1 Traditional transmission theories of teaching ignore alignment. A common method of determining students' grades depends on how students compare to each other ('norm-referenced'), rather than on whether an individual's learning meets the objectives ('criterion-referenced'). In the former case, there is no *inherent* relation between what is taught and what is tested.
2 Some administrative requirements (such as reporting in percentages, and grading on the curve) and resource limitations (that dictate large classes with mass lecturing and multiple-choice testing) make alignment difficult.
3 Lack of knowledge. Many of these matters may not have occurred to teachers. Others might like to use the principle but they don't know how to.

These points are addressed throughout this book. We shall see how the principle of alignment can be applied to the design of most units.

Summary and conclusions

Research into student learning

It is only in recent years that learning researchers have studied learning as it takes place in institutions, by students. There is now a body of theory called 'student learning research' that directly relates to practice, the strands of constructivism and phenomenography being the two most influential. Both emphasize that meaning is created by the learner, constructivism focusing particularly on the nature of the learning activities the student uses. We generically refer to appropriate learning activities as comprising a 'deep' approach to learning, and inappropriate learning activities as a 'surface' approach.

Surface and deep approaches to learning

Surface and deep approaches to learning are not personality traits, as is sometimes thought, but reactions to the teaching environment. Good teaching supports the deep approach and discourages the surface, but much traditional practice, for a variety of reasons, has the opposite effect. The 3P model depicts the classroom as an interactive system in which student characteristics and the teaching context mutually determine on-going deep or surface learning activities, which in turn determine the quality of learning outcomes.

Levels of thinking about teaching

The 3P model helps to put in place three common theories of teaching, depending on what is seen as the main determinant of learning: (a) what students are; (b) what teachers do; and (c) what students do. These factors are in ascending order of abstraction, and define 'levels' of thinking about teaching. At level 1, the teacher's role is to display information, the students' to absorb it. If they don't have the ability or motivation to do that correctly, or in sufficient quantity, that is their problem. At level 2, the teacher's role is to explain concepts and principles, as well as to present information. For this teachers need various skills, techniques and competencies. Here the focus is on what the teacher does, rather than on what the student is, and to that extent is more reflective and sophisticated. At level 3, the focus is on what the students do: do they engage the appropriate learning activities? That is what the teacher is to encourage. The task is two-fold:

1 To maximize the chances that students will use a deep approach.
2 To minimize the chances that they will use a surface approach.

That is the secret of good teaching. And that is what the rest of this book is about.

Constructive alignment

Constructive alignment is a design for teaching most calculated to encourage deep engagement. In constructing aligned teaching, it is first necessary to specify the desired *level* or *levels* of understanding of the content in question. Stipulating the appropriate verbs of understanding helps to do this. These verbs then become the target activities that students need to perform, and therefore teaching methods need to encourage, and the assessment tasks to address, in order to judge if or how well the students have been successful in meeting the objectives. This combination of constructivist theory and aligned instruction is the model of *constructive alignment.*

Further reading

On student learning from a phenomenographic perspective

Higher Education Research and Development, 16(2), June 1997. Special issue: Phenomenography in higher education.
Marton, F. and Säljö, R. (1976) On qualitative differences in learning – I: Outcome and process, *British Journal of Educational Psychology,* 46, 4–11.
Marton, F. and Booth, S. A. (1997) *Learning and Awareness,* Hillsdale, NJ: Lawrence Erlbaum.
Marton, F., Hounsell, D. and Entwistle, N. (eds) (1997) *The Experience of Learning,* Edinburgh: Scottish Academic Press.
Prosser, M. and Trigwell, K. (1998) *Teaching for Learning in Higher Education,* Buckingham: Open University Press.

The article by Marton and Säljö (said to be the most cited in the educational research literature) set the approaches to the learning paradigm in train. Marton and Booth bring phenomenography up to date, but the book is for specialists; Prosser and Trigwell demonstrate the implications for teaching arising from the phenomenographic framework, and this book is in a sense a parallel to the present book, which operates from constructivism.

On student learning from a constructivist and systems perspective

Biggs, J. B. (1987) *Student Approaches to Learning and Studying,* Hawthorn, Vic.: Australian Council for Educational Research.

Biggs, J. B. (1993) From theory to practice: a cognitive systems approach, *Higher Education Research and Development*, 12, 73–86.

Schmeck, R. (ed.) (1988) *Learning Strategies and Learning Styles*, New York: Plenum.

Steffe, L. and Gale, J. (eds) (1995) *Constructivism in Education*, Hillsdale, NJ: Erlbaum.

The first two items bring the cognitive psychology paradigm to student learning, the last two are fairly recent summaries of the constructivist position generally and how it applies to education. Schmeck's book is not restricted to constructivism but is eclectic, containing useful summaries of the European, Australian and North American work on student learning, and for that it is unusual.

On applying student learning research to teaching

Biggs, J. B. (1996) Enhancing teaching through constructive alignment, *Higher Education*, 32, 1–18.

Dart, B. and Boulton-Lewis, G. (eds) (1998) *Teaching and Learning in Higher Education*, Camberwell, Vic.: Australian Council for Educational Research.

Ramsden, P. (1992) *Learning to Teach in Higher Education*, London: Routledge.

The first paper outlines the theoretical basis of constructive alignment with an illustrative example. Dart and Boulton-Lewis contains a collection of papers that address teaching issues from the general student learning paradigm. Ramsden's approach is his own, but derives much from phenomenography, Chapters 1 to 7 giving rather more detail on the history and development of the student learning paradigm than is given here, and how it may be applied to teaching.

3

Formulating and clarifying curriculum objectives

The goal of most teachers would be that their students 'understand' what they teach them. However, what is meant by 'understanding' is not always very clear. The aim of this chapter is to clarify different levels of understanding and convert them to curriculum objectives, as appropriate to the content and level of the unit. A useful tool for doing this is the SOLO taxonomy, which when applied to particular content can specify objectives in terms that are clear both to us and to our students. The objectives contain criteria for the desired learnings, which the assessment tasks are designed to address, thus linking objectives and assessment. Such criterion-referenced assessment steers students' attention to what is to be learned, while their performance tells us how well they have learned it, and how effective our teaching has been.

What do we mean by understanding?

Most teachers would probably agree that they 'teach for understanding'. They don't want their students just to memorize, they want them to *understand*. The trouble is that 'understanding' can mean very different things.

I can 'understand' what *chat* means in French, but not 'understand' the sentence '*Le chat est assis sur la natte.*' My understanding is basic indeed, but is still 'understanding'. Then I can 'understand' the idea contained in a sentence, but miss the meaning of the theme of the text in which the sentence is embedded. I can 'understand' abstract concepts and principles, but here too ambiguity reigns. To say I 'understand' the law of supply and demand means what: that I can tell someone what the law is, that I can solve textbook problems on supply and demand, that I can make wise market decisions and make lots of money?

Entwistle and Entwistle (1997) conducted a series of studies on what students meant by 'understanding', and then asked them how they attempt to understand when preparing for examinations. The students described the experience of understanding as *satisfying*, it was good to have the feeling that you understood at last. It also felt *complete*, a whole, as previously unrelated things were suddenly integrated. The experience was *irreversible*, what is now understood cannot be 'de-understood'. Students thought a good practical test of understanding was being able to explain to someone else, or being able to adapt and to use what had been understood.

These are pretty good definitions of sound understanding that go way beyond the word and sentence levels. They probably fit most teachers' requirements: you want students to interrelate topics, to adapt and use the knowledge so understood, perhaps to explain it to others and, it is hoped, to feel satisfied and good about it.

Unfortunately, when it came to exam time, these excellent indicators of understanding evaporated. Students attempted to understand in ways that they thought would meet assessment requirements. Understanding then took on much less desirable forms. Five different forms of understanding were distinguished:

1 Reproduces content from lecture notes without any clear structure.
2 Reproduces the content within the structure used by the lecturer.
3 Develops own structure, but only to generate answers to anticipated exam questions.
4 Adjusts structures from strategic reading of different sources to represent personal understanding, but also to control examination requirements.
5 Develops an individual conception of the discipline from wide reading and reflection.

Only the last form of understanding, described by a small minority of students, is anything like their own definitions. All others focus on examination requirements. Entwistle and Entwistle find this 'worrying', because it means that in most cases the examinations actually prevented students from achieving their own personal understandings of the content. Many of these students were in their final year, just prior to professional practice, yet we find the assessment system pre-empting the very level of understanding that would be professionally relevant. Worrying indeed.

To use our learning in order to negotiate with the world and to see it differently involves understanding of a high order. It is the kind of understanding that is referred to in the rhetoric of university teaching, yet it seems to be discouraged in practice.

Understanding and institutional learning

In fact, the longer most undergraduate students (not all – not the Susans) stay in most tertiary institutions, the less deep and the more surface oriented they tend to become, and the more their understanding is assessment related. The tendency is almost universal: Australia (Watkins and Hattie 1985; Biggs 1987a), the UK (Entwistle and Ramsden 1983), Hong Kong (Gow and Kember 1990). Learning tends to become institutionalized.

Although students have excellent ideas about what understanding means in real life, in practice understanding becomes whatever they see will meet assessment requirements. Much assessment practice appears to reward retelling, retold knowledge eludes conceptual change and students lose 'ownership' over their learning and become alienated from it: 'Most of all I write what "they" like me to . . . when I get the piece of paper with BA (Hons) on it then I will write the way I want, using MY ideas.' (An arts undergraduate quoted in Watkins and Hattie 1985: 137).

Large classes that pre-empt in-depth teaching, jam-packed curricula that simply attempt too much and the apparatus surrounding accreditation – the reporting of assessment results, concerns about security – all make assessment for in-depth understanding difficult. Under these conditions, it seems understandable that only a few students acquire the sort of understanding that changes perspectives.

The reasons for most of these forces for non-understanding, and how they can be circumvented, will be discussed in due course. First, we should clarify what we do mean by understanding; then we can explicitly foster it in our teaching methods, and test for it in our assessment methods.

Performances of understanding

The Harvard Project Zero Team (Gardner 1993; Wiske 1998) focused on the higher levels of understanding in high school science. They came up with the idea that if students 'really' understood a concept they would *act differently* in contexts involving that concept, and could use the concept in unfamiliar or novel contexts. That is, real understanding is *performative*, which echoes the constructivist or level 3 view that learning changes students' perspectives on the world.

The challenge then is to conceive our teaching objectives in terms of students *performing* their understanding, rather than in getting them to declare it verbally. This also implicates teaching. In Project Zero, students are required to show their understanding by interacting 'thoughtfully' with a novel task, reflecting on appropriate feedback given to them to see how they can improve. That is how students learn complex tasks outside the classroom – just watch how they learn a computer game – but in the classroom, many performances students are required to undertake are simply routines, adequate for handling common assessment tasks, but not for the deep reflection needed in handling novel situations.

The difference between meeting the requirements of institutional learning and real understanding is illustrated in Gunstone and White's (1981) demonstrations with physics I students. In one, two balls, one heavy and one light, were held in the air in front of the students. They were then asked to predict, if the balls were released simultaneously, which one would hit the ground first, and why. Many predicted that the heavy one would 'because heavy things have a bigger force' or 'gravity is stronger nearer the earth' (both are true but irrelevant). These students had 'understood' gravity well enough to pass HSC (A level) physics, but few understood well enough to answer a fairly simple real life question about gravity. They could correctly solve problems using the formula for g – which doesn't contain a term for the mass of the object falling – while still reacting in the belief that heavy objects fall faster. They didn't *really* understand gravity in the performative sense. And the reason for that is almost certainly because their teaching and assessment didn't require them to.

Really to understand is to have one's conceptions of phenomena changed. These physics students hadn't changed their common-sense conceptions of gravity, but had placed alongside them a set of statements and formulae about physical phenomena that would see them through the exams. Their experienced world remained pre-Newtonian. Really to understand physics, or mathematics, or history, is to *think like* a physicist, a mathematician, a historian, and that shows in how you behave. Once you really understand a sector of knowledge, it changes that part of the world; you don't behave towards that domain in the same way again.

Verbal or 'declarative' levels of understanding will suffice for some purposes: for example, to explain what gravity, or the three laws of motion, are about. But is this why we are teaching these topics? Is it for acquaintance, so that students know something about the topic, and can answer the sorts of stock questions that typify examination papers? In that case, declarative understanding will suffice. Is it to change the way (sooner or later) students can understand and control reality? If that is the case, then a performative level of understanding is implicated.

In teaching the laws of motion, the Project Zero researchers required students to predict what will happen in a novel situation such as the following, and to explain why: 'During a space flight, the astronauts discover that moisture is condensing and forming snow. They decide to have a snow fight. Describe what happens.' The kind and level of understanding involved in handling this problem is analogous to that required in higher education, whether academic or professional. Graduates need to face new problems and interact with them, not only competently, but thoughtfully. Predicting, diagnosing, explaining and solving non-textbook problems are what professionals have to do, so this is what university teachers should aim to get their students to do, particularly in higher years. Building such performances of understanding into the course objectives, aligning teaching to them and designing assessment tasks that confirm that students can or cannot carry out those performances is a good way to start.

A framework for understanding understanding

So far we have been talking about the end-point, 'real' understanding. However, understanding develops gradually, becoming more structured and articulated as it does so. Undergraduates will not attain the level of precision and complexity of the subject expert, but we want none to retain the plausible misunderstandings that marked Gunstone and White's physics students' understanding of gravity. What is appropriate in the first year is unacceptable in the final years.

We thus need to define understanding in ways that do justice to the topics and content we teach, as appropriate to the year level taught, much more specifically than was outlined in the objectives column in Figure 2.2. The task is to define what is acceptable for each stage of the degree programme, given a student's specialization and degree pattern. That is a highly specific matter that only the teacher and subject expert can decide, but a general framework for structuring levels of understanding helps teachers to make those decisions, and it also provides a basis for discussing levels across different years and subject areas. Once a sound understanding of the basic structural framework is achieved, adapting it to particular unit or course objectives is straightforward.

The SOLO taxonomy is based on the study of outcomes in a variety of academic content areas (Biggs and Collis 1982). As students learn, the outcomes of their learning display similar stages of increasing structural complexity. There are two main changes: *quantitative*, as the amount of detail in the student's response increases; and *qualitative*, as that detail becomes integrated into a structural pattern. The quantitative stages of learning occur first, then learning changes qualitatively.

SOLO, which stands for Structure of the Observed Learning Outcome, provides a systematic way of describing how a learner's performance grows in complexity when mastering many academic tasks. It can thus be used to define curriculum objectives, which describe where students *should* be operating, and for evaluating learning outcomes so that we can know at what level individual students actually *are* operating.

To illustrate, let us take some content with which you are all familiar. It is set as an assessment task (Task 3.1):

> *What are approaches to learning? How can knowledge of approaches to learning enhance university teaching?*

In a few sentences, outline your answer to this question. **Stop reading any further until you have completed the task**. Then turn to Task 3.1 and try to evaluate your own response and against the model responses.

Task 3.1: SOLO Levels in Approaches to Learning question and why

The following levels of response could be observed (not, it is hoped, the first three responses).

1 Prestructural

'Teaching is a matter of getting students to approach their learning.'

This response could have been written by someone with understanding at the individual word level, but little understanding of what was discussed in the previous chapter. Prestructural responses simply miss the point, or, like this one, use tautology to cover lack of understanding. These responses can be quite sophisticated, such as the kind of elaborate tautology that politicians use to avoid answering questions, but academically they show little evidence of relevant learning.

2 Unistructural

'Approaches to learning are of two kinds, surface, which is inappropriate for the task at hand, and deep, which is appropriate. Teachers need to take this into account.'

This is unistructural because it meets only one part of the task, defining what approaches to learning are in terms of just one aspect, appropriateness. It misses other important attributes – for example, that they are ways of describing students' learning activities and what might influence them – while the reference to teaching adds nothing. Unistructural responses deal with terminology, getting on track but little more.

3 Multistructural

'Approaches to learning are of two kinds, surface, which is inappropriate for the task at hand, and deep, which is appropriate. Students using a surface approach try to fool us into believing that they understand by rote learning and quoting back to us, sometimes in great detail. Students using a deep approach try to get at the underlying meaning of their learning tasks. Teaching is about getting students to learn appropriately, not getting by with short cuts. We should therefore teach for meaning and understanding, which means encouraging them to adopt a deep approach.'

I couldn't agree more. The first part is quite detailed (but could be more so); the second part is also what good teaching is about. What's the problem? The problem is that this response does not address the key issue: *how* can knowledge of approaches enhance teaching? Not *that* they can enhance teaching. This response, if elaborated more fully, would constitute what Bereiter and Scardamalia (1987) call 'knowledge-telling': snowing with a bunch of facts, but not structuring them as required. Students see the trees but not the wood. Seeing trees is a necessary preliminary to adequate understanding, but it should not be interpreted as comprehending the wood.

4 Relational

'Approaches to learning are of two kinds . . . [etc.] The approaches come about partly because of student characteristics, but also because students react differently to their teaching environment in ways that lead them into surface or deep learning. The teaching environment is a system, a resolution of all the factors, curriculum, assessment, teaching methods and students' own characteristics. If there is imbalance in the environment – for example, a test that allows students to respond in a way that does not do justice to the curriculum, or a classroom climate that scares the hell out of them – the resolution is in favour of a surface approach. What this means is that we should be consistent . . .'

And so on. Here we have an explanation. Both concepts, approaches and teaching, have been integrated by the concept of a system; examples have been given, and the structure could easily be used to generate practical steps. The trees have become the wood, a qualitative change in learning and understanding has occurred. It is no longer a matter of listing facts and details: they address a point, making sense in light of their contribution to the topic as a whole. This is the first level at which 'understanding' in an academically relevant sense may appropriately be used.

5 Extended abstract

I won't give a lengthy example here. The essence of the extended abstract response is that it goes beyond what has been given, whereas the relational response stays with it. The coherent whole is conceptualized at a higher level of abstraction and is applied to new and broader domains. An extended response on approaches to learning would be a 'breakthrough' response, giving a perspective that changes what we think about them, and their relationship to teaching. The trouble is that today's extended abstract is tomorrow's relational. Marton and Säljö's original study was such a breakthrough, linking approaches to learning to systems theory was another, but now both are conventional wisdom.

The examples illustrate the five levels of the taxonomy. Uni- and multistructural levels see understanding as a quantitative increase in what is grasped. These responses were deliberately constructed to show that the higher level contains the lower level, plus a bit more. The 'bit more' in the case of multistructural incorporates the unistructural, then more of the same – a purely quantitative increase. The 'bit more' in the case of relational over multistructural involves a conceptual restructuring of the components, the recognition of the systems property as integrating the components, while the next shift to extended abstract takes the argument into a new dimension. SOLO describes a hierarchy, where each partial construction becomes the foundation on which further learning is built. A neat example of how teachers' conceptions of learning fit SOLO is given by Boulton-Lewis (1998).

This distinction between knowing more and restructuring parallels two major curriculum aims: to *increase knowledge* (quantitative: unistructural becoming increasingly multistructural); and to *deepen understanding* (qualitative: relational, then extended abstract). Teaching and assessment that focus only on the quantitative aspects of learning will miss the more important higher-level aspects. Quantitative conceptions of teaching and learning address the first aim only, so that the deepening of understanding is left to Susan's predilections for spontaneous deep learning activities. The challenge for us is to highlight the qualitative aim in the objectives, and support it by both teaching and assessment methods. Then Robert's understanding is likely to be deepened too.

How SOLO is used to construct particular objectives is developed in a later section, after we have clarified the kinds of knowledge we are looking for.

Understanding of what? Kinds of knowledge

Knowledge is the object of understanding, but knowledge comes in various kinds. *Declarative*, or propositional, knowledge refers to knowing-about things, or knowing-what: knowing about what Freud said, knowing what the terms of an equation refer to, knowing what kinds of cloud formations can be distinguished, knowing what were the important events in Shakespeare's life. Such content knowledge accrues from research, not from personal experience. It is public knowledge, subject to rules of evidence that make it verifiable, replicable and logically consistent. It is what is in libraries and textbooks, and is what teachers 'declare' in lectures. Students' understanding of it can be tested by getting them to declare it back, in their own words and using their own examples. If you use SOLO, you can classify the levels of their understanding, right up to extended abstract.

Functioning knowledge is based on the idea of performances of understanding. This knowledge is within the experience of the learner, who can now put declarative knowledge to work by solving problems, designing buildings, planning teaching or performing surgery. Functioning knowledge requires a solid foundation of declarative knowledge, at relational level at least, but it also involves: (a) knowing how to do things, such as carrying out procedures or enacting skills ('procedural' knowledge); and (b) knowing when to do these things, and why ('conditional' knowledge).

Procedural knowledge on its own is skill-based, lacking the high-level declarative foundation; it is a matter of getting the sequences and actions right, knowing what to do when a given situation arises, having the right competencies. Conditional knowledge incorporates both procedural and higher-level declarative knowledge at a theoretical level, so that one knows when, why and under what conditions one should do this as opposed to that. The combination turns procedural knowledge into functioning knowledge, which is flexible and wide-ranging. The relationship between these

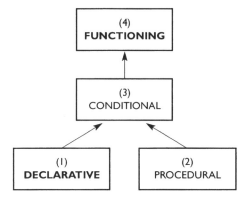

Figure 3.1: Relationships between different kinds of knowledge

kinds of knowledge is given in Figure 3.1. In sum, functioning knowledge (4) involves declarative knowledge (1) (the academic knowledge base), procedural knowledge (2) (having the skills) and conditional knowledge (3) (knowing the circumstances for using them). These distinctions relate to what our curricula should be about – and we have to get the distinctions straight.

To illustrate how straight we have to get them, consider how Leinhardt *et al.* (1995) put 'professional' knowledge in actual opposition to 'university' knowledge:

- *Professional knowledge* is procedural, specific and pragmatic. It deals with executing, applying and making priorities.
- *University knowledge* is declarative, abstract and conceptual. It deals with labelling, differentiating, elaborating and justifying.

It seems that would-be professionals are trained in universities to label, differentiate, elaborate and justify, when what they need out in the field is to execute, apply and prioritize!

Leinhardt *et al.* are making much the same point as did Entwistle and Entwistle (1997): the forms of understanding which university accreditation and assessment procedures encourage are not those that are professionally relevant. The rhetoric is right, but in practice the university focuses on declarative knowledge, which students often see as irrelevant, and hence worthy of only a surface approach.

Traditionally, teaching for the professions has involved declarative knowledge (1), with a skills component as procedural knowledge (2) taught separately in practice (the parentheses refer to Figure 3.1). The problem here is that integrating the two domains is then left up to the student. If the target is *functioning* knowledge (4), however, the theoretical (declarative) knowledge needs to be developed to relation/extended abstract levels in order to provide both the knowledge of the specific context and the conditional knowledge (3) that enable the skills to be performed adequately.

It is a matter of integrating several domains of knowledge, a task for which problem-based learning is particularly well suited (see Chapter 10). But however we do it, in designing our objectives we should be ensuring that by the exit level at graduation, students' knowledge is alive and functioning.

Getting the curriculum in focus

Why use curriculum objectives?

At this point, we should distinguish between goals or aims of teaching (in this context 'aim' and 'goal' are synonymous) and curriculum objectives. All teachers have an overall aim or goal: 'to teach for understanding' is such an aim; 'to produce general practitioners with a concern for treating the whole patient in the community context' is a more specific aim, but it is still an aim.

An objective is much more specific; it not only refers to content topics, but contains a *criterion* for the level of learning required, and that the assessment tasks can address (hence 'criterion-referenced assessment'). A 'performance of understanding' is an example of an objective.

Objectives are unpopular with some educators. They recall the bad, old days of behavioural objectives, which many once thought trivialized education (e.g. MacDonald-Ross 1973). Behavioural objectives were born from an exclusively quantitative conception of teaching and learning, which meant that when objectives were defined it was in quantitative terms, in units of knowledge (see Chapter 2, p. 22), while the assessment process amounted to counting the number of items acceptably performed. Teaching meant 'teaching to the test' (Popham and Husek 1969; Cohen 1987). The alignment was excellent, but what was aligned was a very narrow band of essentially low-level and fragmented activities.

With constructive alignment, on the contrary, objectives are defined not just in terms of content, but in terms of the level of understanding applied to that content. The focus is not just on *what* students know, which is when teaching to the test becomes highly suspect, but on *how well* they know it.

But can complex learning be specified in advance to the degree required by curriculum objectives? Is it not like the drunk who only looks for his lost keys under the street light? That is, what is interesting and important is what you can't see, not what you can.

To make the objectives up-front and salient is not to exclude other desirable but unforeseen or unforeseeable outcomes. The most interesting research is that which yields the unintended and unforeseen. Thus, being clear about what we do want in no way pre-empts us from welcoming unexpected outcomes from our students' learning. In fact, higher-level activities are open-ended, as indicated by verbs like 'generalize', 'solve unseen problems', 'develop a theory to explain why . . .' Particular outcomes are here unspecified, it is only the process that is specified, and that allows for surprises in plenty. It is very important that our assessment procedures encourage students to surprise us – pleasantly, of course – and that our grading procedures are sufficiently flexible to allow us to give them credit when they do (see Chapter 9). Asking them questions to which we already know the answers, when they know that we know, is not only unnatural, it is asking to be bored rigid when assessing students' performances.

So we are not being rabid behaviourists, nor are we being too closed or restrictive in thinking of objectives in terms of the activities we want our students to perform. Specifying objectives in this way gives us the best of both worlds. We are making it very clear in what direction we want to go, but if a student wants to go further and explore the hinterland, that is even better.

The relation between curriculum objectives and assessment

In aligned teaching, assessment after teaching has been completed is conducted to tell us how well students have learned what we intended them to learn, and at what level. This *criterion-referenced* assessment is not to be confused with *norm-referenced* assessment, the function of which is to compare students' performances with each other. Norm-referenced assessment should not apply in normal teaching, as elaborated in Chapter 8.

The curriculum objectives form the central pillar of teaching a unit or module, as we saw in Figure 2.2; they express what we want the students to understand after we have taught the unit, in a range of acceptability that is reflected in the grading system. Some students' understandings will be inadequate, in which case they fail. The understanding of some others will be passable, but no more than that. Yet others will display better understandings. A few, but the more the better, will have an exemplary understanding and control over what we have taught them.

The aim is to specify these levels of understanding in advance and embody them in the objectives. That is what we are going to do now.

Steps in defining objectives

We might start by clarifying what objectives are, and what they are not. The following is not an objective, although it is sometimes mistaken for one:

> Introduce the topic in terms of its relation to last week's lecture. Elaborate for about 15 minutes (No more! Watch the clock!), then the video *Coronary Occlusions: Part 2*. Get the students to converse in pairs, getting them to specify the links between the video's position and my lectures. Summarize and round off.

This is a great way to remind the teacher how to conduct the class, but it is not an objective. Objectives are concerned with the students' learning activities, not the teacher's teaching activities.

Neither will it do simply to say that 'at the end of this unit, students will be able to understand the concept of muscle tone and its relation to functional activity' (taken from the objectives for an occupational therapy unit). But what does it *mean* 'to understand' the concept of muscle tone. What learning activities are involved? What *level* of understanding are the students to achieve? The following further steps are needed.

1   *Decide what kind of knowledge is to be involved.* Are the objectives to rate as declarative knowledge only: knowing about phenomena, theories, disciplines? Or functioning knowledge: requiring the student to exercise active control over problems and decisions in the appropriate content domains? The objectives should be clear as to what kind of knowledge you want and why.

2   *Select the topics to teach.* Selecting the actual topics to teach is obviously a matter of specific content expertise and judgement. You, as the content expert, are best able to decide on this, but note the inevitable tension between coverage and depth of understanding.

There is almost always strong pressure to include more and more content, particularly perhaps in professional faculties where outside bodies validate courses. Each panel member thinks his or her own specialism is absolutely vital, and must be given 'adequate' (= intensive) treatment. Committees tend to resolve matters by including the lot, to the detriment of the students' learning. The same thing is likely when teachers share the teaching of a unit; all see their own topic as the most important. Over-teaching is the inevitable result. We need always to bear in mind that:

> The greatest enemy of understanding is coverage – I can't repeat that often enough. If you're determined to cover a lot of things, you are guaranteeing that most kids will not understand, because they haven't had time enough to go into things in depth, to figure out what the requisite understanding is, and be able to perform that understanding in different situations.
>
> (Gardner 1993: 24)

If we conceive the curriculum as a rectangle, the product of breadth times depth remains constant. Take your pick. Breadth: wide coverage and surface learning giving disjointed multistructural outcomes. Or depth:

fewer topics and deep learning giving relational and extended abstract outcomes. Do you want a curriculum 'a mile wide and half an inch deep', as US educators described the school mathematics curriculum following the abysmal performance of US senior high school students in the recent Third International Mathematics and Science Study (quoted in Stedman 1997)? Or do you want your students *really* to understand what you have taught them?

In fact, the area of the curriculum isn't quite constant. Good teaching increases the area, maintaining depth. But there are limits, and there is little doubt that most courses in all universities contain more content than students can handle at little more than the level of acquaintance. However, when modes of assessment go no deeper than acquaintance, such as may happen with short answer or multiple-choice, the students are out of trouble and the problem remains invisible (see Chapter 9).

3 *The purpose for teaching the topic, and hence the level of knowledge desirable for students to acquire.* Why are you teaching this particular topic? Is it simply to delineate boundaries, to give students a broad picture of what's 'there'? Is it to inform on a current state of play, to bring students up to date on the state of the topic or discipline? Is it to stockpile knowledge, of no perceived use for the present, but likely to be needed later? Is it to inform decisions that need making now? These purposes imply different levels of understanding.

Declarative knowledge in a professional education programme may be taught for various reasons:

(a) As general 'cultural' content, as in the liberal arts notion of an educated person; e.g. a business management student must take an arts subject for 'broadening'. There is no functioning knowledge involved here.
(b) As content specifically related to the profession; e.g. the history of Western architecture in an Architecture degree. This is important background for architects to have, but again there may be little direct bearing on functioning knowledge.
(c) As content which does bear on functioning knowledge, but is not a key priority. In this case, students might be taught the basic outlines and where to go for more details as the need arises.
(d) As content which definitely bears on everyday decision-making. High-level declarative knowledge is now not enough, but it is an essential foundation for functioning knowledge. In the past, the declarative knowledge alone has often been taught, its application being left to the students.

All these different purposes for teaching a topic or subject unit require careful thought as to coverage and depth. The curriculum is not a plateau of topics, all covered to the same extent, but hills and valleys. In an international phone call, you don't chat about the weather. We need similarly to prioritize our classroom communications.

Usually, we spend more or less time on a topic according to its importance. That is one way of addressing the issue, but what we really mean by priority is that important topics should be *understood at a higher level* than less important topics. An important topic should be understood so that students can use it, or solve problems with it. With less important topics, acquaintance may be sufficient. We can signal importance by allocating a level of understanding for each topic. This is discussed below.

4   *Putting the package of objectives together and relating them to assessment tasks so that the results can be reported as a final grade.* We now have a package of objectives that specifies the content and level of understanding that we address in our teaching, and that students will attempt to learn. The question remains: how do we assess these separate objectives so that we can derive a single grade category for each student?

Of the above steps, 1 and 2 are ones that teachers themselves can address, bearing in mind the points made above. Step 4 is a matter of assessment strategy, which is addressed in Chapter 9. Step 3 is what remains for this chapter: how to define our priorities as levels of understanding.

Setting up criterion-referenced objectives

We now look at how we may delineate the ranges of understanding we need in teaching our units, and define our priorities in terms of levels of understanding for different topics. The levels of understanding can be described as verbs in ascending order of cognitive complexity that parallel the SOLO taxonomy. This gives us a wide range of levels that can be adapted to the levels appropriate to particular units, from first to higher years.

High-level, extended abstract involvement is indicated by such verbs as 'theorize', 'hypothesize', 'generalize', 'reflect', 'generate' and so on. They call for the student to conceptualize at a level extending beyond what has been dealt with in actual teaching. The next level of involvement, relational, is indicated by 'apply', 'integrate', 'analyse', 'explain' and the like; they indicate orchestration between facts and theory, action and purpose. 'Classify', 'describe', 'list' indicate a multistructural level of involvement: the understanding of boundaries, but not of systems. 'Memorize', 'identify', 'recognize' are unistructural: direct, concrete, each sufficient to itself, but minimalistic. Figure 3.2 illustrates the point visually. A relevant component is depicted as $\mathbf{|}$, so that unistructural has one of them, multistructural several, relational integrates them with a concept or structure, and extended abstract generalizes them to a new area. With each step,

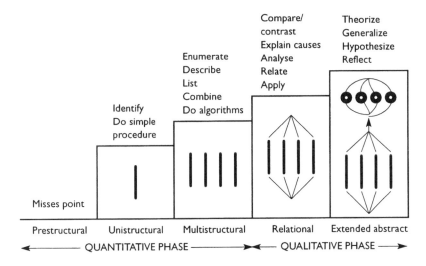

Figure 3.2: A hierarchy of verbs that may be used to form curriculum objectives

typical verbs are associated that might be useful in formulating curriculum objectives:

The verbs in the staircase are general, indicating what each family, from lowest to highest, might look like. Particular content areas and topics would have their own specific verbs as well, which you would need to specify to suit your own unit. The following questions need addressing:

- Why are you teaching the subject? To acquaint students with the topics within an area, or as a central plank in their understanding (see pp. 44–6)?
- Is it an introductory or advanced subject? In first-year subjects taught for acquaintance, an extended abstract or theoretical level of understanding is likely to be too high for even an A grade. The answer also varies according to why students are enrolled: a pass in anatomy I might be defined differently for students in first year medicine, and for students in a diploma in occupational therapy.

These decisions will fall within any range definable by the four SOLO levels, which can refer to specific terminology, to theories and to principles. This is a broad range, and it helps to subdivide the SOLO categories. This can be done in any way that suits. An example follows, with (a) and (b) referring to simple and complex levels, respectively, within each category:

Unistructural
(a) simple naming, terminology;
(b) focusing on one conceptual issue in a complex case.

(b) is clearly more abstract and higher level, but is unistructural in that only one feature is given serious consideration.

Multistructural
(a) a disorganized collection of items, a 'shopping list';
(b) 'knowledge-telling': a strategy used in essay-writing in which the student 'snows' the marker with masses of detail, often using a narrative *genre* inappropriately but with the desired effect (Bereiter and Scardamalia 1987).

(a) is a simple list, which may nevertheless be adequate for some purposes, while (b) may well address abstract content, and be quite impressive in its way, although in most cases the structure is simplified and wrong (see p. 38).

Relational
(a) understanding, using a concept that *integrates* a collection of data;
(b) understanding how to *apply* the concept to a familiar data set or to a problem.

(a) is a declarative understanding, (b) functioning, which requires (a) for the application to work. Many tertiary objectives require this distinction. We see an example from physiotherapy in Box 9.3.

Extended abstract
(a) relating to existing principle, so that unseen problems can be handled;
(b) questioning and going beyond existing principles.

(a) is probably the highest level in most undergraduate work, with (b) a surprising bonus if it occurs. (b) is often called 'post-formal', the sort of understanding required to do postgraduate research (Collis and Biggs 1983).

As SOLO gives a good sense of the hierarchy in learning, it may be a useful guide for defining the grading categories as appropriate to one's own subject (Biggs 1992a). Individual teachers can use it or not as they wish to derive their own categories. Some will find their own experience sufficient in itself.

However the levels are derived, they need to be delineated clearly, and verbs help in doing that. In particular, the use of verbs to structure the objectives emphasizes that learning and understanding come from student activity. Practically speaking, verbs are concrete, easy for you to handle and for students to understand, and they can be related to all stages of teaching: objectives, teaching/learning activities and assessment tasks. The discipline would determine what verbs would be appropriate. A useful exercise would be to list some of the key verbs in your teaching of a particular unit, at those levels you designate (see Task 3.2).

I have suggested the letter grades A, B, C, D here. Other systems refer to

---

Task 3.2: Devise a grading scheme for a focus unit

Define grading categories in terms of levels of understanding that you think are appropriate to your grading system. Letter grades are used here (A to D), but write in whatever terms you use (HD, D, Credit, P . . .). Figure 3.1 suggests some general verbs to help you, see also the text (pp. 47–9) and Figure 4.1.

A (or   ):_____

_____

_____

B (or   ):_____

_____

_____

C (or   ):_____

_____

_____

D (or   ):_____

_____

_____

Is it clear what you are trying to get the students to learn? How could you know if they have learned it?

---

high distinction, distinction, credit, pass or to number grades 1 to 7, or 1 to 9. The degree itself might be graded first class honours, upper second, lower second, third and/or pass. The question of grading categories is dealt with in full in Chapter 9.

The easiest step to decide is: what is *minimally acceptable?* That becomes D. This will almost certainly contain a *mix* of categories of verb: correct terminology, a certain amount of coverage, declarative understanding at a multistructural level for important topic concepts, but some room for misunderstandings with regard to more complex, or more fringe, concepts.

The cocktail of verbs you decide here is obviously a matter of judgement, which can't be taken from a book, not even this one. But aim to define a *certain quality* of performance: a 'D-ness', if you like, that marks minimum acceptability.

Next, define A: what does the sort of performance look like that you would describe as *the best you could hope to expect* in this unit, for this level, for these students? What does 'A-ness' comprise? Being original, using novel examples, relating to first principles, high levels of declarative understanding, demonstrated mastery over concepts and techniques . . . I don't know, you'll have to work that out to suit the unit. But the smorgasbord of high-level, relational and extended abstract verbs will certainly help you to do that.

Having now defined the limits, barely acceptable and marvellous, you can fill in the remaining categories of 'B-ness' and 'C-ness' (or whatever grading categories you use). I have put it like that, as 'X-ness', to emphasize that there is a flavour, a *quality*, that defines categories of performance, that can be captured with the mixture of verbs as applied to the unit content. The content defines *what* to teach, the verb to *what level* it is to be understood. In Chapter 5 we see that the verbs also suggest *how* it might be taught.

The categories should not be defined in terms of ranges of marks along a continuum, such as 'high distinction is 85 per cent and above'. Quantitative definitions of a grade make true criterion-referencing extremely difficult. Because the target of 85 per cent is a heterogeneous sum, students have little idea as to what being 'highly distinguished' means in terms of their understanding of the subject matter. What qualitative difference can there be between 84 and 85 per cent? But we are told there is a whole grade of difference: one is highly distinguished and the other only distinguished. What this tells students is to scramble for as many marks as they can rustle up. Any dispute about grading then becomes a niggling quibble about a mark extra here, a mark extra there. This is demeaning for both student and teacher.

In the case of defining grades qualitatively, the grade itself tells students something meaningful about the nature of their learning. A dispute over grading becomes a one-on-one seminar on the nature of their learning, why the level of their understanding falls short and what they would have to do to demonstrate that it be graded higher. This is altogether a more fruitful, meaningful and dignified encounter, in which some new learning might actually take place.

This chapter on deriving objectives has involved discussion of assessment-related issues, which is closely implicated in a criterion-referenced system. We therefore revisit some of these issues in Chapters 8 and 9, while Chapter 10 contains an example of deriving objectives that you might find helpful.

Summary and conclusions

What do we mean by understanding?

While teachers universally 'teach for understanding', there are institutional obstacles that prevent them from doing so; especially, but not only, in overcrowded curricula and in assessment systems. 'Understanding' is a word of many values; we express one meaning, we assess another. In making our objectives clear it is essential that we unpack and make explicit the meanings we want our students to address. The very highest levels of understanding that we want students to display by the end of a degree programme – and in some cases very much before the end – are seen as 'performative'. Students need to understand what we teach them to the extent that a particular sector of their world has changed, and is now coming under their control.

A framework for understanding understanding

We need a way of describing how understanding grows and unfolds. As understanding develops, it becomes more structured and articulated, as described in the SOLO taxonomy. In learning a new topic, understanding moves through a quantitative phase, from uni- to multistructural, which involves finding out more and more facts. These are the 'bricks' of understanding, which form more or less elaborate and original working structures at the relational and extended abstract levels. SOLO provides a framework for formulating teaching objectives.

The object of understanding is knowledge. It is important to distinguish several kinds. Declarative (propositional) knowledge refers to knowing about things, and at the higher levels is about understanding theory in the abstract; it is independent of the experience of the learner. Functioning knowledge involves the academic declarative knowledge base, but also the procedural skills, and conditions and circumstances for using them; it needs to be brought within the experience of the learner. These distinctions are important in sorting out what students need to understand, as in know about; and what students need to understand, as in put to empowered use.

Getting the curriculum in focus

Before deciding particular objectives we need to:

1 Decide what kind of knowledge is to be involved.
2 Select the topics to teach. But beware: 'The greatest enemy of understanding is coverage . . .'

3 Decide the purpose for teaching the topic, and hence the level of knowledge desirable for students to acquire. We need to prioritize, by requiring that important topics are understood at a higher level than less important topics.

4 Put the package of objectives together and relate them to assessment tasks so that the results can be reported as a final grade.

Prioritizing objectives is done in terms of the verbs related to each level of understanding: important topics are assigned a higher level of understanding than less important. The SOLO taxonomy is useful for providing a 'staircase of verbs' that can be used selectively to define the ranges of understanding needed. Using verbs to structure the objectives emphasizes that learning and understanding come from student activity, while, practically speaking, verbs can be used to align objectives, teaching/learning activities and assessment tasks.

Setting up criterion-referenced objectives

To define each grading category (A to D) qualitatively, the following steps occur:

1 Decide what is *minimally acceptable*. That becomes D. There will be a mix of categories of verb, allowing for low-level verbs and poorly enacted high-level. Aim to define a *quality* of performance, a 'D-ness', that marks minimum acceptability.

2 Define *the best performance you could hope to expect* in this unit. What is the nature of 'A-ness'? A smattering of extended abstract verbs, perhaps.

3 Define the remaining categories, B and C, using the mixture of verbs and content topic. The topic defines *what* to teach, the verb to *what level* it is to be understood.

Qualitatively defined grades tell students something meaningful. A dispute over grading becomes a seminar on the nature of their learning, not a demeaning quibble over mark-sized trivia: more on that in Chapters 9 and 10.

Further reading

Biggs, J. B. and Collis, K. F. (1982) *Evaluating the Quality of Learning: the SOLO Taxonomy*, New York: Academic Press.

Biggs, J. B. (1992) A qualitative approach to grading students, *HERDSA News*, 14(3), 3–6.

Boulton-Lewis, G. M. (1998) Applying the SOLO taxonomy to learning in higher education, in B. Dart and G. Boulton-Lewis (eds) *Teaching and Learning in Higher Education*, Camberwell, Vic.: Australian Council for Educational Research.

Toohey, S. (1999) *Designing Courses for Universities*, Buckingham: Open University Press.

The first goes into the derivation of SOLO in detail, the second focuses specifically on using SOLO for defining grading categories and objectives. Toohey is concerned with designing courses, rather than curriculum objectives for units, but similar principles apply, and it is in any case important that there is consistency across units within the same course.

4

Setting the stage for effective teaching

Effective teaching means setting up the teaching/learning context so that students have every encouragement to react with the level of cognitive engagement that our objectives require. There are several aspects to this: motivation, climate and the elicitation of the specific teaching/learning activities that are likely to lead to the outcomes we want. The last question, what teaching methods to use, we leave to Chapters 5 and 6. The present chapter is concerned with the two preliminary issues: getting students to agree that appropriate task engagement is a good idea (otherwise known as 'motivation'), and the kind of climate we create in our interactions with our students.

The two faces of good teaching

In Chapter 3 we set our objectives by tying levels of understanding to the cognitive activities, expressed as verbs, most likely to realize those objectives. The function of teaching is to activate those verbs with appropriate teaching/learning activities, or TLAs. That is one face of good teaching: to encourage students to use a deep approach. The second face of good teaching is to discourage students from using a surface approach. To do this, we need to identify any factors in our own teaching that might have this effect, and eliminate them.

There is a range of verbs from high to low cognitive level that need to be activated in learning our unit. The highest would refer to such activities as reflecting, theorizing and so on, the lowest to memorizing, and in between are various levels of activity. When using a deep approach, students use the full range of desired learning activities; they learn terminology, they memorize formulae, but move from there to applying these formulae to new examples, and so on. When using a surface approach, there is a shortfall; students handle all tasks, low and high, with low-level verbs ('two pages of writing etc. . . .'). The teaching challenge is to prevent this shortfall from occurring, or to correct it where it has occurred. This situation is depicted in Figure 4.1.

Cognitive level of learning activities

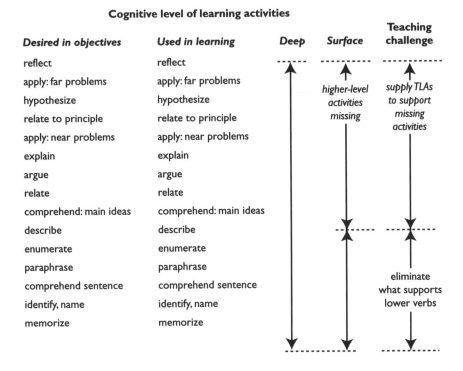

Desired in objectives	Used in learning	Deep	Surface	Teaching challenge
reflect	reflect			
apply: far problems	apply: far problems		higher-level activities missing	supply TLAs to support missing activities
hypothesize	hypothesize			
relate to principle	relate to principle			
apply: near problems	apply: near problems			
explain	explain			
argue	argue			
relate	relate			
comprehend: main ideas	comprehend: main ideas			
describe	describe			
enumerate	enumerate			
paraphrase	paraphrase			eliminate what supports lower verbs
comprehend sentence	comprehend sentence			
identify, name	identify, name			
memorize	memorize			

Figure 4.1: Desired and actual level of engagement, approaches to learning and enhancing teaching

Supporting the full range of activities, the deep approach, is what the rest of this book is about. Preventing the surface approach is the main thrust of this chapter. This is a matter of finding out: first, what in our teaching actually discourages students from engaging the set learning tasks at the appropriate level of cognitive activity; and, second, doing our best to eliminate those factors (see Figure 4.1). These negative aspects of teaching are as much affective, related to feelings, as they are cognitive. They are to do with motivation, and the sort of learning or classroom climate we create in our relationships with students.

The costs and benefits of getting involved

Level 1 thinking sees motivation as a substance that students possess in varying quantities, good students having lots, poor students little or none. Level 3 thinking sees motivation as an outcome of teaching, but that is after engaging the task. What about motivation in the initial sense, of deciding whether or not to engage the task at all? Two factors make students (or anyone) want to learn something:

1 It has to be important; it must have some *value* to the learner.
2 It must be possible to do the learning task; the learner has to *expect success.*

No one wants to do something he or she sees as worthless. Neither do people want to do something, however valued, if they believe they have no chance of succeeding. In both cases, doing the task will be seen as a waste of time.

This common-sense theory of why students do or do not learn is called the *expectancy-value* theory of motivation, which says that if anyone is to engage an activity, he or she needs both to value the outcome and to expect success in achieving it (Feather 1982). Value and expectancy are said to 'multiply', not add, because both factors need to be present; if either one is zero, then no motivated activity occurs.

Expectancy-value theory is particularly relevant in the early stages of learning, before interest has developed to carry continued engagement along with it. The following true incident illustrates this clearly:

> When we got to the Psych I lectures, the Stats lecturer said 'Anyone who can't follow this isn't fit to be at University'. That was the first message I got. I *was* having difficulty with Stats and so I thought, maybe he's right, maybe university isn't for me. I liked the rest of Psych but couldn't handle the Stats and had to withdraw.
>
> Next year, funny thing, I did Maths I and we came to probability theory, much the same stuff that I'd bombed out in last year. But the lecturer there said 'Probability is quite hard really. You'll need to work at it. You're welcome to come to me for help if you really need it . . .'
>
> It was like a blinding light. It wasn't *me* after all! This stuff really was *hard,* but if I tried it might just work. That year I got a Credit in that part of the subject.
>
> (A mature age student, quoted in Biggs and Moore 1993: 272)

This story has important implications for understanding what motivates students.

What makes students expect to succeed, or to fail?

This student initially had been led to believe she had no chance of success. Her first teacher attributed success to ability, she perceived she was not succeeding, so she naturally concluded she didn't have the ability needed. As this was something beyond her control, she concluded she had no chance of ever succeeding. Her second teacher attributed success instead to effort, which is something the student could control. With that came the liberating realization that what was certain failure could now be possible success. So she engaged the task, and did in fact succeed. The reasons for that transformation are very instructive.

With a history of successful engagement with content that is personally meaningful, the student both builds up the knowledge base needed for deep learning and, motivationally, develops the expectations that give confidence in future success: what are known as feelings of self-efficacy and 'ownership' ('I can do this; this is my thing'). The most direct way expectations of success are instilled is on the basis of previous success, but only if the conditions that are believed to lead to success remain unchanged. If a student believes that a particular success was due to factors that might change, and that are uncontrollable, such as luck, or dependence on a particular teacher, belief in future success is diminished.

Westerners and Asians differ significantly in their attributions for success and failure. Westerners tend to see success as being attributable more to ability than to effort, while ethnic Chinese see effort as more important. This is possibly one reason why Chinese students do so well in international comparisons of attainment (see Chapter 7).

Norm- and criterion-referenced assessment send different messages about likely future performance. In norm-referenced assessment, students see the game as competitive; to get a high grade they have to beat other students, which puts a premium on the importance of relative ability as determining the outcome. In criterion-referenced assessment, students see the situation as a designated learning experience; to get a high grade they have to know the goals and learn how to get there, with a premium on attributions involving effort, study skill and knowing the right procedures. The results of norm-referenced assessment depend on the abilities of other students, over which there is no control, while in criterion-referenced assessment, they depend on each student learning the appropriate knowledge and skills: the ball is in the student's court.

These attributions are also sensitive to teacher feedback, as the student's story on learning statistics makes very clear. The maths I teacher made students see that it was up to them. Feedback about process also encourages belief in future success, which again is easier with criterion-referenced assessment: 'This is what you did, this is what you might have done, this is how to get a better result.' How does norm-referenced feedback, such as 'You are below average on this . . .' help? What does Robert do with *that* information? This is not to say that some students don't want to be told where they stand in relation to their peers, but that information has little to do with teaching and learning. It is nice to be told that you're cleverer than most other students, but not very helpful for learning how to improve your performance. To be told, directly or indirectly, that you're dumber than most others is simply destructive.

Task 4.1: What messages of success and failure do I convey to my students?

Hopeful messages: *success is due to ability, failure to lack of effort or skill.*

Hopeless messages: *success is due to luck, failure to lack of ability.*

Think back on some recent communications to students – such as comments in class, body language, handling questions, writing comments on assignments, describing what it takes to succeed, descriptions of tasks, readings and so on. Do you think you convey hopeful, or hopeless, messages? Write down a couple of telling examples:

1   _____

_____

_____

_____

2   _____

_____

_____

_____

To instil expectations of failure, as did our statistics lecturer with consummate skill, is easy to do. This is classic blame-the-student stuff: attributing success to ability, and failure to lack of ability, or to some other entity that lies fixed within the student. A very valuable act of self-reflection as a teacher is to monitor what you say, how you say it and what comments you write in students' assignments. What does the subtext say about future failure?

Task 4.1 asks you to think of the hopeless and hopeful messages you might convey.

What creates value?

Next, we look at the second term in the expectancy-value formula. What makes a task worth doing? How can we enhance the value of the task to the students? The general answer is clear enough: make their work important to them. Work can be important in various ways, each one producing a familiar category of motivation:

- what the outcome produces (extrinsic motivation);
- what other people value (social motivation);
- the opportunity for ego-enhancement (achievement motivation);
- the process of doing it (intrinsic motivation).

1   *Extrinsic motivation.* When students are motivated extrinsically they perform the task because of the value or importance they attach to what the outcome brings. There are two subcategories:

(a) *Positive reinforcement,* where the student performs in order to obtain something positive following success, such as a material reward.
(b) *Negative reinforcement,* where the student performs in order to avoid something negative, a punishment, that would follow failure or non-engagement.

The student's focus in both cases is not on the process, or even on the product, but on the consequences of the product: obtaining reward (e.g. a pass) or avoiding punishment (a failure). The quality of learning is usually low under extrinsic conditions, particularly negative reinforcement. The task itself is instrumental; the focus of attention is on getting what you want, or on not getting what you don't want, the task only something to be got out of the way. Extrinsic motivation is a standing invitation to students to adopt a surface approach. Negative reinforcement is worse than positive, because if the learning is not successful, punishment is implicated, which introduces a range of side issues.

2   *Social motivation.* Students learn in order to please people whose opinions are important to them. If the processes of studying, or the fruits of a good education, are valued by other people important to the student, education may take on an intrinsic importance to the student. This is very evident in some families, particularly Asian families, who have a high regard for education. In these circumstances, children are likely to accept that education is a good thing, to be pursued without question. Motivation here is not focused on material consequences, and social motivation is a good precursor for intrinsic motivation itself. We can usually trace the beginning of our interest in something to someone else who exhibited that interest to us. We then want to be like him or her. This is the process called 'modelling', where the models are admired and readily identified with. University teachers can be models, as was evident in the Oxbridge tutorial system, and often still is in postgraduate supervision. At the undergraduate level today, cult figures and peers are more likely to be the models, which academically speaking is not likely to be so fruitful.

3   *Achievement motivation.* Students may learn in order to enhance their egos by competing against other students and beating them. It makes them

feel good about themselves. This can often lead to high achievement, and tends even to be associated with deep learning (Biggs 1987a), but the aims of deep learning and of achievement motivation ultimately diverge. The one is concerned with handling the task as appropriately as possible, the other as *grade-effectively* as possible. Achievement motivation in the raw is not a pretty sight, killing collaborative learning. Other students are competitors, not colleagues; key references are hidden or mutilated. Achievement motivation needs competitive conditions in which to work, and while that suits the minority of students who are positively motivated by competition, it actually damages the learning of those who perceive competition as threatening. Achievement motivation, like anxiety, changes the priorities of students, because content mastery plays second fiddle either to winning or to avoiding the appearance of losing. More students are turned *off* and work less well under competitive conditions than those who are turned on and work better.

4 *Intrinsic motivation.* Here there are no outside trappings necessary to make students feel good. They learn because they are interested in the task or activity itself. They do mathematics for the intellectual pleasure of problem-solving and exercising their skill, independently of any rewards that might be involved. The point is to travel rather than to arrive. Intrinsic motivation drives deep learning and the best academic work.

Such motivation has a long history in the individual, which includes successful and rewarding engagement previously in the same content area. Susan does not turn up at university to study mathematics without a long and successful previous involvement in mathematics; she not only has a solid background of content knowledge, but that extra spark that causes her to question, to wonder, to hypothesize alternatives. She is already motivated; she presents few problems to teachers.

The problem is created by students who are like Robert was initially. They will have their own largely pragmatic ways of valuing their studies, but these values will be broad, lacking the focus on particular topics that interest creates. Their motives will derive from the meal-ticket, parental and other social pressures, possibly a generalized need for status, perhaps lack of other employment alternatives. Of course they want to graduate, in the long term, but that is marginally related to the here-and-now of getting involved with an academic task. In the absence of an immediate felt need, it has to be created, and that is where selling the cost-benefits positively is so important. How can one create the value in the task if it is not already felt by the students?

We are quickly back to assessment. A common cry is that students will not spend time learning a topic if they think it is not going to be assessed. Therefore, the word goes out that the topic *will* be assessed, and so they had better study it. This is a double-edged strategy. If that is the topic's only value, then this is an excellent way of *de*valuing it. The subtext says: 'The only value of this topic is that I have decided to test you on it!'

In a criterion-referenced or aligned system of instruction, this does not happen. The reason why the topic is being tested is because it was thought important enough to be overtly included in the objectives in the first place. The fact that it is there establishes its value, even if the student at this stage cannot see why. Our conclusion must be: *unless assessment tasks mirror the official curriculum they will erode it.* Assessing outside, or below, the curriculum gives irrelevant or counter-productive tasks a false value, such as 'saying who said what on two sides of paper'.

It also depends on the kind of climate that has been created. I was told of one teacher who informed his senior undergraduate class: 'You're going to hate the next couple of weeks; I know I am. I see absolutely no point in this form of linguistic analysis, but there it is, it's in the syllabus and we've got to cover it.' Amazingly, the student who told me this had found that topic to be the most interesting part of the course, and was designing a dissertation proposal around it! Susan can of course cope with this kind of thing; she has her own reasons for valuing the topic. But Robert, who has nothing but the teacher's word for it, will see the topic as valueless, hence not worth learning, except for the most cynical of reasons.

Using social motivation is a far superior strategy to the assessment ploy to get the students going initially: for example, by displaying enthusiasm for the subject. Teachers who love their subject, and show it, can be inspirational. The fact that here is someone who does perceive great value in it will cause the students to be curious, to seek some of that value.

Students need to find academic activities meaningful and worthwhile. Nowhere is this clearer than in problem-based learning, where real-life problems become the context in which students learn academic content and professional skills. Learning all the necessary knowledge leading to the diagnosis and treatment of a patient is manifestly a worthwhile activity for a medical student, and learning is usually very enthusiastic (see Chapter 10 below).

We can sum up this section on motivation by saying that teachers might worry less about motivating students, and more about teaching better. When they teach in such a way that students build up a good knowledge base, achieve success in problems that are significant and build up a feeling of 'ownership' over their learning, motivation follows good learning as night follows day. It is a matter of getting the causes and the effects right. 'Motivation' is best dealt with by avoiding what not to do. This is where the expectancy-value model is useful. Devaluing academic tasks by encouraging cynicism destroys motivation.

Teaching better is what the book as a whole is about. Establishing a productive classroom climate is taken up in the next section.

The teaching/learning climate

Individual teachers, like institutions as a whole, create a learning *climate* through formal and informal interactions with students. This climate is about how we and they feel about things, and that naturally has positive or negative effects on students' learning. McGregor's (1960) distinction between theory X and theory Y assumptions about human trustworthiness is a good way to characterize that climate.

Theory X and theory Y climates

Teachers operating on theory X assume that students cannot be trusted. They don't want to learn, they will cheat if given the slightest opportunity, and so they must not be allowed to make any significant decisions about their learning. They need to be told what to do and what to study, attendances need to be checked every lecture, invigilated examinations must make up most of the final grade, self- and peer-assessments are quite out of the question, deadlines and regulations need to be spelt out, with sanctions imposed for failing to meet them.

This way of thinking leads very quickly to a working climate based on anxiety: put the fear of God into them, then they'll shape up. Theory X is essentially a blame-the-student model of teaching, and with that goes all the other baggage associated with the level 1 view of teaching.

Teachers operating on theory Y assume that students do their best work when given freedom and space to use their own judgement, that while bureaucratization of the classroom and of the institution may be necessary to run a tight ship, it may be counter-productive for good learning. Consequently, theory Y driven teachers take the opposite view on such matters as take-home assessment tasks, self- and peer-assessment, class attendance, allowing students freedom to make their own decisions and so on. You give the benefit of the doubt. Sure, some students may be more likely to cheat when assessed on projects than in invigilated exams, but the educational benefits outweigh that risk. Theory Y is a meta-theory that is compatible with the level 3 view of teaching: the main thing is to support student learning, rather than to beat student deviousness.

I have described pure cases here. An all theory X environment would be intolerable for students, while all theory Y would be near impossible to run efficiently. Elements of both exist in the learning climates we create, but in our individual philosophies we tend to lean more towards one theory or the other. Our leanings may be because of our personalities, our own educational history, but most of all, it is hoped, because of our worked out philosophy of teaching. We should create the sort of learning climate that we believe strikes the right balance for optimal learning, given our conditions, our subject and our own students.

The way we learn translates into action at virtually all levels of student–teacher interaction. For example, when I told colleagues at the University of Hong Kong, where English is the official language medium of instruction, that I allowed students to use Cantonese in group discussions, because group interaction was then much livelier, a not uncommon reply was: 'But they could be discussing the Happy Valley race results for all you know!' True, they could have been. On the other hand, they could have been engaged in fruitful learning. It is a question of balancing trust, risk and value. Theory X produces low trust, low risk but low value, while theory Y produces high trust, high risk but high value – if it works. This book is about making it work. It can, as the following extract from an erstwhile theory X teacher suggests:

> The biggest point I have learned from this course is my biggest flaw as a teacher, that is, I did not trust my students to be able to behave themselves . . . [or to be] capable of being responsible for their own learning . . . I made numerous rules in class for them to follow so as to make sure that they 'behaved', did all the preparations and planning for them, giving them mountains of homework and short tests to make sure that they revise for their lessons and so on – all rooted from my lack of trust in them! And I dared to blame them for being so passive and dependent when all along I helped to encourage them to be so!
>
> (BEd student, University of Hong Kong)

How climate affects learning

The effects of classroom climate on student learning come about in several ways. Cognitively, theory X restricts the range of potentially useful ways of learning, particularly self-directed learning, as the above quotation illustrates. Affectively, theory X generates negative feelings, which distract from proper task engagement, directly encouraging a surface approach. The aim is to get the task out of the way. Theory X generates two counter-productive emotions in particular: anxiety and cynicism.

Anxiety, produced, for example, by intimidation, sarcasm, threats of failure or heavy use of sanctions, simply creates an intense need to get out of the situation. The student's behaviour is therefore directed towards that end, rather than towards proper task engagement. Anxiety makes a mess of a student's priorities.

Cynicism works in a more coldly cognitive way. Perceptions that the teacher is somehow degrading the task, or belittling students by requiring them to behave in a demeaning manner, evoke cynicism, the reaction to which is a deliberate decision not to engage the task honestly. If the teacher doesn't take the task seriously, why should the student? There are many ways in which teachers convey cynicism:

- Showing lack of interest or dislike of a topic ('You'll hate this, but we've got to cover it!').
- Playing games with students when they can't play back, such as setting facetious distractors in multiple-choice test items.
- Theory X by numbers: for example, drawing a line after word 2000 in a 2000 word limit essay, and marking only to that point. One can attribute all sorts of theory X subtexts to this practice, from a blame-the-student theory to the delirious joy of exercising power. But the consequence is that the student's work is devalued. The student had exceeded the limit surely in order to make the argument more clearly. This is telling the student not to bother with making cases in future, just to list isolated points within the word limit.
- Discounting grades or marks for being late, or some other offence. Subtext: meeting a deadline is more important than trying to create a product of quality. This practice makes genuine criterion-referencing impossible. Issues of learning should not be confused with issues of discipline.
- Busywork: insisting on trivia, making quality performance secondary to bureaucratic demands or to personal convenience.

This last category is extremely wide: for example, refusing to accept student criticisms or suggestions as to content or teaching method, assessing for trivial content, being 'too busy' to attend to reasonable student requests. As a teacher educator and a staff developer, I have to mention our own particular occupational hazard and come-uppance: not practising what we preach. As one student quoted to a teacher educator: 'Faculties of Education should not be advocating things for teachers or schools that they are not capable of practising themselves' (Fullan 1993).

Time stress: coverage. A particular source of both anxiety and cynicism is time stress brought out by an obsession with coverage. There are too many topics, yet each is taught with equal emphasis. Students are grossly overloaded, pre-empting deep engagement with any topic. There are many reasons why students are subjected to time stress:

- lack of coordination between teachers in setting assignment deadlines;
- insisting on the prime importance of what you teach yourself;
- lack of knowledge or even concern about the students' perspective on the workload;
- shared teaching, and particularly shared assessment, where each teacher thinks his or her own contribution the most important;
- generally, a lack of care and forethought in designing the curriculum initially.

Deep engagement in a task takes time. If you don't provide the time, you won't get deep engagement.

Climate and direction: summary

Let us bring the two sections on motivation and climate together. A theory Y climate is a necessary but not a sufficient condition for the cultivation of positive motivation. The teacher must further demonstrate that the task is intrinsically worthwhile and valued.

Expectations of success and failure depend critically on what students are most likely to attribute their success and failure to. How these attributions are built up is partly cultural, partly upbringing and partly what goes on in the classroom. Communicating the message that failure is due to factors that aren't going to go away, and that aren't controllable (such as low ability), is to instil an expectation of future failure. Attributing failure to factors that can be changed, such as lack of the appropriate skills (these can be taught), or insufficient effort (this can be increased next time), helps to remove the crippling incapacity that failure may induce. Likewise, attribution of success to a special interest, or competence, is likely to increase feelings of ownership and hence positive motivation. Attributing success to luck or to help from someone is likely to decrease feelings of ownership.

Finally, a theory Y climate does not necessarily mean a disorganized teaching/learning environment. An organized setting, with clear goals and feedback on progress, is important for motivating students, and for the development of deep approaches (Hattie and Watkins 1988; Entwistle *et al.* 1989). Knowing where you are going, and feedback telling you how well you are progressing, heightens expectations of success. Driving in a thick fog is highly unpleasant.

Improving teaching by avoiding the negatives

No doubt there are many other ways in which teaching can encourage surface learning, but the previous section gives the general idea. The first step towards improving teaching is to find out the extent to which these surface-inducing features exist in your own teaching, and who controls them. Those that are under your own control can be minimized or removed, while those that are under the control of others you may or may not be able to do something about.

Finding out what might be wrong

Three possible sources could provide information on what might be encouraging students to react with a surface approach:

1 Your own reflections on your teaching.

2 The students themselves.
3 Informed advice from a colleague in the role of 'critical friend', or from a staff developer.

Much can be achieved by self-reflection. We can reflect on objectives, on alternative TLAs and on different modes of assessment, which is exactly what this book is hoping to encourage. The *Approaches to Teaching Inventory* (Prosser and Trigwell 1998; see also Chapter 11) is a very useful instrument for clarifying your conceptions (views) of teaching and how consistent your practices are with those conceptions.

However, there are limits to what we can ourselves see as wrong with our own teaching. We are likely to be blind to the more personal aspects, the kind of learning climate that we establish with our students. For example, what we intend as humour might come across as sarcasm; attempts at being friendly, as patronizing. Both are fertile breeding grounds for anxiety and cynicism. We need someone to tell us such things.

Our students are probably the most direct source of this kind of information. It is after all their perceptions that structure the intention to use a surface approach. Obtaining student feedback is best done anonymously, providing you are capable of putting up with the jibes of the facetious, and the negativism of the genuinely disgruntled. You can use an open question: 'What aspects of my teaching do you like most? What would you like to see changed?' A positive note is better than: 'What do you see wrong with my teaching?' You might as well walk around with a 'kick me' sign on your backside.

A structured questionnaire, in which you specifically ask about aspects on which you want feedback, allows for positive as well as critical feedback. Aspects of teaching that are likely to lead to surface approaches are listed in Table 4.1, while constructing a questionnaire to suit your context forms part of Task 4.2.

Another perspective on teaching can come from colleagues. In this respect, a 'buddy-system' is useful, in which two teachers in the same department, who trust each other, visit each other's classes as critical friends. They will need a common framework, and a common set of assumptions about what is good teaching, to do this well. This procedure needs to be entirely separated from summative evaluations of teaching that might influence decisions on contract renewal, or promotion. All but the most exceptional department heads are therefore excluded from this exercise.

Yet another perspective is provided by a professional development or teaching and learning centre, if your university has one. Staff developers have the expertise to act as critical friend, and to provide important insights on all stages of teaching where your own perspective might be limited.

Table 4.1: Aspects of teaching likely to lead to surface approaches

---

Motivation

1 Conveying expectations of a low probability of success:

- Oral and written comments suggesting failure is due to lack of ability, success due to luck or other factors outside the student's control; not suggesting how a poor result might be remedied.
- Norm- rather than criterion-referenced assessment.
- Lack of clear direction, no feedback, no milestones of progress.

2 Conveying low evaluations of tasks, cynicism:

- Playing games with students at a disadvantage, especially in the context of assessment ('funny' multiple choice alternatives; busywork).
- Displaying personal dislike of content being taught.
- Assessing in a trivial way: low-level tasks requiring memorizing only, marking only to the literal word limit, discounting grades for non-academic or disciplinary reasons, assessments not based on content taught.
- Emphasizing rules and regulations beyond their functional utility. *Subtext*: rules are more important than learning.
- Not practising what is preached. *Subtext*: you lot can do it, but it's not worth me doing it.

The learning climate

3 Aspects suggesting theory X:

- Negative reinforcement, use of anxiety to 'motivate'.
- Blame-the-student explanations of student behaviour.
- Time stress: failure to consider or appreciate student workload, no time available to students for reflection.
- Students given little input in decisions that affect them.
- Anxiety: engendered by harsh sanctions, bullying, sarcasm, lack of consideration of students' perspective, work/time pressure.
- Cynicism: engendered by students feeling that you are not playing straight with them, that you don't actually believe in what you are telling them.

What can be set right?

Having found out what the problems are, the next step is to minimize them. Some problems may be located in your own personal style of teaching, which is what we are concerned with here. Others will lie in the institutional system, which will be addressed as they arise in following chapters. Of those that reside in yourself, some will be within your own power to remove, but others may not. The present task is to look at those aspects of our teaching that we can control.

Table 4.1 summarizes the aspects of your personal teaching that might

---

Task 4.2: How can I improve my teaching? Eliminating the negative

Construct a questionnaire for your students to complete that will tell you what you should know, but would probably prefer not to know, about your teaching. The focus is on those aspects that are likely to lead to surface approaches. What this really means is: what is it about your teaching that students might react to negatively, but for the right reasons? Table 4.1 is a source of possible foci. You might regroup under subheadings that you worry about. For example:

- *Interaction with students in class.* Do they feel free to answer questions? Do they perceive you as censorious, sarcastic . . .
- *Direction.* Are they clear about expectations of what to do: for example, in completing assignments? Carrying out group discussions . . .
- *Commitment.* Do they perceive you as playing straight, practising what you preach . . .

And so on. There are many headings you could use. There are some points about giving questionnaires to students:

1 Avoid the 'kick me' approach. Try to work your questions positively; they can then rate them negatively if they wish. For example, don't ask: 'When I ask questions in class does my manner make you feel anxious? Very anxious/anxious/not very anxious/not at all anxious.' But rather: 'How do you feel when I ask questions in class? Very glad to be asked/somewhat glad/anxious/very anxious.'
2 Use open-ended questions at the end, so that they can tell you things that you didn't think to ask about.
3 They should be anonymous. Even making it optional could distort the results.

---

lead to surface approaches. You might care to tailor a questionnaire or interview based on those aspects that you think may be an issue in your own teaching (see Task 4.2).

The list comes under the two headings, motivation and learning climate, although they do interrelate. Some of these things I list here as leading to surface learning, and therefore to be removed, you might think to be necessary, however regrettable they might be, such as deducting marks for late submissions of assignments. I would make two points. The first is that while the problem of late submission, for which this is a common solution, is a real one, there are alternative solutions. It is a matter of being consistent, which raises the second point.

Theory X and theory Y are meta-theories, like the level 1, level 2 and level 3 views of teaching. That is, they provide an overall framework that generates consistency across most teaching decisions. If you are committed to level 3, then it follows that you need to structure a predominantly theory Y learning climate, where student learning is the top priority. This means using such features as criterion-referenced assessment, time for reflection, trying to eliminate anxiety and cynicism and adopting the principles and practices of constructive alignment. Some teachers are more committed than others, of course, and will lay more or less stress on different aspects of their learning climate, but basically we are dealing with a package.

Given that, the first set of decisions is to remove those aspects of your teaching that are actually encouraging surface approaches in students, but of which you are unaware. Using some form of reflection, with appropriate student and peer feedback, it would be possible at least to lessen some of the things that are not right with your teaching.

Discouraging surface approaches and creating the right climate is setting the stage for effective teaching. The next and more important step is to develop those TLAs that actually promote deep learning. We take up that theme in following chapters.

Summary and conclusions

The two faces of teaching

Effective teaching involves maximizing the chances that students will engage the full range of verbs needed to achieve the desired outcomes. When students use a surface approach they engage only at the lower end of the range. The teaching challenge is therefore to prevent the shortfall of higher-level cognitive activities. There are thus two facets to teaching: identifying and removing those features of our teaching that encourage the use of those surrogate lower-level verbs, and supporting what might encourage students to use the legitimate higher-level verbs instead. Much of the trouble of the first kind lies in the affective area: motivation and classroom and institutional climate.

The costs and benefits of getting involved

Motivation has two meanings: it refers to initiating learning, and to maintaining engagement during learning. To initiate learning, students need to see the cost-benefits: that engaging in learning has evident value, and that engagement is likely to realize that value. Value accrues to a task for a variety of reasons: extrinsic, where the consequences are desirable, because they either bring something we want or avoid something we don't want; social, where the value comes from what other important people think; achievement, where the value is ego-enhancement; intrinsic, where we don't even think to ask where the value comes from.

Some of these aspects of value are difficult to do much about, others you can. If you must use extrinsic reinforcement, let it be positive rather than negative; you can show enthusiasm for what you teach and act as a role model; you can use norm-referenced assessment if you want to get the juices of high need achievers flowing, or you can use criterion-referenced assessment if you want to address the *learning* needs of students. But you cannot require students to be intrinsically motivated, except by teaching properly.

The teaching/learning climate

The quality of the relationship set up between teacher and students, or within an institution, is referred to as its climate: the way the students feel about it. A theory X climate is based on the assumption that students cannot be trusted, a theory Y climate on the assumption that they can. If level 1 and level 3 views of teaching describe two cognitive views of teaching, theory X and theory Y climates are their affective counterparts.

If students cannot be trusted, tight formal structures with sanctions for non-compliance need to be established. Anxiety and cynicism are the result, both leading to surface learning. Anxiety distracts students: the point is to avoid the threat, not to engage the task deeply. Cynicism simply devalues academic work in the students' eyes: If you have to have all these rules, rewards and sanctions to get people to work, then it cannot be worth much.

Improving teaching by avoiding the negatives

The two big questions for any individual teacher are: What do I believe in, a theory X or a theory Y climate? What am I doing, unwittingly, that might be creating the opposite climate to what I want? Teachers trying to implement aligned teaching must answer the first question with theory Y. Information on the second question may come from one's own reflections, from the students, from informed advice such as that of a colleague, or of a staff developer. Each source provides a different perspective, but reliance on your own reflections isn't likely to be a productive source of information on those aspects of your teaching of which you are unaware. These can be supplemented with questionnaires, observations and interviews, their focus on aspects of teaching discussed in this chapter. The factors that are likely to lead to poor motivation and surface learning are summarized in Table 4.1.

Further reading

On expectancy-value theory of motivation

Feather, N. (ed.) (1982) *Expectations and Actions*, Hillsdale, NJ: Erlbaum.

On classroom climate

McGregor, D. (1960) *The Human Side of Enterprise*, New York: McGraw-Hill.

On both

Biggs, J. and Moore, P. (1993) *The Process of Learning*, Sydney: Prentice Hall of Australia.

Further reading for this chapter is a tough one. There is plenty of theoretical material on motivation, but readers who don't know this literature already will have no time to read it now and transform it into functioning knowledge. Feather's book is there for those who would like to delve further. Most of the work on climate is directed either at school classroom level or at big business. The recent literature addressed to business persons is hairy-chested achievement motivation stuff, not level 3 oriented at all. The exception is McGregor's original work on theory X and theory Y, which is well worth reading, but it needs translating into the tertiary context. The general principles of both foci of this chapter are given a more in-depth treatment in Biggs and Moore.

5

Good teaching: principles and practice

Now the stage has been set, we look at the action. Successful teaching is like a construction site – it *is* a construction site – on which students build on what they already know; it requires much activity, interaction with others and self-monitoring to check that everything is proceeding according to plan. The teacher's role varies, from highly directive, specifying procedures and correcting errors, to supervisory, to consultant, to group leader. The role adopted defines the nature of different teaching/learning activities (TLAs), each of which is best suited to achieve a different purpose. We visit a range of teacher-directed, peer-directed and self-directed TLAs. The focus in this chapter is on TLAs suitable for classroom situations of around 40 students or fewer, and in the next chapter, on TLAs for large classes.

Characteristics of rich teaching/learning contexts

In Chapter 1 good teaching was defined as 'getting most students to use the high cognitive level processes that the more academic students use spontaneously.' Traditional teaching methods – lecture, tutorial and private study – do not in themselves provide much support for higher learning processes. They work for Susan, but leave Robert floundering with a pile of lecture notes; a lot of trees but no wood. The challenge for teaching, then, is to select teaching activities that will encourage Robert to reflect, to question, to analyse and to do those other things that Susan does anyway.

Our search for good rich TLAs might well start by looking at good teaching/learning environments. Some general principles of good teaching emerge, which we illustrate in this chapter for the situation of up to about 40 students in the class, and in the next for the special case of the large class.

Not so long ago, I attended an educational research conference: a mammoth event, comprising 40 parallel sessions over five days. There were hundreds of studies relevant to the question of what contexts seemed to support good learning, and what didn't. I attended as many as my spinning head would allow, and then read the abstracts of all the rest. On the flight back home, four factors floated into my head, and I haven't been able then or since to find any instance in the literature that gainsaid them. They are as follows (Biggs and Moore 1993):

1 A well structured knowledge base.
2 An appropriate motivational context.
3 Learner activity.
4 Interaction with others.

Constructing a base of interconnected knowledge

The first two, a well structured knowledge base and an appropriate motivational context, are recyclable, being at the same time prerequisites of good learning and outcomes of it. The need to know more arises from knowing a lot already; that's how the burning questions are defined. Answering them leads inevitably to deeper knowledge still. The better you have learned, the better you will learn. When that happens to students we call it deep learning, and when to teachers we call it research.

Sound knowledge is based on *interconnections*. Everything that has been written so far in this book about understanding, deep learning, the growth and development of knowledge and intrinsic motivation reiterates this. Understanding is itself the realization that what is separate in ignorance is connected in knowing. Cognitive growth lies not just in knowing more, but in the restructuring that occurs when new knowledge becomes connected with what is already known.

Four general precepts arise out of this recognition.

Building on the known

The physics professor is greeting the new intake of freshers, still glowing from their A level successes.

'Now. You remember the physics you were taught in sixth form?'
  Two hundred heads nod enthusiastically.
  'Well forget it. You're here to learn *real* physics, not the baby stuff you were taught at school!'

That took place many years ago (in my old university), but it illustrates an attitude that is arrogantly anti-intellectual, a perfect example of how not to teach. Teaching builds on the known, it must not reject it. In deep learning, new learning connects with old, so teaching should exploit interconnectedness: make the connections explicit ('Last week we . . . Today, I am taking that further . . .'), choose familiar examples first, get students to build on their own experiences, draw and explain parallels while teaching, use cross-references, design curricula that draw out cross-connections . . .

Maximizing structure

Connections are best drawn hierarchically, not horizontally, reconceptualizing so that what are seen as differences at a subordinate level are related at a superordinate level. Let us take as an example the concept of motivation from the previous chapter. Extrinsic and intrinsic motivation have different, sometimes opposite, effects on learning; one is associated with poor learning, the other with high-quality learning. Two different phenomena. Not so: each is incorporated within expectancy-value theory. The different effects are not because they are different forms of motivation, but because the student reads the value component in a different context.

In all curricula, there must be many specific concepts that seem irreconcilably different to students, but which are best seen as different exemplars of the same higher principle. It is the trees and the wood all over again. In teaching, we should see that the shape of the wood becomes clear; that the students understand what the nodes in the structure are.

One can maximize the chances of students coming to grasp the structure in many ways. New information should not be just dumped on the learner, in rambling lessons, or in poorly constructed texts. Good teaching always contains a structure, hidden away, but there to be found.

In some circumstances, it is appropriate to present the structure upfront. An 'advance organizer' is a preview of a lecture that mentions the main topics to be dealt with, and the overriding conceptual structure to which they may be related (Ausubel 1968). The student then has a conceptual framework from the start: as material is introduced, it can be fitted into place. For example, a diagram based on expectancy-value theory could be used as such an organizer for a lesson on motivation.

A 'grabber', on the other hand, elicits interest in the topics to follow. Whereas the advance organizer is *conceptual*, the grabber is *affective*, based on interest and familiarity. Both have their place.

Some teachers fall into the trap of talking down to students with an in-your-face conceptual structure, all answers and no questions. Lessons that are *too* well structured encourage students simply to take on board the given structure and memorize that, thereby establishing one of the lowest of the forms of understanding mentioned by Entwistle and Entwistle (1997; see p. 34). The student must do the structuring in the end; it's what the student does that is important. The challenge is to strike the right balance between presenting students with chaos on the one hand, and with cut-and-dried conclusions on the other, where all the interesting conceptual work has been done. The question of how much structure to present, given your students and their existing knowledge base, comes through reflective experience.

Using error constructively

In the course of knowledge construction, students inevitably create misconceptions, which need to be corrected. But, first, you have to find out what they are, by *formative assessment*. This does not necessarily mean formal testing, although trial runs on final assessments can be useful, but probing students' knowledge as it is being constructed, so that any misunderstandings can be set right, literally in the formative stage. To do this requires a theory Y climate, where students will feel free to admit error. If they think they might be graded on the result, they will be very defensive.

In a tutorial or group session where the tutor is censorious, or sarcastic, students will keep quiet, preferring not to make themselves vulnerable. This is independent of any particular teaching method. In an otherwise fine problem-based course at a particular university, one tutor completely wrecked the process. The aim is for students to pose questions, and follow up plausible answers to a given problem. This they do by reference to theory, past experience, similar cases etc., asking questions and testing possible answers in discussion. But in this particular case, the tutor replied to every question put to her, all-knowing and sneering: 'That's for me to know, and for you to find out!' The students in this group gave up asking questions, and problem-based learning acquired a bad name. So did the tutor, but she deserved it.

Some teachers feel awkward about drawing attention to students' errors. In wanting to create a theory Y climate, where students can feel free to explore possibilities and ask far-out questions, these teachers allow misconceptions to pass uncorrected or even unquestioned.

The dilemma is: do I correct mistakes and risk discouraging students from expressing their understandings in public? Or do I let them go uncorrected in the interests of maintaining a productive working atmosphere? Not to correct is abdicating from an important teaching function. One technique is to smile encouragingly, with 'Yes, not bad. Can anyone else elaborate on that?' This signals that there is a problem, and that we are getting on to a better reply, but not exactly what the problem is. The answer must lie in the interpersonal chemistry, the rapport, that a teacher can create, so that public correction is cheerfully accepted and appreciated (see also Anderson 1997).

Japanese teachers use a technique Hess and Azuma (1991) call 'sticky probing', which to Westerners might seem a little drastic. A single problem is discussed for hours by students, with the teacher adjudicating, until a consensus acceptable to teacher and students is reached. The focus of the probing is a particular student's error, which the teacher believes would be instructive to unpack and reconstruct publicly, with the student the focus of public correction. Japanese students, however, don't appear to see this as a punishment for making a mistake, but as part and parcel of learning.

Learning from error thus presents two problems:

- to get students to expose their erroneous thinking without risk of ridicule, loss of face or low grades;
- to correct them nicely.

How one resolves this dilemma is obviously a very individual matter, but it does need addressing.

Maximizing students' awareness of their own knowledge construction

Constructing a knowledge base is done not by the teacher as master-builder, but by the students using the materials supplied both by their teacher and by their experience. That being so, the students need to be aware of what they are doing, and to check how well they are doing it.

Monitoring the 'construction site' is another name for those study skills that involve self-management, including self-assessment. This is best discussed under the heading of self-directed TLAs (below).

Learner activity and interaction

The last two characteristics of rich teaching/learning contexts, learner activity and interacting with others, provide some general principles of teaching, and a basis for classifying TLAs.

The fact of activity

Being active while learning is better than being inactive: activity is a good in itself. Wittrock (1977) outlines one study in which students were required to learn from text in increasing forms of activity: reading silently, underlining important words, writing out the key sentences containing those words, rewriting sentences in one's own words and the most active, teaching someone else the material. There was a strong correlation between extent of activity and efficiency of learning.

In quite a different vein, MacKenzie and White (1982) devised an excursion on coastal geography in which each of the objectives was linked

---

Box 5.1: Adventure learning in the School of Law

Nadja Siegel, lecturer in law at Queensland University, is the winner of the law section of the Australian University Teaching Awards. Through adventure learning she tries to develop in students the skills they will need to apply professionally . . . She creates activities with an element of risk – physical, social or emotional – so that the experience is more real. Crossing a river using blocks as rafts, with one team missing equipment, forces them into deciding whether to adopt a competitive or cooperative approach. But she says adventure learning is not just games . . . 'You really need to be aware of how you're using the activity and be able to direct the students' experiences to the focus of their learning . . .'

Source: *The Australian Higher Education,* 26 November 1997.

---

to quite dramatic actions, such as chewing mangrove leaves, wading through a muddy swamp, jumping across rock platforms and so on. Recall on a written test three months later was near perfect. Spiegel describes a similar approach of 'adventure learning' to legal studies (see Box 5.1).

There are two factors at work here. The first is a matter of attention and concentration. Activity simply heightens arousal, which makes performance more efficient. Even physical exertion has quite dramatic effects on mental performance. Typically, four minutes of brisk exercise, such as running or pedalling on an exercycle, improves performance in such tasks as mental arithmetic, after which time performance worsens in the unfit, continuing to improve in the fit (e.g. Tomporowski and Ellis 1986). Getting the adrenalin to flow increases alertness. This is one very good reason for breaking up long periods of lecturing with interspersed activities (see Chapter 6).

The second factor is that activities should be keyed to academic objectives. For example, the role of salt in the ecology of mangrove swamps was an objective, so chewing mangrove leaves for their salt content was integral to that objective. Cooperating in building a raft is relevant for team management (Box 5.1). Declarative and functioning knowledge are linked, reinforcing each other.

We learn through different sense modalities, and the more one modality reinforces another, the more effective the learning. It is like trying to access a book in a library. If all you know is the author, or the title, or the publisher, or the year of publication, you could be in for a long search, but the more those 'ors' become 'ands' the faster and more precise the search becomes. Just so in accessing or remembering what has been learned. The more TLAs tie down the topic to be learned to multiple sensory modes, the better the learning.

Table 5.1: Most people learn . . .

10% of what they read
20% of what they hear
30% of what they see
50% of what they see and hear
70% of what they talk over with others
80% of what they use and do in real life
95% of what they teach someone else

Source: Attributed to William Glasser; quoted by *Association for Supervision and Curriculum Development Guide 1988.*

Table 5.1 puts this very neatly. Don't take the percentages mentioned too literally, but the messages are clear, simple and basically right. Some sensory modalities are more effective for learning than others; the more they overlap, the better; and best of all, you learn through teaching. The practicalities and logistics of that we shall be exploring later.

Think of learning as stored in three memory systems (Tulving 1985):

- *Procedural* memory: remembering how to do things. Actions are learned.
- *Episodic* memory: remembering where you learned things. Images are learned.
- *Semantic* memory: remembering meanings, frequently from statements about things. Declarative knowledge is learned.

When we learn something, each system is involved; we learn what we did, where it was and how to describe what it was. However, they are not equally easily accessed. Actions are easiest to remember (do we ever forget how to ride a bicycle?), and semantics, what was actually said, are hardest. That sequence probably reflects the sequence of biological development: first actions, then images, then semantics. Be that as it may, recalling the context or the actions can often bring back the semantics; once we picture where we learned it, we are more likely to recall what it was that we were supposed to have learned. It's like accessing the book in the library. Thus even learning straight declarative knowledge, the stuff of academia, is best done in association with a rich store of images. The adventure learning studies do exactly that.

The kind of activity

Some activities are more relevant to our course objectives than others. Not only do MacKenzie and White's and Spiegel's adventure learning contexts provide powerful images to associate with declared objectives, those contexts require relevant actions; the TLAs address the objectives.

Lecture rooms might offer less scope for activity than wilderness areas, but the same principles apply. Students can be required to do more than just listen and take notes, but to do things that directly address what we want them to learn. One activity resource is increasingly plentiful in tertiary classrooms: students. The kinds of activities that are elicited when students interact with each other greatly increase our options even in large classes, as we see in the following chapter. The problem is not a shortage of possible TLAs, but selecting those that will do what you want them to do, in your teaching context. For some purposes, lecturing is better than problem-based learning; not many, perhaps, but there are some. So any TLA is chosen because:

1 It is the most suitable for realizing your objectives.
2 It is practical to use within your context and resourcing.

A classification of TLAs

Let us simplify by classifying TLAs according to who is in major control. TLAs can be *teacher*-directed, *peer*-directed and *self*-directed. Each typically elicits a different kind of engagement from the learner.

1 *Teacher*-directed activities include most formal teaching situations: lectures, tutorials, laboratories, field excursions etc. These TLAs are by far the most common in undergraduate teaching, for obvious and very good reasons, but they are not the only valuable ones. Some, of course, are quite subject specific, others suitable across subjects.
2 *Peer*-directed activities include both formal TLAs that the teacher may have initially set up and then left to the students to run, and activities set up by the students outside the classroom. Teachers may initiate peer activities, and then withdraw so that the role of peers becomes increasingly important, but retain control in report-back sessions, and in orchestrating conclusions.
3 *Self*-directed activities include all independent learning and study activities. Flexible learning provides an instance where the context and materials are set up by the teacher, but the learning itself is self-directed.

Each kind of TLA best addresses a particular form of learning.

• Teacher-controlled activities are best suited to dealing in depth with a topic; the teacher is the expert and can correct misconceptions and present the 'official' view. These TLAs are particularly useful for focusing on prioritized content; imparting, explaining and clarifying information; providing feedback; deepening understanding through interaction with students.
• Peer-controlled activities are particularly useful for elaborating, broadening understanding, providing different viewpoints and perspectives and obtaining self-insight by comparison with others like oneself.

- Self-controlled activities are useful for developing in-depth understanding, monitoring and self-assessment, and independent learning. Self-direction is surely included in most tertiary aims, and is surprisingly under-utilized, despite the rhetoric and despite recent increases in class size.

Teacher-directed TLAs

Lecturing and class teaching

Lecturing is the standard tertiary method. The subject matter expert tells the students about the major topics that make up the discipline or professional area, and what the latest thinking is. The assumption is that the flow of information is one-way, student contribution usually being limited to questions and requests for clarification. Elaborating the material, removing misconceptions, applying to specific examples, comparing different interpretations, are left to the complement of the lecture, the tutorial.

Lecturing is used over an enormous range of class size. In classes of about 12 students and fewer, most teachers change from a straight lecturing style and become more interactive, deliberately eliciting contributions from the students, while for their part, the general run of students begin commonly to participate at about 12 in a group, the more so as the group becomes smaller. Of course, there are large individual differences in how teachers react to class size, some managing to teach 40 and more in an interactive way; and by the same token, there are students who will happily respond interactively with a large audience looking on. There is, however, no doubt that class size has a crucial influence on teaching style.

The distinction between expository and interactive teaching is basic. Expository teaching is one-way, involving minimal interaction from students. It is appropriate whenever the teacher wants to tell the students something from a position of expertise. It is endemic in large classes, however, not because it is the most appropriate way to teach, but because many see it as the *only* way. We see in the next chapter that there are in fact many alternatives to lecturing. Interactive teaching is two-way, occurring in smaller classes.

The presentation

The class presentation is a more interactive version of the lecture more suited to small-class delivery. All the principles of good teaching apply: structuring, using the knowledge base, a suitable climate and so forth.

It is essential that the presentation has an implicit structure. This is where some 'inspirational' lecturers need to be careful. They talk well, they have brilliant ideas on the run, all the better for their freshness and spontaneity. They like students to ask unplanned questions, so they can think up answers on their feet: the lightning *riposte*, that's the stuff of good teaching! Possibly in some cases, but probably not in most. There could be a role confusion between stand-up comic and serious academic.

Nevertheless, there is an important *improvisational* nature to expert teaching. Research into teaching expertise has emphasized two apparently opposed aspects: teaching as management, and teaching as improvised conversation. One requires meticulous planning and preparation, the other on-the-spot responding to events as they occur (Berliner 1986; Biggs and Moore 1993: Chapter 16). The conversational metaphor is misleading if it suggests that spontaneity is marred by tiresome pre-planning and schedules. Unfortunately, you don't get relevant and high-level spontaneity without content knowledge, preparation and experience.

Good improvisation is crucial in making the best of interactive teaching: questions and comments from students can be the basis for rethinking and reconstructing new and exciting ideas, if the ball is picked up and taken in the appropriate direction. The experience gives the phrase 'the social construction of knowledge' real meaning. Papers have originated that way.

Dealing with student questioning
An important skill for the presentation is dealing with student questioning. This requires a knowledge of topic structure that is sufficiently rich and flexible that you can recognize the students' perspective of it, and their access to it. It is a matter not only of having expert knowledge of your subject – that goes without saying – but of having 'pedagogic content knowledge' (Shulman 1987), which is jargon for understanding your students' perspectives on that knowledge; how they see it, and how their contributions can be orchestrated in harmony with your own expert knowledge.

Questions may be of different kinds. Important distinctions are:

- Convergent or divergent. Convergent questions are asked with a correct answer in mind, divergent are genuinely seeking student input.
- High-level or low-level. High-level questions probe the high-level verbs: theorizing, reflecting, hypothesizing. Low-level questions seek factual answers, and tend therefore to be convergent.

Convergent questions are, however, not necessarily low level. Socratic questioning is a case in point. The teacher goes around the class asking questions that lead subtly to an answer the teacher already has in mind. This comes across as the social construction of knowledge: all contribute and agree on the picture the individual answers have painted.

Divergent questions are obviously useful for probing student experiences and incorporating them as examples of the case-in-point, and for student reflection. Divergent questions are best for high-level learning activities, but they can just lead to aimless rambling, and that needs controlling. In professional programmes, where the students have hands-on experience, there is a wealth of functioning knowledge to be tapped, located in a conceptual structure and generalized. But it can also be extremely boring and unproductive. Good questioning skills are required.

High-level questions need *wait time* if they are to be answered satisfactorily. Thinking takes time, and high-level thinking takes more time than low-level thinking. Whether out of fear of silence, impatience or just bad judgement, the fact is that in most classrooms nowhere near enough wait time is allowed (Tobin 1987). Ellsworth *et al.* (1991) allowed tertiary students unlimited time to answer and found they averaged nine seconds to answer a convergent question, and over 30 seconds to answer a divergent question. The quality of response increased the longer students took. You might feel embarrassed by 30 seconds of silence, so work out ways of not being embarrassed.

Concept maps

Concept maps were designed both to present a structure and to find out how students see the structure (Novak 1979). This makes it a very flexible device. It can be used by teachers for both teaching and assessment purposes, and by students for organizing their ideas: for example, for reviewing the semester's work, for planning and writing essays or for clarifying difficult passages.

In creating concept maps, students singly or in groups can be presented with a central concept or principle, and they then generate subconcepts that relate to it, or the subconcepts can be supplied. A taught unit could be the target. They then arrange the subconcepts, either drawing them or arranging cards on which they have been written, in a way that makes best sense to them, the distance between subconcepts reflecting their perceived degree of interrelation. Lines are then drawn linking sub- and central concepts, with a brief explanation of what the link or relationship is. It is not necessary to use cards; once the nominated concepts are decided, they can be written directly on to a sheet of paper, and the connecting relation lines drawn in.

Creating concept maps is a learning experience for the students, helping them to structure their thinking explicitly, and, at the same time, the resulting maps give an indication of how the student sees the way in which individual concepts relate to each other. They can therefore be used for assessment purposes. Concept maps present an overall picture, and as holistic representations of a complex conceptual structure, are best evaluated by judging the complexity of the arrangement, and the correctness of the interrelations, rather than by analytic 'marking' (see Chapter 9). They can be used as feedback, to see how teaching might be adjusted, or as part of the final assessments of student learning, or as study aids by the students themselves.

Let us look at two concept maps of the previous chapter (Task 5.1). These maps might be the work of students, or the teacher (in this case the teacher posing as student). A good strategy would be to get students to tell their versions, then for you to tell yours (or mine), and they can compare. It may well be that some students will come up with a different central focus, which could be as good as or better than that intended. Comparing different versions could result in some interesting learning all round.

In one study with first-year science and agricultural students, Santhanam *et al.* (1998) obtained mixed results. Students saw the value of the procedure but not its relevance: they thought memorization was the best approach to study in the first year, and so did not adopt concept mapping in their own studying; a depressing finding, which signifies that students are getting the wrong cues from the teaching or assessing contexts (see also Ramsden *et al.* 1986).

Think-aloud modelling

When presenting new tasks or problems, it can be very helpful for the teacher to think out loud while handling it, so that the students are clearer about what they are supposed to be doing. The teacher is doing the self-analysis and reflection publicly, letting the students know how an expert does it, so that eventually they do so themselves. Many teachers think aloud for their students automatically, but many others do not. Modelling is handy whenever you get the inevitable: 'What are we supposed to do?'

In written tasks, using an overhead projector is an advantage because it enables you to face and interact with the class while at the same time thinking out loud, showing your notes and revisions, and mistakes, as you go. A writer can think out loud while planning, composing and revising, thus demonstrating the purposes of the various techniques that academic writers use. Students are brought face to face with processes and possibilities that they themselves would not think of, and if the class is not too large, the students can call out contributions to the ongoing composing or problem-solving process. In large classes, you could nominate the front two rows to do this.

The tutorial

The tutorial is meant to complement the large lecture. In the lecture, the expert delivers the information, the learners are passive. In the tutorial, the students should do much of the work, the tutor's role is to see that they do. They should set rich tasks, ask probing questions, challenge

Task 5.1: Two concept maps of Chapter 4

Look at these two maps and see what you think. How would you evaluate them?

(a)

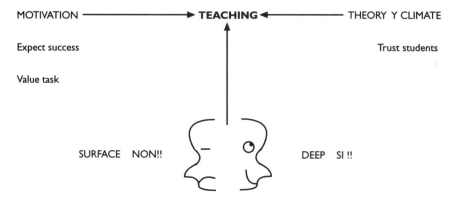

THE TWO FACES OF TEACHING

(b)

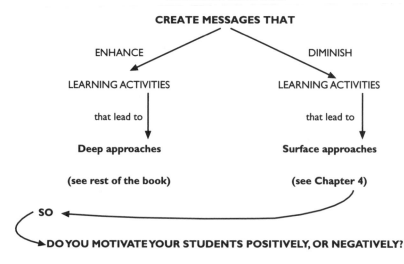

HOW DO YOU SEND THESE MESSAGES?

CLIMATE, personal relations with students, practice what you preach.
ASSESSMENT PRACTICES, comments, feedback, criterion-referenced.

HOW DO YOU FIND OUT *WHAT* YOU DO?

SELF-MONITORING, REFLECTION?
FROM STUDENT FEEDBACK?
FROM PEERS, STAFF DEVELOPMENT?

What I think is given below.

Analysis of concept maps (a) and (b)

Map (a) sees 'teaching' as the central focus of the chapter, with 'motivation', a 'theory Y climate' and encouraging deep and discouraging surface as being essential for good teaching. 'Motivation' comprises expecting success, and a task that is valued, while 'trust' is the essential characteristic of a theory Y climate.

This is a distorted simplification. The give-away is the overall structure: a 'starburst', a central focus (which isn't quite correct, the focus isn't teaching as such) and subconcepts radiating out from it. There are no connections between each of the subconcepts, which makes it multistructural at best, in SOLO terms. What it says is that 'Teaching is this, and this, and this . . .' One more thing: it picks up the words of a subhead, 'the two faces of teaching', and makes that a dominating feature without explaining what those two faces are. Then the map itself is about the smiling face only: success, value, theory Y. In fact the message of the chapter is that motivation also has a dark side: expecting failure, devaluing, theory X. Which way are you as a teacher going to go? How will you find out? What will you do about it when you have found out? Map (a) completely misses these points, and shows that the chapter has been misunderstood; the student who created this one is in need of conceptual therapy.

Map (b), on the other hand, links this chapter with the rest of the book, then goes on to say what the chapter is about, addressing those questions that (a) glossed over. The central focus is that messages that students receive from the teaching context affect their learning activities. Aligned teaching is one part of that; reflecting on the sorts of messages we send that discourage appropriate learning is the other part.

misconceptions, manage the proceedings appropriate to the students' levels of understanding and chair the proceedings. Students see 'good' tutorials as those that promote active learning, where tutors are able to set up a good theory Y atmosphere, to facilitate good debate, to open out the quieter students, to quieten the already too open and to provide a *focus* for discussion and interaction that requires students to prepare in advance (Anderson 1997).

Tutors should therefore be aiming to seek elaboration and criticism of given interpretations, and to develop different interpretations and applications of lecture material. Particularly valuable are the opportunities for students to see how others interpret the material, and to judge, with discreet adjudication from the chair, what are the best interpretations so that misconceptions are also corrected. Tutorials in the sciences often deal with public problem-solving, which calls for other skills.

If these are the aims, tutorials often do not achieve them. Students 'are often silent and often ill-prepared, and the tutor often finds himself giving a lecture' (Collier 1985: 7). A poor tutorial is one where the students are inactive. This can be because of group size. As the group exceeds about 12 or so, the tutor increasingly will take centre stage. It is difficult to see how 'tutorials' of 30 and 40, as happens now in many universities, can possibly do what they are supposed to do. Other universities solve the problem by scrapping tutorials, thereby creating other problems.

Inadequate preparation, poor tutoring or even the decision to go 'democratic', so that all the questions come from the floor, can result in the tutor conducting a question and answer session, with the tutor as instant expert delivering an off-the-cuff and inexpert lecture. This situation is perhaps more likely where tutors are junior, insecure and desperate to impress. It is obviously important that tutors should be given clear training and guidance as to the purpose of tutorials and how to conduct them. In particular, tutorials must be understood as the complement, not the supplement, of the lecture.

One-to-one tutoring
The classic tutorial situation derives from Oxbridge, where it was once the main teaching method. The Oxbridge model is too expensive for wide use in today's universities, but good one-to-one teaching may arise in two contexts: in the early stages of senior undergraduate and postgraduate supervision, and in some forms of interactive software, which could be used in flexible learning. Indeed, the paradigm for many computer games, where the computer responds to the player's last response, thereby increasing the level of difficulty as skills are mastered, is so effective as to be addictive. To create all this motivation in an academic cause should be a major aim of educational technology. In general, this guided conversational style of tutoring is highly effective, but it requires deep and flexible knowledge on the part of the tutor to anticipate the tutee's responses.

The seminar

The seminar is usually a student presentation on a topic each student has researched. With senior or graduate students, these can be very effective, particularly if combined with peer assessment of the presenter (see

Chapter 8). Unless this is conducted carefully, however, the seminar can become a surface approach to teaching, particularly in undergraduate years. It seems all very student-centred, but all the teacher need do is to allocate the topics and then sit back; the presentation can also do the work of the assessment. The major, if not the only, beneficiary is the presenter, and then only with respect to learning the topic presented. What the audience gets is yet another lecture given by someone with even more hazardous lecturing skill.

Laboratories, excursions

These are usually intended as 'hands-on' experiences and are subject-specific as to intent and design. However, MacKenzie and White (1982) point out that, if the excursion is not to become 'a bus tour', the activities need to be specifically and overtly linked to the declarative knowledge they relate to. Similar considerations apply to the lab.

Peer-directed TLAs

There is much evidence that student–student interaction, both formally structured and spontaneous, can enrich learning outcomes (Collier 1983; Johnson and Johnson 1990; Topping 1996). The following outcomes are likely in effective student–student learning interactions.

- *Elaboration of known content.* Students hear of different interpretations, things they themselves hadn't thought of. This facilitates:
- *Deriving standards for judging better and worse interpretations.*
- *Metacognitive awareness of how one arrives at a given position.* How did he arrive at that conclusion? How did she? How did I get to mine? Which is better?

The metacognitive aspects are sharpened because students readily identify with each other's learning in a way they do not do with top-down teacher-directed learning (Abercrombie 1969).

Then there are the motivational and social outcomes:

- Interacting with peers is usually more interesting than listening to lectures
- Increased self-concept, communication skills, self-knowledge ('I can teach!').
- Getting to know other students better, out of which friendships may arise.

There are very many ways in which student–student interaction can be utilized.

Peer groups (other than tutorial)

In the School of Experimental Psychology at the University of Sussex, there is an interesting mixture between student-led tutorials and teacher support. Students give a brief 15-minute presentation that has been assessed by the teacher beforehand, each tutorial has assigned questions for discussion and each student must put to the group at least one point in the lectures that he or she didn't understand. Beyond that, the students run the main proceedings themselves, except that it was found useful for the teacher to turn up for the last ten minutes. This has a good effect on morale, and allows unresolved issues to be put to the teacher (Dienes 1997).

Buzz groups are *ad hoc* groups of students that are given a question or topic to discuss in the course of a class. The success of this technique, and of many multi-person group structures, depends on the size of the class, and making *absolutely sure* it is clear to them what they have to do. Putting the question or topic in writing is highly advisable.

If the architecture permits, students can be allocated to groups of ten or so in the same room, but it can be awkward where lecture rooms are tiered, with fixed seats. Try outside under the trees. When the groups have reached their conclusions, one person speaks to the plenary session on their behalf, making sure that spokesperson is nominated in advance. When reporting back, individuals then need not feel shy about saying something others might criticize: it comes from the group.

Syndicates and jigsaw are developments of the buzz group.

Syndicate groups

These are formed out of a class of 30 or so divided into four to eight students each (Collier 1985). Each group has an assigned task. The heart of the technique is the intensive debate that is meant to go on in the syndicates. The assignments are designed to draw on selected sources as well as on students' first-hand experiences, so that everyone has something to say. The syndicates then report back to plenary sessions led by the teacher to help to formulate and consolidate the conceptual structures that have emerged from each group. Collier reports that student motivation is very high, and that the higher-level skills are enhanced, as long as they are assessed. Otherwise, students tend to ramble. The system has to be aligned.

Jigsaw

This is somewhat similar, except that the groups are more clearly allocated subtasks, and the plenary is to put the finished subtasks back together to solve the main task. This is a good way of getting a complex task handled where every person has had some active input into the solution. The downside is that each group only gets to see the fine-working of its own subtask, and may miss the whole. Again, assessment is the answer: the assessment task must address the whole (concept maps are useful here, as they are what the whole complex is about, not just the subconcept).

Problem-solving groups

Abercrombie (1969) worked with medical students in problem-solving groups. Her groups consisted of ten or so students, and the task was diagnosis, mostly using X-ray plates as stimulus material; the questions found on what was the subject of the X-ray, and what it might mean. The principle is applicable to any situation where students are learning to make judgements, and where there is likely to be a strong difference of opinion. Students have to construct a hypothesis where the data are insufficient to reach an unambiguous conclusion. Different individuals typically seize on different aspects of the data, or use the same data to draw different conclusions, so that astonished students find themselves at loggerheads with others equally convinced of the correctness of their own interpretations. The shock of that discovery can be powerful, forcing students to examine closely the basis of how they arrived at their own conclusions. Students taught in this way made better diagnoses, based more firmly on evidence, and they were less dogmatic, being more open to consider alternative possibilities (see also Abercrombie 1980).

In all group work, the students must have sufficient background to contribute, either from reading enough to have an informed discussion, or where the topic relates directly to personal experience. Above all, the group leader needs to be able to create the right sort of atmosphere so that students can discuss uninhibitedly. Some teachers find it hard not to correct a student, or not to be seen as the expert, and the one to arbitrate in disputes. But to become expert arbitrator kills the point of the exercise, as students then tend to sit back and wait to be told what to think.

As to the optimal size of a group, there is no set answer as it depends on the nature of the group task, and on the group dynamics. The principle is that each member should feel responsibility and commitment. The larger the group, the more likely it is that 'social loafing' will take place, one jerk leaving it to the others to do the work. Interestingly, this is a Western phenomenon. In ethnic Chinese groups, members work *harder* in larger groups (Gabrenya *et al.* 1985). This issue of group size and contribution is important when using group tasks for assessment purposes (see Chapter 9).

Learning partners

Students select, or are assigned, a 'partner' for the unit. This technique is particularly useful in large-class teaching and is elaborated in Chapter 6.

Learning cells are dyads formed not so much for mutual support but for working jointly on a problem or skill. The justification is simply that students work better when working in pairs (McKeachie *et al.* 1986). This is particularly useful in laboratory situations, learning at the computer terminal or question and answer on set tasks, as in reciprocal questioning.

Reciprocal questioning
Students are trained to ask 'generic' questions of each other following the teaching of a piece of content (King 1990). Generic questions get to the point of the content; in SOLO terms they are relational. For example:

- What is the main idea here?
- How would you compare this with . . .?
- But how is that different from . . .?
- Now can you give me a different example?
- How does this affect . . .?

King compared these kinds of questions with equal time open-ended discussion, and while the latter often gave longer answers, they were almost all low level. On critical thinking, and high-level elaboration, the questioning groups were far superior. Reciprocal questioning emphasizes that when you are getting students to interact in order to reach specific cognitive objectives, make sure there is a clear, and high-level, agenda for them to address.

Other forms of *peer teaching* specially suitable for large-class teaching are described in the next chapter.

Self-directed TLAs

The aims of all tertiary institutions would refer, implicitly or explicitly, to the development of self-management skills. When the basic bodies of knowledge, and knowledge relating to professional practice, are changing as rapidly as they are, it no longer makes sense to teach students all those things they will need to know in their professional careers. While there are still vestiges of the old 'fill-up-the-tanks' model of education (see Chapter 10), our aims at least recognize that the old model is impractical. Students should be taught how to learn, how to seek new information, how to utilize it and evaluate its importance, how to solve novel, non-textbook, professional problems. They will need high-level metacognitive skills, and an abstract body of theory on which to deploy them, so that they can judge reflectively how successfully they are in coping with novel problems, and how they may do better (Schön 1983). Action learning for life, if you like (see Chapter 1).

We are dealing with three levels of self-directed learning.

Generic study skills

Study skills are ways of managing time and space. For example:

- keeping notes and references neatly and systematically so that they can be found when needed
- apportioning time, and keeping track of deadlines, so that all topics and subjects are given adequate time, and in proportion to their importance.

Generic study skills might be thought to be the job of high school, or of the counselling or learning assistance centre. Certainly they seem to be well learned in the university of hard knocks: adults are very much better at such foresight, organizing and planning than are students straight from school (Candy 1991; Trueman and Hartley 1996), and women are better than men (Trueman and Hartley 1996). Teaching generic study skills, particularly long-term planning, has positive effects on performance (Hattie *et al.* 1996).

Study skills that relate to learning particular content

These skills include:

- underlining/highlighting the key words in a passage;
- reading for main ideas, not details;
- taking notes properly, by capturing the main idea of several sentences in own words, rather than copying every second or third sentence;
- using concept maps to derive a major structure;
- composing essays according to a pre-planned structure; using review and revise, not first drafts.

But consider this experiment. Ramsden *et al.* (1986) taught study skills to first-year undergraduates from a variety of faculties, focusing on reading and note-taking, examination preparation and writing skills. The effects were the opposite of what was intended: in comparison to a control group, the students increased their use of *surface* approaches. Subsequent interviews with the students revealed that they believed that to be successful in the first year you needed to retain facts accurately, so they selected from the study skills course just those strategies they believed would help them to memorize better. You will recall that first-year students rejected concept maps for the same reason (Santhanam *et al.* 1998). Students get these ideas from hints dropped in lectures, and particularly from non-aligned assessment tasks.

Chalmers and Fuller (1996) recommend that teachers embed useful study skills in their teaching so they are not only teaching *what* they want their students to learn, but *how* to learn it. They suggest sections of strategies for *acquiring* information (note making, memorizing, skim reading), strategies for *working with* information (explaining ideas, organizing ideas, writing summaries), strategies for *confirming* learning (handling assessment tasks) and so on. These are adapted to suit the particular unit or course content.

The same applies to other study skills, such as the well known heuristic SQ4R, used for reading text (Thomas and Robertson 1982):

- *Survey.* What's it about? What are the headings, subheadings, figures etc.?
- *Question.* Formulate questions to be answered after reading.
- *Read* the text with a view to answering the questions.
- *Reflect.* How does it relate to what you already know? Are your questions answered? What else should it have said?
- *Recite* the important facts, quotes, that you'll need.
- *Review.* Can you answer the questions in future?

SQ4R is as good as the use to which it is put. If the students think they need factual answers to simple questions, that's what they'll get from SQ4R. However, if the teacher models the method to the class, showing how to focus on themes and main ideas, and how to extract them from text, it can be helpful. It has to be done in interaction with particular content, where the teacher can explain the main ideas, and why they are important.

In sum, study skills are part of the teaching system and therefore should be supported by the context in which they will be used. It then becomes clear why those strategies are useful. Building knowledge is so much more effective when the tools needed for building are used on the spot, thoughtfully.

Metacognitive learning skills

Finally, there are those self-management skills that are focused on what the learner does in new contexts, which is the ultimate aim of university teaching. Perkins (1991) characterizes the difference between the study skills of the previous section and those of this as the difference between 'going beyond the information given' (BIG) and 'without the information given' (WIG). In BIG teaching, direct instruction is followed by thought-oriented activities that challenge students, so that they come to apply, generalize and refine their understanding: conventional teaching at its best. WIG teaching goes beyond direct instruction in that the students are encouraged by questioning and support to find their own way out, as in the best examples of problem-based learning (see Chapter 10).

So, in WIG, we are not dealing with heuristics or other specific study tips, but with managing the problems and questions that have not been previously addressed:

- This is a 'fuzzy' problem; how can I reformulate it in a way that relates to first principles, and leads to good solutions?
- What do I know that might be relevant? What problems like this have I met before? What did I do then?
- How can I find out further information? From where? How do I test it?
- Let's try this solution, does it work? How could I improve it?

These constitute a different order of question, using both generic and content skills, in order to organize and conceptualize what is known (BIG), prior to reconceptualizing it (WIG). The verbs involved here are mostly open-ended: planning, theorizing, hypothesizing, generating. However, there is also a strong monitoring side, a watching brief over what is going on and the testing of outcomes for adequacy.

Evaluating one's own work, of prime importance in everyday professional life, is one skill that graduates feel their university education least prepared them to do (Boud 1986). Self-evaluation or self-monitoring skills therefore need to be addressed. They are already implicit in properly aligned teaching. We return to the development of this fundamental skill in the following chapters.

Summary and conclusions

Characteristics of rich teaching/learning contexts

If we are to devise and implement effective TLAs, it makes good sense to see what there is in common between contexts in which good learning takes place. We find that they embody the construction of a good knowledge base, the perception by students of a felt need to learn and student activity, including social interaction. The power of a teaching method or TLA depends on the extent to which it embodies these characteristics.

Constructing a base of interconnected knowledge

A powerful knowledge base is complex in structure and error-free, built on accessible interconnections. Creating such a base involves, for teaching purposes: building on the known, making use of students' existing knowledge, emphasizing structural interconnections between topics and confronting misconceptions students may have. These points should infuse teaching whatever the particular method, and can be helped with such techniques as advance organizers and concept maps to outline overall structure. Most important is to maximize students' awareness of their own knowledge construction, largely by placing them in situations that require them to self-monitor and self-direct their own learning.

Learner activity and interaction

Knowledge is constructed through learner activity and interaction. Activity has several roles. The fact of being generally active in and of itself provides general alertness and efficiency; TLAs using different sensory modes of learning provides multiple access to what has been learned.

Learning may be directed by teacher, peers or self. Each agent best serves different purposes. These agencies of direction provide a convenient way of classifying TLAs.

Teacher-directed TLAs

Lecturing is the main TLA at university, although there are plenty of interactive modifications: student questioning, think-aloud modelling, concept mapping and – to anticipate the next section – use of student– student interaction.

Other teacher-directed sessions include the tutorial, in which student– student interaction addresses those verbs that the related lecture could not permit; the seminar, which is nominally teacher-directed although most of the work is done by students; laboratories and excursions, providing selected first-hand experience for students, but requiring good teacher guidance to be successful.

Peer-directed TLAs

Student–student interaction brings a different range of outcomes: elaboration, awareness of others' interpretations, deriving standards of acceptability and metacognitive awareness. Student–student interaction can take many forms. Different results emerge according to the group structure and purpose. Peer teaching and learning partnerships are particularly well suited for high student–staff ratios and are considered in the next chapter.

Self-directed TLAs

Self-directed learning is what university is ultimately about. There are three levels:

1 Generic study skills that apply to managing and organizing one's time and space.

2 Study skills that relate to learning particular content: of being given information and then proceeding paradigmatically beyond it.
3 Metacognitive learning skills of high generality that enable one to handle new situations where teacher-provided information is lacking.

In traditional university teaching, the teacher has been directly concerned with none of these, 1 being the province of school or specialist intervention, 2 and 3 being learned by osmosis. That position is no longer tenable: students need contexts that require independent thinking; and that allow them to flex their metacognitive muscles.

Further reading

On good teaching/learning contexts and principles of good teaching

Biggs, J. and Moore, P. (1993) *The Process of Learning*, Sydney: Prentice Hall Australia, Chapters 16 and 17.
Jackson, M. (1997) But learners learn more, *Higher Education Research and Development*, 16, 101–10.
Ramsden, P. (1992) *Learning to Teach in Higher Education*, London: Routledge, Chapter 6.

Biggs and Moore describe rich learning contexts and the conditions for good learning, and summarize research on expert teaching. Ramsden deals with six key principles of effective teaching. Jackson is a senior academic proactive in advancing teaching. His title comes from Comenius: 'The main object is to find a method in which teachers teach less but learners learn more . . .' Exactly.

On good teaching practices (on lecturing, see next chapter)

Brown, G. and Atkins, M. (1988) *Effective Teaching in Higher Education*, London: Methuen.
Chalmers, D. and Fuller, R. (1996) *Teaching for Learning at University*, London: Kogan Page.
HERDSA News. The newsletter of the Higher Education Research and Development Society of Australasia. There are three issues a year, each containing at least one highly practical article of the 'It worked for me, why don't you have a go?' variety.
Race, P. and Brown, S. (1993) *500 Tips for Tutors*, London: Kogan Page.

Just a sample of the many books on good teaching practice. The 'tips for . . .' genre contains useful collections of procedures, but you must use your own judgement as to their applicability to your own problems. There is a grave danger of falling into the level 2 mode: tell me what are good teaching techniques and I'll use them. Chalmers and Fuller remind you to teach students how to handle the information you are teaching them.

On using groups

Abercrombie, M. L. J. (1980) *Aims and Techniques of Group Teaching*, London: Society for Research into Higher Education.
Collier, K. G. (1983) *The Management of Peer-group Learning: Syndicate Methods in Higher Education*, Guildford: Society for Research into Higher Education.
Johnson, D. W. and Johnson, R. T. (1990) *Learning Together and Alone: Co-operation, Competition and Individualization*, Englewood Cliffs, NJ: Prentice Hall.

The first two are very practical accounts of using groups effectively. Johnson and Johnson is the latest edition of a classic on setting up cooperative learning groups.

6

Enriching large-class teaching

The lecture is the standard method for teaching large classes. Its strengths lie in communicating (a) information and (b) the teacher's personal interpretations, but it makes demands on concentration that drastically undermine its value if not properly handled. This chapter suggests how the lecture can be made more effective, using periodic pauses, changes in activity that clarify and elaborate the lecture content, and active review by students. Other large-class TLAs are peer-directed, such as learning partners, various kind of group work both in an out of class and peer teaching; and self-directed, particularly in conjunction with teacher-prepared flexible learning materials used on- or off-campus. Class size, although constraining, is no reason to abandon the principle of alignment. It is a different context for learning, not necessarily a worse one.

The ubiquitous lecture

In the early 1970s, a celebrated lecturer, a Dr Fox, did a circuit of several US university medical faculties. He was hugely successful wherever he went. The student ratings were highly positive, praising him particularly as an inspirational teacher, and a master in total command of his subject matter. It turns out that Dr Fox was a professional actor, whose only knowledge of the field was supplied by a *Reader's Digest* article (Ware and Williams 1975). This study has been used:

1 To call student ratings of teaching into question, on the grounds that a clever presentation can mask real deficiencies in substance.
2 To support the idea that lectures may motivate, and even inspire, students.

Both conclusions are inappropriate.

Very few teachers are professional actors, or have any training in public speaking. The normal class lecture is not a one-off event with a billed guest speaker, but the regular method of teaching throughout the semester. The majority of academics do not have the personal gifts, or the rhetorical skills, to be able to perform centre stage, inspiring students day after day. Those who think that they can do so are likely to be deluding themselves. My point is not that large-class lecturing should be subcontracted to professional actors, but to seek how we can best use the situation, one teacher/many students, more realistically.

We look at ways of enriching the teaching of large classes from two points of view: (a) examining ways of increasing the cognitive range of the lecture; and (b) looking at alternatives to the lecture for handling these high student–staff ratios. First, let us see what the lecture can do, and what it cannot do.

Advantages and limitations of the lecture

One attraction of the lecture is that it accommodates large fluctuations in student numbers. It has therefore become the method for all seasons. It is assumed that if you know your subject, and do not have any speech defects, you can deliver a passable lecture. That assumption needs examining closely.

Classic reviews of the lecture method were conducted by Bligh (1971) and McLeish (1976). Bligh reviewed nearly a hundred studies comparing lecturing with other methods, mostly group discussions or reading, and found the following:

1 Lectures are as effective as other methods for *teaching information*, but not more effective. Forty studies suggested that unsupervised reading is better than lecturing.
2 Lectures are quite ineffective for stimulating *higher-order thinking*. Examples of the latter included: amount of outside reading, considering more than one authority, problem-solving, decision-making, application of principles, creativity, undertaking higher degree work. Of 26 studies reviewed, not one favoured the lecture over other methods on any of these highly desirable criteria.
3 Lectures cannot be relied on to inspire, or to change students' attitudes favourably. One study did favour the lecture, but that only reiterates the point that while exceptional orators might inspire (see Box 6.1, part 2), most teachers do not, while believing that they do.
4 Students like really good lectures, but as a rule prefer well conducted group work.

So, if lectures do not inspire students, and are only as good as other methods for passing on information, how can they be justified? What can the lecture do that books and groups cannot?

Many university teachers, through their research and scholarship, have developed a *perspective* on their field of expertise that is not to be found in textbooks. Textbooks – regrettably – do not usually have an 'angle', a perspective, but are more often a multistructural list of things that every first-year student might ever need to know. Who better to provide a critical perspective on that bland display of knowledge than the teacher at the cutting edge of the topic, and in person? Through sheer publication lag, textbooks are well over a year out of date, and active researchers are not. The best defence of the lecture, particularly in senior undergraduate years, thus lies not in doing what other media do as well or better, but in exposing students to the most recent developments in the field, and to the ongoing workings of a scholarly mind. But it has to be a *scholarly* mind.

The *unique* contribution of the lecture thus derives from the nexus between research and teaching. This role is most recognizable today in supervising research students. In the undergraduate years, sheer student numbers have weakened that role of active scholar-cum-mentor, but not entirely. It is still possible to provide that personal perspective on knowledge, both on the process of constructing and validating knowledge and on interpreting the outcome. Heaven forbid that teachers have reached the demeaning point where all that remains is to tell students content that they can read more effectively.

In short, the teacher should be an agent for *transforming* knowledge, helping students to interpret and to construct their own knowledge, not a passive substation that relays preformed messages to them. The teacher is as it were a master craftsman, the student an apprentice in the craft of scholarship. This is where modelling might come in, and where the word 'inspire' becomes relevant.

The lecture is therefore as good as the lecturer, not as crowd-pleaser, but as scholar. So, if you want to use the lecture as your predominant method, the question is: can you offer your students something that the textbook or other sources cannot? If the answer to that is in the negative, and you are not a highly skilled orator, you should if you can use the lecture sparingly. Box 6.1 gives examples of two successful lecturing styles.

Psychological constraints

Many of the lecture's limitations arise from certain facts about human learning:

1 Sustained and unchanging low-level activity lowers concentration. Sitting listening to a lecture is such an activity. Yet it requires concentrated effort to follow lecture content.

Box 6.1: Two prize-winning approaches to lecturing

1   Conceptualization through questions and relevance

Judy Cowie, lecturer in economics at the University of Adelaide, and National CAUT Fellow 1996, pioneered the 'Adelaide method', where workshops and tutorials are held before lectures, so that students can approach lecture material with increased confidence. Ms Cowie never presents textbook material in lectures and allows question-and-answer time, even with hundreds of students . . . relating key concepts to newspaper articles and television reports.

Source: The Weekend Australian, 26–27 July 1997.

2   Conceptualization through infectious enthusiasm

Dr Alastair Greig, lecturer in sociology, Australian National University, won The Australian University Teaching Award in the social science section, with the 'highest student approval ratings the panel had seen' – and with a Glaswegian accent so broad 'my students think I stepped off the boat yesterday'. His style is described as 'infectiously enthusiastic'. He starts each lecture with appropriate cartoons, poems, or songs and distributes typed lecture notes 'so students . . . can concentrate on listening.'

Source: The Australian Higher Education, 26 November 1997.

---

2 The attention span of students under these conditions can be maintained for about 10 to 15 minutes, after which learning drops off rapidly (see Figure 6.1).
3 A short rest period, or simply a *change* in activity, after about 15 minutes leads to a restoration of performance almost to the original level (see Figure 6.1).
4 A brief period of consolidation after prolonged learning greatly enhances retention. Getting students to review at the end of the lecture what has been learned leads to much better and more lasting retention than simply finishing and dismissing the students (see Figure 6.2).
5 The low-level outcomes usually gained from the lecture are in large part due to the unbroken activities of listening and note-taking.

Figure 6.1 shows, first, the rapid drop-off in attention and therefore in effective learning as a function of time into the lecture, then the recuperative effect of a rest or change of activity after about 20 minutes. That '20 minutes' might be 10, 30 or even longer. It depends on the students, the skill of the lecturer, the pace of the lecture, the difficulty of the material, the use of educational technology (which involves a change of activity), the time of day and so on. But the basic point remains: do not talk longer than

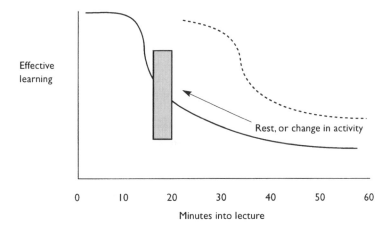

Figure 6.1: Effect of rest or change of activity on learning
Source: after Bligh 1971

15 or 20 minutes without a pause, unless you are certain you still have their attention. When you do pause, get the students to change their activity.

Figure 6.2 suggests that you should *consolidate* what has been dealt with in a learning session if it is to be retained for a significant period of time. In the original study on which the figure is based, the consolidation was determined by asking students about the lecture content at the end of the lecture. They were required *actively to review* what they had just learned. That does not mean that you tell them what you have just told them, as in

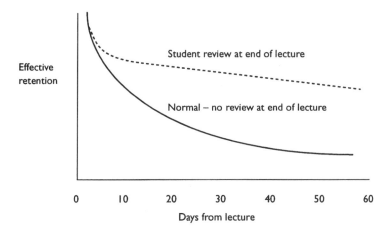

Figure 6.2: Effect of testing at end of lecture on retention
Source: after Bligh 1971

the conventional summary (although you can do that too), but getting *them* to tell you, or a neighbour, what you have just told them. They need to be active in reviewing what they have been exposed to in the previous 50 minutes or so.

Interposing breaks with a different focused activity during the lecture, and active review after, helps to lift the quality of learning outcomes, as in point 5 above.

We arrive yet again at the fundamental premise of this book: it's what the student does . . . And that is the basic problem with the lecture. Both teacher and students see the lecture as a matter of teacher performance, not of learner performance. It is a perception that has to be changed.

In sum, while lectures can convey information to students, the usual form – talking on the one hand, listening and note-taking on the other – does not get students to think critically or creatively, nor does it motivate them. Yet as budgets get tighter, and student–staff ratios larger, the lecture is likely to become even more entrenched.

Think of the large-class situation as a *plenary session* rather than as a 'lecture'. This carries the strong suggestion that there are other ways of using the time than listening to the chair endlessly talking. When we talk about lectures being scheduled, we really mean the time slot is fixed, the large plenary session. What happens within that slot need not be lecturing. The question is how to use the time most usefully. There are two rather different aspects to this:

- *managerial,* dealing with large numbers of people at a time;
- *educational,* using that space for effective learning.

Management skills for large-class teaching

Management issues are paramount in large-class teaching (see, for example, Gibbs *et al.* 1984; Brown and Atkins 1988; Gibbs and Jenkins 1992; Davis and McLeod 1996a). Davis and McLeod define large-class teaching from two points of view:

- *the teacher's,* when the group size, about 40 students or more, prevents the use of strategies that depend on close contact;
- *the student's,* when the individual begins to feel anonymous.

This implies two almost contradictory sets of management strategies:

1 'Close contact' strategies won't work, so that specific 'large-class' strategies will need to be acquired.
2 The anonymity the students feel needs to be counteracted.

Paradoxically, we use large-class techniques so that students don't feel that they are in a large class. In meeting this challenge, we are cheerily assured that large-class teaching isn't just making the best of a bad job, but holds its 'own delights and advantages. [Large classes] actually allow a teacher to achieve quite easily some things that are more difficult to achieve in small groups' (Davis and McLeod 1996a: 3). This is an important realization. On the other hand, large-class teaching is difficult, and requires rather more self-assurance and experience on the part of the teacher. It is quite irresponsible to allocate the largest classes of first years to the least experienced and junior staff members, as so often happens.

Following are some suggestions for managing large classes. Many of the skills needed are different from the presentation skills mentioned in Chapter 5.

Preparatory

Large classes need much more meticulous preparation than small classes. The larger the class, the slower things get done. A spur of the moment change of direction, perhaps in response to a student question, highly desirable and manageable with a group of 30, becomes perilous with 200.

Preparation includes planning the academic content and the management procedures, and preparing mentally. Most people find large-class teaching more of a 'performance', with greater possibilities of stage fright, than teaching smaller classes. Even experienced teachers need time beforehand to collect themselves.

Academic structure
You should make the purposes of each session clearly explicit well in advance. Is it to outline the boundaries or coverage of the topic/unit, to go in depth into a particular topic or series of topics, to make a case or argument in depth, to use as an outline or summary session or to challenge previously accepted points? The students should be told the purpose.

Materials
Notes, handouts, overhead transparencies etc. need to be organized before the class, ready to be used. If you are using overheads and you suddenly decide to change the order it can be fatal. Don't sort material on the run.

Procedural rules
This slow heaving hulk needs to be carefully directed, otherwise it will crush your plans. Establish your procedural rules at the outset, in writing where appropriate: signals for silence, signals for starting and stopping; if you are going to use buzz groups, who is to discuss with whom, who is to be spokesperson on report back. How do you bring them back to order when

it's time? Davis and McLeod suggest playing lively music to accompany discussion; when it stops, it's back to the lecturer. Establish the rules in the first session.

Questioning
In such a large group, questioning needs quite different procedures from those in a small group. Some teachers allow questions only at the end of the lecture, some at any time, some only one-to-one afterwards. Do the students know your rules/expectations about questioning? Are you going to pause and ask: 'Any questions?' How are you going to deal with the forest of hands; or with the clown who always asks questions to class groans? What about those students who irritatingly wait behind to ask you a terrific question that should have been aired in class, or to point out that the deadline won't work because . . . These are whole-class matters. You should discuss these issues and allow a procedure for questions.

Dealing with questions requires 'large-class' technique. Questions provide a welcome break that many students perceive as chat-to-neighbour time, while the nerd has a heart-to-heart with the lecturer. To prevent this, the whole class must be included and involved. This means *distancing* yourself from the questioner, not doing the personable thing and leaning towards the questioner. Move back so that the questioner is part of the class, and the question then becomes a whole-class question. Repeat the question loudly into the microphone, while looking at the 'U', the back and side rows, not the 'T', the front and middle rows, from whence the question almost certainly came. In a very large class, it may be better to ask them to write down their questions and pass them up to the front, rather than shouting them at you. You could take them on the spot, or answer them in the introduction to the next session.

Starting the lecture

Again, the size and buzz of a large class makes different demands on getting started smoothly.

- Don't just sail straight in: signal that class has started and wait for quiet.
- Start with a proper introduction: 'Following from last week when we . . . What we are going to do today . . .' Then *brief* them (Gibbs *et al.* 1984): explain what the lecture is supposed to be doing that some other activity cannot. Why lecture when the topic is in the textbook? Because you are going to do something the textbook can't. Tell the students what that is; what they should be getting from this particular lecture.
- Preview with an overhead giving the subheadings of the lecture, and some explanation of the sequences of subheadings, or a diagram if that is appropriate.

Structuring the lecture

The structure of the lecture is ideally a reflection of the structure of the topics or content being taught. Brown and Atkins (1988) refer to several lecture structures:

1 *Classical*, where the lecture addresses several broad areas, each of which is subdivided. This is the easiest method of structuring, and 'potentially the most boring' (Brown and Atkins 1988). If not prepared and structured properly, it can become a rambling monologue: 'I'll tell them about this, then that, and then wind up.' It is in this situation that one needs to be very clear about structure both for oneself and for the students. The topic structure needs to be clearly emphasized, and keyed in to the subdivisions.
2 *Problem-centred*: a problem is presented and alternative solutions are suggested. It could be left with alternatives there for students to sort out, as in the most teacher-directed versions of problem-based learning (see Chapter 10), or the lecture could be closed with an argument for one of them.
3 *Comparative*: two or more theories, views, perspectives etc. are offered and compared. Students need to know the different theories or positions first.
4 *Thesis*: a position is taken and then supported with evidence, argument, hypothesis.

Whatever the structure, explain it specifically on an overhead, or handout.

Delivering the lecture

Following are a few points to watch during lecturing.

- Eye-contact students while talking; no head buried in notes.
- Ensure clarity: project the voice, check it can be heard at the back. Cordless radio mikes are best.
- Focus on the 'U' rather than the 'T' of the geography of the lecture room, as when asking or repeating questions. Susan and her friends tend to sit along the front row and up the middle, Robert and his friends at the back and down the sides. Focus on grabbing Robert; you will automatically include Susan.
- Any points you want students to get verbatim in their notes, signal and dictate, or put on an overhead. Allow sufficient time.
- Clear visual aids, notes, handouts. Handouts are important in large classes.
- But provide handouts at the beginning or the end of the lecture, so students can collect them on entry or exit. If possible, organize the schedule at least a week ahead so that the end of the previous session can

be used for handouts. Distributing handouts during class (of 100+ say) is messy and time-wasting.

- Consider tape-recording the lecture and making cassettes available in the library, possibly with a clear copy of your own notes. This is particularly useful for international students who may have difficulty in comprehending and keeping up with note-taking. It is best not to record live, but in your office using good equipment.
- When changing activities, explain why: Gibbs calls this 'flagging'. For example, in the event of a break, don't just say 'OK, stop. Get up and stretch.' They and you will look and feel silly. Rather: 'We've been hard at it for 20 mins. We'll all feel better for a break. Stretch, yawn and walk around a bit. I'm going to. OK, we've got one minute.' The same applies to all changes in flow or activity.

Personalizing the class

One of the features of large-class teaching that students dislike most is the impersonality; it is a short step from there to a cold theory X climate. How you handle that is a personal matter, but the following are possibilities (Davis 1993).

- Stand in front of the lectern, not behind it, which also means don't read from your notes. Walk about, up and down the aisles if feasible. Get students to leave a few rows empty, so you can move along them. Such ploys give the impression of accessibility, not distance. Stand still, however, when delivering important points.
- If the session is a whole-class activity, such as lecturing, do not in your friendly wandering allow yourself to be seduced by a *sotto voce* conversation with a nearby student, in answer to a quick informal question. It must be treated as a question coming from the whole class (see above).
- At the beginning of the class get neighbouring students to introduce themselves to each other. These may or may not lead to formal learning partnerships (see below).
- Get students to complete a short biographical questionnaire, with names, reasons for taking the unit, hobbies etc. You can then refer to students by name occasionally, and select examples to illustrate points in your lectures to match their interests. They'll feel good about that, even though everyone won't get a mention.
- Arrive early, and/or leave late, to talk with students. Let them know you'll be there. Similarly, make your hours of availability in your office known, and keep those times sacred. Some teachers may be comfortable with inviting groups of students, in circulation to cover everyone, to coffee.
- Where tutors mark assignments, make sure you read a sample, and discuss in class. Let them know you are not delegating entirely.

- Use humour and topical references. (But be careful where there are large numbers of international students, who are likely to be confused by topical references, colloquialisms and culturally specific jokes: see Chapter 7).

These points focus on what the teacher does. We now focus on the more important issue of what the student is doing.

Active learning in the large class

There is nothing wrong with someone with expert knowledge explaining important and useful aspects of that knowledge to someone else. In normal communication, if the listener's attention seems to wander you do something to haul it back: a brush of eye contact, a question. Listeners, for their part, can clarify difficult points as they go, comment on aspects that strike them and do something with that knowledge as they proceed, such as think of their own examples, make sure their notes are sufficient for structuring good recall later on, or for explaining it someone else.

In a small class, these props for understanding are relatively easy to arrange. The challenge is to arrange them when there are hundreds of people listening.

The teacher's task, the students' tasks

We teachers have one task, sharing our recent thinking in an erudite and stimulating lecture, but the students have two: to comprehend what they are hearing, and to write their notes and commentary for later reference.

Many students find it difficult to do both tasks, so they alternate them. This results in a 'copy-delete' strategy. They listen to one sentence, and while writing the gist of that one down, the lecturer is saying at least two more, and these sentences are missed. Using this inefficient note-taking strategy, students have on record less than a third of the ideas that make up the lecture. And with only a fraction of the trees, they have to reconstruct the whole wood. Students need a chance not just to check that their notes are accurate, but more importantly to see that their notes actually do address the plot. They need time to reflect on the bigger picture.

The solution is simple: separate comprehension time from recording time. Give them a time-slot to check their notes. Gibbs *et al.* (1992) suggest setting a timer to ring every 15 minutes; when it rings, stop talking and get them to consolidate the process the lecture has set in train. If your lectures are such that any stopping point is as good as any other, fair enough, but I would prefer the timer to be audible only to me, to remind me to stop at the next best logical break. Students can then swap notes with their neighbours, discuss differences and rewrite their own notes. They can thus repair the holes in the notes with the main ideas about what has been said, not the sentence by sentence details.

The pause can also be used to engage them in other, higher cognitive level, activities that use the content:

• For reflecting on what they think they have just learned individually, or in pairs, telling each other what they saw as the most important point in the preceding 15 minutes of lecturing.
• Each student writes down a question or a comment sparked by the previous 15 minutes. See if a neighbour can respond. They can hand in their question/comments sheet at the end of the session; it will be useful for feedback (and for attendance check).
• You put a question on a transparency. They discuss with a neighbour.
• You set a problem for them to work on, either individually or in pairs.
• You answer their questions.
• You get a break, to reflect on any points that might need clarifying or elaborating, to sort out notes or just to catch your breath.

Near the end of the lecture, you might allow five minutes for the students to tell their neighbour or learning partner what they think was the thrust of the session. This achieves the active review, and also gives them a different perspective to think about, other than their own interpretation of yours.

Linking diagrams and key points can be achieved by handouts using *Powerpoint* or other presentational software, so that overheads can be copied and distributed, with the overheads reduced so that three or so can be placed down one half the page, and the students can write their notes and comments beside each. This gives students accurate basic notes and diagrams, but requires them to search actively for the main idea, and put it in their own words with an example or two. Chalmers and Fuller (1996) recommend the integration of the two sets of task, the teacher's and the students', by actively incorporating note-taking into the lecture.

Self-addressed questions

Any particular lecture is only one episode in a long story. You can help students to focus on the story rather than just on the episode by seeing that they have the schedule of lecture topics at the commencement of the unit, then getting them to respond to self-addressed questions (Fleming 1993), such as:

(a) What do I most want to find out in the next class?

Before each class the students have to read around this question, and note down their responses. Five minutes or so before that session is due to finish, ask them to address the next questions:

(b) What is the main point I learned today?
(c) What was the main point left unanswered in today's session?

These are then handed in, with names. The actual writing is a matter of very few sentences per question, and they can be read in a couple of minutes. The answers can be used as formative assessment both for them and for you – and as an attendance check. The cumulative record gives a very good, and quick, indication of the development of students' thinking through the course.

This forces students actually to *do* the pre-reading, and to reflect on it, as in question (a). Question (b) can tell you something about their learning and your teaching: if some quite minor aside is seen as 'the main point' either you or they have a problem. The last question allows you to address misconceptions derived in today's class in next week's class, and to discuss differences between what you and they saw as the important points. All this provides students with feedback on how their thinking is in line with other students', and with your own. For this purpose, only a sample need be read. Question (b), called 'the three-minute essay', can also be used for assessment purposes, graded or ungraded.

These are not of course the only questions that could or should be asked. You can no doubt think of others that would better suit your objectives.

Techniques of informed note-taking, pauses, swapping lecture notes with neighbours, discussing key questions and so on, taken singly or in combination, meet many of the objections raised about the lecture, both improving the efficiency of the lecture itself, by keeping students alert and their notes relevant, and getting students involved in the high-level activities the lecture itself usually does not evoke. In particular, the interspersed activities address monitoring, structuring and consolidating the information presented in the lecture.

Student–student interaction in the large-class setting

The preceding activities are teacher-directed, with incidental use of students interacting with each other. As we saw in the previous chapter, peer interaction leads to valuable outcomes of its own: elaboration of knowledge, awareness of standards of knowing, reflection leading to metacognitive awareness and various social benefits such as improved social skills and self-concept. Students also like learning from peers.

Learning partners

The suggestion for forming partnerships comes from the teacher, but then students choose their own, usually one other person. Partnerships are not so much for working towards a goal, such as a group assignment, but for mutual support. The larger the class, the more likely that students will feel alienated. They need someone to talk to: to share concerns, to seek clarification over assignment requirements, to check their own insecure interpretations of procedure or of content (Saberton 1985).

Partners could be matched by the teacher: alphabetically, or on the basis of the way students complement each other (high performing/at risk, international/local, mature age/straight from school, those with access to desirable resources/those with little access). Alternatively, students could choose their own partners, and that probably is the best way. Partners then agree to sit next to each other in class, and to consult out of class, exchanging telephone numbers, e-mail etc. It may be desirable for them to (officially) collaborate on assessment tasks: we deal with that issue in Chapter 9. Partnerships that do not work because of the personal chemistry should be reformed. Some students may prefer to remain loners; that should be respected. They may come round later.

Learning partners permanently sitting next to each other makes life much easier for you when implementing the kinds of note-swapping, active review and so on mentioned above. It is also easier for two students to seek clarification from you than one. Your out-of-class time in dealing with queries is halved.

Peer teaching

There is no single best method of teaching, 'but the second best is students teaching other students' (McKeachie *et al.* 1986: 63). Peer teaching is a very powerful method of learning that is greatly under-utilized, although it is highly effective for a wide range of goals, content and students of different levels and personalities, and is easily adapted for large-class teaching, transforming a class of 500 students into 500 teaching assistants. The research on peer teaching finds that both tutor and tutee benefit academically, the tutor more than the tutee. The tutor is also likely to have increased social skills and attitudes to study and self (Goodlad and Hirst 1990; Topping 1996). The reasons are clear:

- The content to be taught is viewed not from one's own perspective, but from that of someone whose conceptions of the topic to be taught are different and less satisfactory.
- The teacher reflects on how he or she learned the topic, which means that peers, being closer to that process and more aware of the traps and difficulties than the expert, can teach more empathically.

- The teacher 'owns' the material, publicly taking responsibility for it and its validity. There is heavy loss of face if teachers get it wrong. So they are more careful about getting it right.

Such are the presumed benefits of peer tutoring in terms of enhanced learning and development of tutoring skills that two New Zealand tertiary institutions give course credit for peer tutoring, the practical work being carried out by tutoring secondary school students (Jones *et al.* 1994). Not education students, destined for a teaching career, but law, science and business students. The assumption is simply that teaching the subject deepens students' cognitive understanding.

Student-led groups
The most common patterns of peer teaching/tutoring are not with pairs but with groups. There are two main types: where the groups comprise students from the same class, and where the tutor is of a higher year level than the tutored.

Same-class groups may be initiated by the teacher, or spontaneously by the students. Both kinds can work very well. A common finding is that, compared to teacher-led groups, student-led groups range wider in their discussion and produce more complex outcomes (McKeachie *et al.* 1986; Tang 1998). However, it is not the technique, but how it runs, that is important. It may be necessary to provide some training and a structured agenda. This is something that individual teachers would need to experiment with in their own circumstances. The cost-benefits of student-led groups in classes with high enrolments are attractive. This arrangement also works extremely well in flexible learning contexts (see below).

Cross-year tutoring is closest to traditional instruction, in that the tutor is either a senior undergraduate or a postgraduate. The most general findings from many studies are that both tutors and tutees like the process, and that achievement of the tutees is little different from that of those conventionally taught (Topping 1996), which is a very positive and cost-effective finding, when you think about it.

Supplemental instruction (SI)
Variously known in Australia as the Peer Assistance Supplementary Scheme or Peer Assisted Study Sessions (PASS in either case), this is a variant of cross-year tutoring that originated at the University of Missouri in 1975. It is now used in over 300 US institutions, 15 British universities and several Australian ones. It is particularly designed to alleviate the problem of large first-year classes.

The tutors are second-year or third-year students who passed the first-year subject exceptionally well, and are judged to have appropriate personal qualities. They are trained to 'model, advise and facilitate' rather than to address the curriculum directly, and are either paid or given course credit. Data involving 295 courses in the USA show improved achievement and higher re-enrolment and graduation rates (National Center for Supplemental Instruction 1994). Outcomes in the UK are likewise encouraging (Topping 1996). At the University of Queensland, over 10,000 students a year have attended PASS, regular attendees averaging a whole grade higher than students who did not attend, while of the students gaining high distinctions, 85 per cent attended PASS (Chalmers and Kelly 1997).

PASS employs two tutors or student leaders per group of 25 first years, and they are paid to attend at least one lecture that the tutees receive (Watson 1996, 1997; Chalmers and Kelly 1997). Leaders receive one full day of training and ongoing weekly meetings with the staff coordinator. Attendance from the first-year class is voluntary, ranging from 20 per cent of the class to over 80 per cent. The agenda is up to the students, frequently involving a review of what has gone on in class that week. No new material is presented; PASS is not in any sense a substitute for other teaching. Following are some of the benefits that students see (Chalmers and Kelly 1997):

- a friendly environment where they can ask 'the dumbest questions';
- weekly study keeps them up to date;
- insight into the range of material other students are covering, and the difficulties they have;
- a mentor can give information and inside knowledge of how they coped;
- international students particularly like the opportunity to discuss without staff present.

Leaders are required to keep a reflective diary, with which they provide feedback to the departmental staff coordinator. This ongoing information is far more useful to lecturers in meeting current problems than end-of-semester course evaluations.

PASS is considered particularly useful in subjects having:

- large classes, particularly when unsupported by other group work;
- highly technical content;
- a failure rate of more than 10 per cent;
- high international student enrolments;
- a service role as a core subject for a number of degree courses.

Spontaneous collaboration

Some student groups are unofficial, formed spontaneously to focus on coping with specific tasks, such as set assignments (Tang 1996). Tang studied spontaneous collaborative learning among physiotherapy students at a Hong Kong university, who after the announcement of an assignment formed their own groups, deciding who would check out what set of references, what ideas might be included and so on. The collaborative effort extends variously through the planning phase of the assignment or project, but the final detailed plan and write-up is conducted individually. Over 80 per cent of Tang's students collaborated to some extent, and those that did showed greater structural complexity (higher SOLO levels) in their assignments. Such a high proportion of spontaneous collaboration may not occur with Western students, but Goodnow (1991) reports on self-formed syndicates at Macquarie University exchanging wisdom on examination questions. An interesting question is how far teachers might encourage, or have any interaction with, these groups (Tang 1993).

Self-directed TLAs and flexible learning

In self-directed study, students learn to meet institutional requirements outside the classroom.

Learning outside the classroom

Learning outside the classroom (LOC) demands the skills of self-management and self-direction that tertiary learning should be encouraging anyway. Formalized instruction outside the classroom was originally called 'external studies', the written word the means for putting such teaching into effect. Out of that came various phases of distance education, leading to what is now called 'flexible learning'. This is assumed to mean off-campus teaching, but it need not. In fact, it provides at the least an important answer to some at least of the problems of large-class teaching; at most, a preview of a brand new tertiary system.

There are three phases in this development of LOC. Each phase was based on assumptions about teaching and learning that rendered regular class attendance unnecessary.

1 *External studies* developed in countries, particularly Australia, where the distances made part-time university attendance impossible for many people. This early phase of LOC was based on a level 1 transmission model; the teaching method consisted basically of detailed lecture notes and assignments that were sent out through the mail. In most cases, students would descend on the campus for a couple of weeks to experience rigorous lecturing and some tutorial work. Final examinations were conducted and invigilated in local centres. In the institution where I taught, every attempt was made to maintain parity between internal and external students. They both had the same syllabus and sat the same examinations, but as the internal students had the benefit of the lectures, they were forbidden the external lecture notes in the interests

of 'fairness'. The administration was obviously unaware of Bligh's (1971) finding that undirected reading is better at passing on information than the lecture itself. Perhaps that is one reason – but only one – why external students usually performed better than the internals.

2 *Open learning*. The next phase was much more sophisticated, commencing with the Open University (OU) in Britain in the 1960s. It was based on level 2 (teacher-centred) and level 3 (student-centred) views of teaching, depending on how it was implemented in particular cases. The OU developed much more interactive materials than lecture notes in the post; the materials made use of innovative and interactive publishing formats, which were often keyed into nationwide television programmes. Regular tutorials, which gave face-to-face contact throughout the year, gave students the opportunity to be more proactive in their learning. The OU had a tremendous influence on the practice of LOC elsewhere. The term 'open' learning itself carries connotations of interactive learning and of access that replace the earlier level 1 transmission view of teaching. The OU model made philosophical assumptions about access to higher education: for example, that degree level standards were possible by adults who had no background in the field of study. This assumption is now widespread throughout the tertiary sector.

3 *Flexible learning*. The third phase of LOC is probably not philosophically so different from open learning, but makes wider use of high-level educational technology, and the teaching/learning options thereby offered. Its proponents certainly see it as a new generation of public learning.

Flexible learning

Beattie and James (1997) distinguish four categories of flexible learning activities, in a framework of descending levels of interactivity.

1 *Real-time teacher-student interaction*. Video- and tele-conferencing offer at a distance much the same kind of interaction that occurs face-to-face.
2 *Computer-mediated communication*. The 'virtual' campus offers enormous library and journal information banks on the Internet, electronic bulletin boards, e-mail. It is difficult to be specific about the nature of the TLAs they might elicit, as they are still developing. One impression is of level 1 information transmission at a stupefying rate.
3 *Pre-packaged learning resources*. These are intended to be used by the learner, mostly alone; this is the closest link with open learning (above). Materials can be quite interactive, requiring a range of high-level learning activities.
4 *Guided experiential activities*. Given that much LOC is with part-time

students in full-time professional jobs, flexible learning offers excellent opportunities for reflective practice and action learning type activities using real job experience.

This classification implies that live teacher–student interaction is prime, the rest substituting for, or supplementing, that. Others see computer-mediated communication technology, particularly involving the World Wide Web, as by far the most important thrust in flexible learning, whether for on- or off-campus teaching (Taylor 1995; Bourner and Flowers 1997; Laurillard and Margetson 1997). Such a development could be radical indeed. Staff in all departments would need the expertise in the technology to teach effectively through distance communication with students and peers, while students, of course, would have to have their own computers, hardship funds being established for those who can't afford it (Laurillard and Margetson 1997). The implications for higher education are immense: much reduced face-to-face contact with further downsizing of academic staff, flexible delivery from prestigious overseas universities possibly eliminating local universities, a total rethink of the function and nature of post-secondary learning (Laurillard and Margetson 1997).

We are far from that situation at present. Many students, not to say teachers, are intimidated by the new electronic technologies. Although students mostly do become comfortable, they and their teachers still feel the need for face-to-face contact. As a supplement to full-time attendance, though, some students appreciate the freedom to manage their own time: 'I try to go to campus twice weekly, but don't have to . . . it frees me up to put more time into my homework' (Beattie and James 1997: 184).

Again, it is not the technology, but how it is used. It can be counterproductive. Some teachers have the idea that 'putting my lecture notes on the Web' is what flexible learning is all about, a surface approach to teaching that can only lead to a surface approach to learning. The phrase 'surfing the Net' is itself ominous: surface indeed, with cut-and-paste here, cut-and-paste there, link up with a few connecting sentences, rewrite some sentences in your very own personalized style, and bingo . . . an assignment that looks really terrific, but contains no original or deep thinking.

There thus appear to be two ways of thinking about flexible learning: as supplemental, or as millennial. In either case, flexible learning offers real opportunities to generate effective and high-quality learning in ways that are economical of the teacher's time despite high student–teacher ratios. However, the evidence so far suggests that interaction with teachers and with other students is as much needed here as when students are lectured to hundreds at a time. Flexible learning shouldn't become the solitary equivalent of the mass lecture, in terms of cognitive engagement. In both cases, it is a matter of realistic and imaginative implementation.

Summary and conclusions

The ubiquitous lecture: advantages and limitations

The lecture has become a generic term for tertiary teaching, an authority it does not deserve. Virtually the only advantage over other methods is that it exposes students in person to a scholar's ongoing thinking. Even then, care is needed. A low-activity task like listening requires concentration; attention diminishes rapidly after 15 minutes or so. The challenge of large-class teaching is to restore the supports for learning that the context diminishes:

1 Interpose changes of activity during the course of the session. It is a very special lecturer who can keep students continually and fully attentive for the whole of the session.
2 Use these breaks to get the students to monitor their notes, and to do some high-level cognitive work with what they have heard.
3 Make sure there is a review activity at the end of the session.

Management skills for large-class teaching

A large class needs carefully planned management. Students must be aware of what to do when changes of activity are required. In large-class teaching you need to learn different management strategies, based on the fact of distance, while overcoming students' dislike of the alienation of being an anonymous face in the crowd. It is a familiar dilemma in the caring professions: reconciling efficient impersonality with the appearance of the personal touch.

Active learning in the large class

To understand a lecture properly, students need to juggle two tasks simultaneously: comprehending the message and recording its gist. Most can't do this adequately, so we should separate the presentation and consolidation sections: then students can focus on the one task, then on the other. Breaks can also be used to ensure that students have good notes, for exchanging interpretations with neighbours, for solving problems and in general for using the content just expounded. The links across lecture episodes can be created with self-addressed questions given out in advance to students. The structure of plenary sessions thus focuses on two basic strategies: presenting content efficiently to students, and getting them to work on it. The two strategies aim at different objectives and can be incorporated in teaching even the largest classes.

Student–student interaction in the large-class setting

The most prolific resource in large classes is the students themselves, and using them appropriately engages a different set of verbs that address a range of objectives scarcely touched by teacher-directed TLAs. Creating semi-permanent learning partnerships can make life easier for both you and them, providing a continually accessible resource for discussing, reciprocal questioning and mutual support in an otherwise anonymous environment. Groups of various kinds extend the range of activities even further. Probably the most powerful is peer teaching, where the research evidence is very strong and positive, for both the learners and teachers. In resource starved times, it is amazing that peer teaching in its various forms, including the use of paid students as in PASS, is not used more widely.

Self-directed TLAs and flexible learning

Learning outside the classroom (LOC) has been identified with external studies, then with distance education and now with flexible learning. These modes reflect different views of teaching, but basically they involve the learner taking responsibility for learning, which after all is what tertiary teaching is about. Flexible learning should actively involve learners, as in the level 3 view of teaching, and although it may be conducted outside the classroom, it is not necessarily conducted off-campus. Flexible learning is still developing, and it is too early to say yet what forms it might take: as a supplement to conventional teaching, or as ushering in the new higher educational millennium.

Matching TLAs with objectives: an overview of Chapters 5 and 6

This and the previous chapter are both concerned with the fundamental question of choosing TLAs that match your objectives. We first looked at some basic principles of teaching, and then at a range of TLAs that can be linked with high-level learning-related verbs. The research relating TLAs to particular verbs is so far incomplete, but personal and collegial experience will help fill gaps. Table 6.1 suggests some TLAs and the sort of learning they are likely to encourage.

The important thing is to be clear about the sort of learning you want, and then to set up TLAs that are most likely to get it. Usually the lecture and the tutorial are the givens, and in practice we bend our objectives to suit. What I am suggesting is precisely the opposite: we tune our teaching

Table 6.1: What activities are teaching methods most likely to elicit?

Each teaching/learning activity	*A form of learning*
Teacher-controlled	
lecture, set texts	reception of selected content
think-aloud	demonstrate conceptual skills
questioning	clarifying, seeking error
advance organizer	structuring, preview
concept mapping	structuring, overview
tutorial	elaboration, clarification
laboratory	procedures, application
excursion	experiential knowledge, interest
seminar	clarify, presentation skill
Peer-controlled	
various groups	elaboration, problem-solving, metacognition
learning partners	resolve differences, application
peer teaching	depends whether teacher or taught
spontaneous collaboration	breadth, self-insight
Self-controlled	
generic study skills	basic self-management
content study skills	information handling (BIG)
metacognitive learning skills	independence and self-monitoring (WIG)

methods to elicit from students the learning activities most likely to produce the desired learning outcomes.

Further reading

On lecturing in large classes

Andreson, L. W. (1994) *Lecturing to Large Groups: a Guide to Doing It Less . . . but Better*, Birmingham: Staff and Educational Development Association.

Bligh, D. A. (1972) *What's the Use of Lectures?*, Harmondsworth: Penguin Books.

Cannon, R. (1988) *Lecturing*, HERDSA Green Guide No. 7, Kensington: Higher Education Research and Development Society of Australasia.

Elton, L. and Cryer, P. (1992) *Teaching Large Classes*, Sheffield: University of Sheffield Teaching Development Unit.

Gibbs, G., Habeshaw, S. and Habeshaw, T. (1984) *53 Interesting Things to Do in Your Lectures*, Bristol: Technical and Educational Services.

Gibbs, G. and Jenkins, A. (eds) (1992) *Teaching Large Classes in Higher Education*, London: Kogan Page.

McLeish, J. (1976) The lecture method, in N. Gage (ed.) *The Psychology of Teaching Methods*, 75th Yearbook of the National Society for the Study of Education, Chicago: University of Chicago Press.

O'Neill, M. (Project Director) *Teaching in Large Classes*. A very comprehensive CD-ROM, showing examples of expert teachers in action at all stages of teaching, from getting prepared for lecture to closing elegantly. Has interviews with novice teachers, expert teachers and students at each teaching stage.

Contact: jfoo@ecel.uwa.edu.au

Concerns about large class teaching are obviously reflected in the plethora of publications on this matter. I have included a large selection so that interested teachers can obtain at least some of those available.

On peer tutoring

Goodlad, S. and Hirst, B. (eds) (1990) *Explorations in Peer Tutoring*, Oxford: Basil Blackwell.

Saberton, S. (1985) Learning partnerships, *HERDSA News*, 7(1), 3–5.

Topping, K. J. (1996) The effectiveness of peer tutoring in further and higher education: a typology and review of the literature, *Higher Education*, 32, 321–45.

The first book provides case studies of peer tutoring. Topping provides a useful classification of different types of peer tutoring and a summary of research results. Saberton's short article suggests how learning partnerships may be set up and used.

On flexible learning

Laurillard, D, (1993) *Rethinking University Teaching: a Framework for the Effective Use of Educational Technology*, London: Routledge.

Laurillard, D. and Margetson, D. (1997) *Introducing a Flexible Learning Methodology: Discussion Paper*, Occasional paper No. 7, Griffith Institute for Higher Education, Griffith University, Nathan, Queensland.

Taylor, J. C. (1995) Distance education technologies: the fourth generation. *Australian Journal of Educational Technology*, 11(2): 1–7.

Laurillard's book discusses general principles, and the second item is a discussion paper for establishing a mixed mode delivery at Griffith University in Queensland. Laurillard has established an e-mail discussion network on this 'strong' version of flexible delivery and invites discussion.

To join, send: 'add occprs-L<your e-mail address>' to maiser@ed-hydra.edn.gu.edu.au Taylor's paper is a much broader discussion of the 'strong' flexible learning position.

7

Teaching international students

Many university teachers report difficulties in teaching international students. These complaints refer not only to deficient language skills, but to learning-related problems that are seen as 'cultural' in origin, such as reliance on rote learning, passivity, teacher dependence, lacking creativity and so on. These perceptions are, like most stereotypes, distortions of the real situation. This chapter reviews some of the evidence for these cultural differences, and how they might affect teaching and learning. We find that teaching international students develops in the same way as teaching generally, from a level 1 'blame-the-student' view of teaching, to an inclusive level 3 view that engages students in effective learning whatever their ethnicity. This is not to say that misunderstandings will not arise when teachers and learners come from different cultural backgrounds, but that an inclusive view of teaching will minimize them.

Who are international students? What kinds of problem do they present?

International students (ISs) are students who have gone to another country in order to enrol full-time in a university course. The numbers of such students in United Kingdom universities have remained amazingly constant. The figure has ranged in the past sixty years from a low of 10.4 per cent in 1939 to a high of 11.6 per cent in 1963 (Perraton 1997). What has varied is the make-up. Students from the EU have risen from 4 per cent of all international students in 1979 to 43 per cent in 1994, students from the Commonwealth having dropped from 54 to 31 per cent in the same time.

British and Australian universities are not becoming more international, but more regionalized. In Australian universities, an average of 8 per cent come from overseas, mostly from Asian countries on the Pacific Rim, and they range from none at all in a few single purpose institutions, to 17 per cent at the Royal Melbourne Institute of Technology (figures from the Department of Employment, Education, Training and Youth Affairs 1998).

Whatever the overall figures, what teachers experience is the student mix in particular classes, and that ranges widely. The proportion of ISs in the humanities is mostly low, but in architecture, business, engineering, para-medical studies and science and mathematics, ISs could be in the majority in some classes. Local teachers are reported as seeing this as a problem for their teaching (see below). While a problem perceived is a problem experienced, need it be so? What is the nature of this seeming problem? What can be done to address it? These are the concerns of this chapter.

'Cultural' problems

American students studying in England, or New Zealand students studying in Australia, are technically ISs, but they are not thought of as presenting any different teaching problems from those already presented by local students. The perceived problems arise with students from a non-Anglo-Celtic background: for example, from African, Middle Eastern or East Asian countries. The problems are thus said to be 'cultural' in origin (Ballard and Clanchy 1997; Harris 1997).

But is this in principle different from the 'cultural' problem when Anglo-Celtic students move from the more protected and passive culture of secondary school to the academic culture of university? At university, class attendance is not compulsory, independent study skills are important and teachers do not sit on you to see you are up to the mark with deadlines and schedules. Many local students find bridging these two distinct teaching cultures difficult. The view taken in this chapter is that, language issues aside, the problems presented by the cultural gap between school and university are different from those experienced by non-Anglo-Celtic ISs in extent, not in kind.

An 'international' student can for present purposes be defined in terms of: (a) differences in *ethnicity* between home and university cultures; and (b) the *kind of problem* experienced. Problems are typically of three kinds:

1 *Social-cultural adjustment.* A major problem experienced by ISs is of course the stress created by adjusting to a new culture. While this is not strictly the concern of the teacher, there is an obligation on the university to supply strong support structures, particularly now that universities are vying with each other for full student fees from ISs – which results in some universities offering bargain basement fees, at the expense of student support services (Harris 1997). Our concern in this chapter is not, however, with the learning problems that flow indirectly from more general adjustment difficulties, but 'how culture itself shapes cognition and learning', and thereby presents problems in teaching and learning (Harris 1997: 78).

2 *Language.* Despite language prerequisites, many ISs undoubtedly have language problems that need attention; you cannot learn if you are not fluent in the language medium of instruction. Who is to deal with these language-related issues: content teachers or language specialists? While most content teachers would say that language for academic purposes is not their expertise or their business, language and learning interact deeply. But more than language is at stake: 'many of the difficulties international students experience in their study derive not from "poor English" (though lack of language competence is in many cases a real problem), but from a clash of educational cultures' (Ballard and Clanchy 1997: vi).

3 *Learning/teaching problems due to 'culture'.* In short, the cultural background of many ISs is thought to make it difficult for them to adapt to the *style* of tertiary teaching adopted in the host country. In particular, many ISs are too teacher-dependent, too uncritical of material they have been taught, prone to rote memorization; they misunderstand the cardinal sin of plagiarism, and lack knowledge of the genres of academic writing (Ballard and Clancy 1997; Harris 1997). How to cope with this is the problem. If it is a problem.

Certainly many Australian university teachers see that it is:

> Students from Malaysia, Singapore, Hong Kong appear to be much more inclined to rote learning. Such an approach does not help problem solving. (Dentistry)

> [Asian students] tend to look on lecturers as close to gods. Often they are very reluctant to question statements or textbooks. (Parasitology)

> . . . it can be difficult to cope, in small [graduate] classes, with overseas students who are reluctant to discuss, criticize reading and express an opinion. (Commerce)

> (Quoted in Samuelowicz 1987: 123–5)

And in the United Kingdom:

> many overseas students now originate in Pacific Rim countries, whose educational cultures characteristically value a highly deferential approach to teachers and place considerable emphasis on rote learning. This approach, of course, promotes surface or reproductive learning, which is at variance . . . with officially encouraged teaching innovations . . . to ensure deep transformational learning.

> (Harris 1997: 78)

There seems to be quite a consensus that there is a lack of 'goodness of fit', to use Harris's term, between the ISs' backgrounds, especially those from

Asian countries, and the style, ethos and task demands British and Australian universities typically make. Possibly it depends on how you look at it.

Teaching across cultures from three perspectives

Let us bring to bear the views of teaching developed in Chapter 2 (pp. 20–24), which were in fact generalized from how expatriate teachers adapt to teaching in a new system (Biggs 1997). In that situation, what often happens first is a kind of colonial phase; the way things are at home is the yardstick by which the new environment is measured, from shopping and TV programmes to students. Here is the initial reaction of an expatriate teacher to teaching Hong Kong:

> I found the deathly silence that preceded the start of the lecture quite unnerving, the more so when my open-ended questions met with no response. I had to plough on, and if, as was likely, I ran out of prepared material, I had to *ad lib* until the scheduled end of the lecture.
>
> (Biggs 1989a: 3)

The students apparently weren't behaving like students should. They just sat there, passively. They didn't even ask questions! This comment, I deeply regret having to admit, reflects pure level 1 blame-the-student thinking. It became the students' fault, not mine, that my teaching was ineffectual.

The next phase is accepting that the new environment has developed its own system, and the teacher's task is to adapt to that. This is level 2 thinking: good teaching involves the teacher doing all the right teacherly things.

The final phase is of course level 3: focusing on getting students to learn. Cultural factors might well mean that there may be different ways of doing this to best effect, but the focus is not on cultural or pedagogic difference, but on the universality of learning processes. The model is by now familiar to you, but let me illustrate how it applies to teaching across cultures (see Figure 7.1). As we ascend the cross-cultural teaching ladder, the differences between our own (Western) educational system and the 'exotic' systems from which our students come become less important. Differences are greatest on the bottom rung, where all we observe are differences between the way ISs behave and how we think students should behave. ISs have to assimilate in accordance with our definition of what constitutes a good student.

Ascend the ladder another rung, and we focus on adapting our teaching techniques to accommodate to the students. We lecture, but speak more slowly, dropping the witty word-play; they are still different but our responsibility is to teach by allowing for the differences. At the top rung, we find that ISs – surprise! – use the same cognitive processes as locals, and if

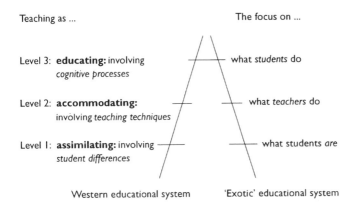

Teaching as ...

Level 3: **educating:** involving
cognitive processes

Level 2: **accommodating:**
involving *teaching techniques*

Level 1: **assimilating:** involving
student differences

Western educational system

The focus on ...

what *students* do

what *teachers* do

what students *are*

'Exotic' educational system

Figure 7.1: The focus in cross-cultural teaching

we aim to engage those processes, teaching ISs is little different from teaching locals.

In the context of teaching across cultures, the three different foci of teaching at each level create convenient labels: teaching as assimilation, as accommodation and as education.

Level 1: teaching as assimilation

Applying level 1 thinking to the situation of ISs, we arrive at a view remarkably similar to that adopted by the governments of countries receiving immigrants in pre-multicultural days: you must assimilate. The focus is on how ISs differ from local students; and because ISs do differ in some ways from local students, it is easy to stereotype them. When that happens, misconceptions and self-fulfilling prophecies occur.

The following generalizations about ISs derive from personal experience (Harris 1997), from research into lecturers' perceptions of ISs (Samuelowicz 1987; Chalmers and Volet 1997) and from recommendations on how to handle ISs (Ballard and Clanchy 1997). Some are supported by evidence, some apply equally to local as to international students, some are simply wrong.

'They rote learn and lack critical thinking skills'

This generalization is typically used to describe students from Confucian heritage cultures (CHCs), such as China, Korea, Japan, Hong Kong and

Singapore. It is one of the definitely wrong ones, yet is one of the most widespread.

This criticism is voiced while CHC students are cleaning up the first class honours and gold medals in huge disproportion to locals in such subjects as architecture, business studies, engineering and science. Do they achieve this on the basis of rote learning? If so, it doesn't say much for our assessment criteria. Or is it that these are the very bright ones, specially selected to study overseas? But then CHC students on their own turf, taught in their own fierce and overcrowded classrooms, consistently outperform Western students, as established both in controlled international comparisons of school performance in maths and science (International Association for the Evaluation of Educational Achievement 1996) and in the more fine-grained studies of Stevenson and his team in China, Taiwan, Japan and the United States (Stevenson and Stigler 1992).

Stevenson focused on elementary schools, and found that CHC students achieved better, with more understanding, than US students for a very good reason: they were taught better (Hess and Azuma 1991; Stevenson and Stigler 1992; Stedman 1997). Baumgart and Halse (in press) compared the levels of thinking assessed in public examinations in Thailand, Japan and Australia (the NSW Higher Schools Certificate), and found the Australian exam relied more on rote memorizing than did the Thai and Japanese equivalents. It thus turns out that when you look at the hard evidence, as opposed to level 1 perceptions, Western countries teach and assess in a way that encourages rote learning more than do many East Asian countries.

It should therefore be no surprise to find that the approaches to learning of CHC students are typically lower on surface and higher on deep than those of Western students, both in their own culture (Hong Kong and Singapore) (Biggs 1991; Kember and Gow 1991; Watkins *et al.* 1991) and overseas in Australian institutions (Biggs 1987a; Volet and Renshaw 1996). A major exception, among dozens of studies, was that Western medical students were higher on deep and lower on surface approaches – but it turned out that these students were taught by problem-based learning (PBL), while the CHC medical comparison students were (then) in a highly traditional medical school (Biggs 1991). That medical school is now committed to PBL.

So where does the 'rote learning' myth come from? It is true that CHC students engage in much repetitive activity and memorization. The culture demands it. Learning the several thousand characters in common use requires more memorization than learning the 26 letters in the Latin alphabet. But memorization in these circumstances is in service to understanding. You learn a communication system in order to communicate with understanding. A CHC saying states that 'repetition is a route to understanding' (Hess and Azuma 1991; Marton *et al.* 1996). But language learners and lovers of classical music anywhere know this. Every repetition of an intense and complex structure offers us the opportunity to increase our understanding of it. Sections begin to fall into place; the big picture unfolds.

Repetition is also used as a strategy to ensure correct recall, and here it works alongside meaning, not against it. Actors learning their lines are an example, as are students studying for an exam. Both need to eliminate any cognitive load involved in verbatim recall so that they can concentrate on the meaning at the time of performance; Tang (1991) refers to this strategic use of repetition as 'deep memorizing'. Neither of these instances, repetition as a strategy of coping with complexity or as a strategy for verbatim recall, has anything to do with rote learning and using a surface approach. Repetitive learning is a well established way of coping meaningfully with the world.

Western educators distinguish between rote learning and meaningful learning (Ausubel 1968), but not so easily between rote learning and repetitive learning. Rote learning is defined in common language as 'the mere exercise of memory without proper understanding of the matter in question' (*Shorter OED*). Hence, we use the term 'rote' memory as characteristic of the surface approach, where it is used deliberately to circumvent understanding.

But that is not what CHC students are doing when they use repetition in order to reduce complexity or to ensure recall. However, Westerners with a level 1 view see only the repetition, which stereotyping labels as mindless rote learning. Thus, Harris's (1997) comment that the educational systems of the Pacific Rim countries strongly promote surface or reproductive learning misunderstands those Pacific Rim countries – unless he means Australia and the USA, in which case the evidence is fairly clear that these systems do just that (Biggs 1991; Stedman 1997; Baumgart and Halse in press). But I don't think Harris did mean this.

'They are passive, they won't talk in class'

This is partially true of CHC students but not of Asians from the Indian subcontinent or of West Indians. Even with CHC students the evidence is contradictory, although the *perceptions* of Western teachers, including my own initially, are definite (see above). Volet and Kee (1993) found that the mean number of contributions in tutorials was no different between Singaporeans and Australians, but that the variance was: local (Australian) students either held the floor or said little, leaving an overall impression that locals did all the talking.

The 'inside/outside' rules, which determine when it is proper to talk, provide a useful slant on this (Scollon and Wong Scollon 1994). Westerners are often puzzled by the contrast between café and classroom behaviour of Chinese students: so demure and shy in the classroom, so noisy and boisterous in the café. The difference lies in what is implicitly defined as 'inside' (appropriate) and 'outside' (inappropriate). Normally, talk inside the class is outside, but outside the class talk is inside. So students tend to be quiet inside the class, but outside even academic talk is inside – hence the spontaneous collaboration noted by Tang (1993). However, if you turn the outside in – for example, by setting up learning partners, which makes it very difficult to attack academic tasks without talking to your partner – talking is now inside, and in my experience is very enthusiastic. Watson (1997) found that Asian (especially female) students attending the student-led tutorial system PASS (see Chapter 6) were much more likely to participate orally than in teacher-led groups, commenting that they particularly appreciated this chance to talk. Evidently, talking was outside in class, but inside in PASS.

There's also the point that it is outside to talk inside the classroom when you're self-conscious about your oral language ability. I would certainly find that to be outside.

'Progressive Western teaching methods won't work with Asians'

So far as Far Eastern (China, Japan, Korea) students are concerned it is a *truism* [emphasis supplied] that, raised in a conformist educational system, they are happier with memorising and reproducing information than with problem-oriented and more active teaching strategies.

(Harris 1997: 87)

This not only shows a fundamental misunderstanding of Far Eastern educational methods (Stevenson and Stigler 1992; Lee 1996), it sends all the wrong signals to teachers of ISs. Thus, too, another expatriate teacher in Hong Kong: 'Students in Hong Kong . . . expect lecturers to teach them everything they are expected to know. They have little desire to discover for themselves . . . They wish to be spoon fed and in turn they are spoon fed' (McKay and Kember 1997: 55). The speaker's self-fulfilling prophecy had served him well, and his students badly, over many years. He was speaking against a proposal to introduce PBL into his department; he lost and PBL won. Several Hong Kong universities now use PBL, where it works as well as it does anywhere else (McKay and Kember 1997; Whitehill *et al.* 1997).

The trouble with these misinformed stereotypes is that they exacerbate any teaching problems. They encourage teachers of ISs to continue lecturing and to assess reproductively, because teaching more innovatively 'would be unfair on the international students'. It would not. It would be unfair to continue lecturing – for everyone.

The issue of using active teaching methods with ISs is quite central, and I return to it in a later section.

'They appear to focus excessively on the method of assessment'

What ambitious student doesn't? The answer is in the principle of alignment: make sure the method of assessment contains the content you want them to learn (see Chapters 8 and 9).

'They don't understand what plagiarism means'

Neither do Western students, to many of whom plagiarism (as opposed to cheating) is a new concept at tertiary level; they simply do not see it as a moral issue or that it undermines assessment (Ashworth *et al.* 1997). Indeed, many software packages actively encourage students to cut-and-paste from CD-ROM or Web sources. The extent of plagiarism in Western universities is enormous – up to 90 per cent of all students plagiarize in some universities (Walker 1998; this article also deals with definitions of plagiarism, and how students, staff and institutions deal with it). The issue of plagiarism may, however, be more complex with ISs from cultures where students are taught that it is disrespectful to alter the words of an expert (Ballard and Clanchy 1997).

What all this suggests, on both local and international fronts, is that teachers need to be extremely clear about what constitutes plagiarism, and what the rules of referencing are. Plagiarism may, however, be difficult to define. Wilson (1997) points out that plagiarism proceeds in stages (that interestingly follow the SOLO levels):

- *Repetition:* simple copying from an unacknowledged source. Not confident of the content area. Unistructural and unacceptable.
- *Patching:* copying, with joining phrases, from several sources. Some general, non-specific, acknowledgement. Weak multistructural and still unacceptable, but harder to spot.
- *Plagiphrasing:* paraphrasing several sources, and joining them. All sources are in the reference list, but page unspecified. Still multistructural and still unacceptable, technically, but it merges towards:
- *Conventional academic writing:* ideas taken from multiple sources and repackaged to make a more or less original and relational type of synthesis. Quotes properly referenced, general sources acknowledged, quite confident of what is being said, the package may be new – but are the *ideas?*

The extended abstract level would include a 'far' transformation from the sources and genuine originality, which the last of Wilson's stages, conventional academic writing, does not necessarily incorporate.

Of these levels, patching is clearly unacceptable, but students writing in a second language (of whatever cultural background) find it hazardous to attempt to 'put it in your own words' when they are not confident in their use of the language. Lack of rhetorical confidence can easily lead to patching, when in fact the student has good *content* understanding. Such cases might need augmented modes of assessment, such as a brief interview. Even the shift from 'plagiphrasing' (unacceptable) to 'conventional academic writing' is not always clear, even to academics. And where that leaves textbook writers I dare not contemplate.

In short, it is not always easy to decide what is plagiarism, after the definite no-noes of repetition and patching. But we can at least be clear about those. *The rules of citation must be made crystal clear.* All too frequently, a level 1 view is taken: good students just *know* what is plagiarism and what is not, and it's not the teacher's job to explain such basics. Not so. It is precisely the teacher's job, no matter what the ethnicity of your students.

'They stick together . . . won't mix with locals'

This is often true, both socially (which is not an issue here) and educationally (which is). Volet and Ang (1998) studied mixed groups and found stereotypes were challenged and attitudes changed positively, yet both locals and ISs preferred like-with-like tutorial groupings next time.

What are your views? Do you deliberately mix ISs and locals in tutorial/ lab groups, or let them decide (which inevitably means unmixed groups)? Or do you do both at different times? Mixed groups means intercultural learning; homogeneous groups probably means better content learning. There are value judgements here which each teacher will have to decide (Task 7.1).

'They do not easily adjust to local conditions'

Wrong, as far as *teaching* is concerned. One characteristic of CHC students is precisely their adaptability. They are very good at spotting cues and picking up coping strategies (Singaporean: Volet and Renshaw 1996; Japanese: Purdie and Hattie 1996; Chinese generally: Watkins and Biggs 1996). Volet and Renshaw's (1996) Singaporean students studying in Australia changed in one year from strategies that were adaptive in Singapore to those that were adaptive in Australia. 'Always aim to get the correct answer' and 'learn lecture material by heart', adaptive in Singapore, dropped from first to last in importance, replaced after a year in Australia by 'evaluate different ideas and give own opinion'. 'Make sure you understand main ideas' was adaptive in both contexts and didn't change.

'They tend to look on lecturers as close to gods'

Authority relations are very different between many Western and non-Western societies. Westerners tend to play down the authority they have,

---

Task 7.1: Mixed or homogeneous groups

If you have a significant number of international students in your class (say the number equivalent to a 'group' size), how do you normally go about arranging the groups (tutorial, discussion/buzz group, lab group etc.): let the students decide, mix at random, deliberately mix ISs and locals, deliberately keep ISs and locals apart?

Why? _____

Do you have any problems in getting ISs to interact in groups? _____

When you have finished this chapter revisit your thinking on teaching ISs. Have your views changed? _____

'which leaves Asians confused as to just who is in charge' (Scollon and Wong Scollon 1994: 22). Asian teachers, on the other hand, usually do not hesitate to make their authority quite clear. CHC teacher–student inter-action is not lubricated with the democratic oil of first names and warm fuzzies; in a hierarchical, collectivistic culture the oil of respect is a more effective lubricant. Many ISs are uncomfortable with being on first-name terms with their teachers. Such issues should not be forced.

The teacher may be seen as a sort of powerful uncle, bought with gifts: 'I'll be a loyal and diligent student; in return, your obligation is to ensure that I pass' (Ballard and Clanchy 1997). Western teachers find gifts embarrassing, and unacceptable if there is an implied bargain. It is difficult, however, to gauge whether or not an obligation is implied. Some cultures, like Korea, have a tradition of bringing gifts to the teacher on a special Teacher's Day. I recall a similar tradition when I taught in an English secondary school, but there was no suggestion of bribery. But maybe I missed something.

On the other hand . . .

While ISs come to our Western system of tertiary education, many come from cultures that have a rich educational heritage, particularly Confucian heritage societies (Lee 1996). Indeed, there is a closer link in those countries between common beliefs, values and socialization practices, and the demands of formal education, than there is in the West (Biggs 1994). Thus, some characteristics of CHC students make teaching them easier, rather than more difficult:

- Success is attributed to effort and failure to lack of effort, whereas Westerners believe success requires ability more than effort, and attribute failure to lack of ability (see also Chapter 4). The CHC bottom line is optimistic – 'If I fail I can do something about it' – whereas attributing failure to lack of ability engenders hopelessness.
- Motivation tends to be complex and stronger than for Western students. Pressures to succeed are collectivist – familial, peer – as well as personal. Socialization practices 'create a sense of diligence and receptiveness that fit uncomfortably into . . . concepts of intrinsic and extrinsic motivation' (Hess and Azuma 1991: 7).
- As a result, CHC students are highly adaptable, as already discussed.

Study strategies, and knowledge of genres and plagiarism rules, are not written in the DNA. They are learned – and can therefore be taught. A major responsibility of teachers is clearly to see that they are taught, whether the students are international or local.

Level 2: teaching as accommodation

The level 2 view of teaching cross-culturally sees the important thing as accommodating to the cultural context. In the case of expatriate teachers, this means learning the teaching techniques that work for that system. In the case of local teachers teaching ISs, it means adapting one's teaching towards meeting the preferred ways of ISs. In both cases, it's what the teacher does that is the important thing:

> Lecturers in Australia teaching classes with half or more students from East Asia are likely to . . . be put psychologically off-balance and become indignant and confused. It will be difficult for the bulk of lecturers to learn good lecturing practice for Asian students. Few academics have interest in learning an alien technology. . .
>
> (Robert M. March, Professor of International Business, University of Western Sydney, Letter to the Editor, *The Australian*, 9 September 1996)

Professor March is suggesting that to teach ISs successfully you have to know what works in their system. To teach aliens, you need to know the right alien technology. Applied to teaching ISs, every local academic may need to learn several alien technologies. However, in the Faculty of

Commerce and Economics at the University of NSW, there are over 80 different mother tongues among the 1800 students. Teachers could not possibly accommodate to such diversity. Practicalities thus force level 1 assimilation. It's the aliens who 'must undergo an intellectual and cultural sea-change if they are to succeed' (Ballard and Clanchy 1997: ix).

Teachers can, however, accommodate to some extent without learning alien technologies. For example, a colloquial and humorous interpersonal style that works very well with the right students is clearly inappropriate with ISs (Burns 1991). Ballard and Clanchy (1997: viii) suggest

> minor modifications in current teaching practice, and in almost all cases the changes should be of benefit to all students . . . The problems of teaching students from other cultures are very often a more acute expression of the common problems of teaching our own students.

Such modifications include the following, some familiar from Chapter 6.

- Tape lectures and make tapes available.
- Speak slowly, avoid colloquialisms.
- Provide as much *visual* backup as possible: overheads, diagrams as advance organizers, notes, handouts.
- Model, using 'think-aloud' to socialize students into desired tutorial and discussion group behaviour; model how you would read material for subsequent discussion.
- Place preferred names on labels in front of people, including you.
- Pair IS with local; the latter introduces the IS to the class.

These are useful management tips, which brings us back to the point made in Chapter 6, that they are not about teaching itself.

In sum, level 2 suggests that teachers accommodate their teaching strategies to their students' cultural expectations. This means minor accommodation in class management techniques; accommodation beyond that, to learning alien technologies of teaching, is impractical.

Levels 1 and 2 are deficit models. The deficit in level 1 belongs to the students: they lack the skills and background to study in our system, language aside. The deficit in level 2 belongs to the teacher in the range of appropriate teaching skills. We examine the deficit model itself below. In the meantime, we might ask: is there not such a thing as good teaching that works anywhere?

Level 3: teaching as educating

To the above question, the answer is 'Yes!' It is to be found at level 3, with what the student does, not with what the teacher does, or what the student is. Neither differences between students nor how teachers teach are universal, but the cognitive processes students use to learn are. The argument is exactly the same as that throughout this book. The strategy is to focus on activating students' learning processes as appropriate to the objectives, as does good teaching anywhere. The means of activating those learning processes, however, could well differ between cultures.

Let us turn to the third stereotype above ('progressive Western teaching methods won't work with Asians'), and to the 'truism' that 'they are happier with memorising and reproducing information than with problem-oriented and more active teaching strategies' (Harris 1997: 87). That argument is disproved if Asians can learn effectively and with enjoyment with our more active teaching strategies.

Whitehill *et al.* (1997) report on the introduction of problem-based learning (PBL) with speech therapists in Hong Kong, noting particularly how the task demands of PBL interfaced with Chinese cultural beliefs. One difficulty was that conflict resolution – argument – was required in PBL: 'To discuss with our dearest classmates is very difficult because we always out of track and shift to another topics but today is quite okay in our discussion and we work in harmony' (Whitehill *et al.* 1997: 137). The problem was to resolve conflict in a culturally acceptable manner. They worked out their own strategies for arriving at consensus: voting, formal debate and seeking further information. They settled on the last strategy, which is the most adaptive. They saw that this strategy led to an appreciation of theory: 'otherwise, it's difficult to make it proof and make other people believe you' (Whitehill *et al.* 1997: 138).

The issue of working with friends – a difficulty when disagreement was present – turned out to be 'one of the most exciting aspects of the course. As one student said, "Problem-based learning gives me a sense of release for I will no longer be like a clammed duck" ' (*ibid.*). Another mentions the positive side of resolving the problem of conflict: 'We are working to our limit, without any reluctance – through cooperation, all our group members have developed deep friendship, sense of trust and confidence. This is very precious' (*ibid.*). As for motivation, students did not mention grades or teacher approval, only their desire to learn to be effective speech therapists. Student ratings of the course were overwhelmingly positive. The only problem is to reconcile this with the 'truism' that these students would have been happier with memorizing.

Tang *et al.* (1997) report the adoption of PBL in six departments at the Polytechnic University of Hong Kong. Full-time students had initial difficulty in adjusting to PBL, having come directly from an extremely teacher-centred and examination-dominated school system. The strategy was therefore to modify PBL, giving more teacher-direction at first than would usually be the case; these ducks too then became unclammed. So there are 'cultural' problems at first, but they are about adapting from a strongly teacher-directed culture (school) to a self-directed one (PBL), not from an 'Asian' to a 'Western' teaching culture. It is a matter of adapting to a context, not a matter of ethnicity.

Another instance where Chinese students were happier with active teaching strategies and problem-oriented assessment than with memorizing is my own use of a learning portfolio at the University of Hong Kong. Fuller details are given in Chapter 10. Briefly, the programme required minimal exposition, student-centred small and large groups, often with no teacher present, and no set questions for the students to answer, the opposite of what these students were used to, and initially wanted. In fact, reactions at first were highly negative: 'Constructivism is fine in the West, but unworkable in Hong Kong!' as several students told me. The following comment points to the 'cultural' issue of teacher-as-leader: 'How am I supposed to do it well when I'm not exactly sure what the professor wants to see in it? . . . though he did say that we can put what means much to us in the portfolio, yet how can I be sure that he agrees with me?' Rather like Volet and Kee's Singaporean students in Singapore, they wanted to be sure of what the teacher wanted – they would then happily supply it, as they had done in the past. Likewise, several students objected to the procedure adopted in plenary report-back following group discussions. My procedure was to list points on the board as the various group leaders summarized their discussions, leaving it to the students to come to their own conclusions. But:

We were not told what we were supposed to have learned.

Lecturer's opinion is not clear enough. Discussions can't draw up a conclusion.

When we are reporting in one big group, our lecturers seem to accept every opinion but seldom criticize them or give a conclusion. Are all our ideas right? This makes me puzzled.

Again, teachers were supposed to give leadership and draw matters to the correct conclusion. There is One Right Way, into which the teacher guides the students (Gardner 1989).

By the end of the unit, however, the students' comments changed drastically:

The reason why our lecturers seldom criticized our opinions for there are no fixed answers. One really has to find one's own way out. There are no fixed routes of becoming an expert teacher . . . That was why they kept throwing us a lot of questions to stimulate our thinking.

Is this last conclusion 'Western' or 'non-Chinese'? Or is it simply a reflective response that is entirely reasonable in that learning context?

The following two comments on the use of the portfolio appear 'counter-cultural'. The first suggests that the learner learns when the teacher isn't necessarily teaching, and the second that there are more things to be thought about than the One Right Way.

Now I do not see the portfolio as an assignment to be handed in, it's rather a powerful learning tool for the learner himself.

I found lots of fun [in making my portfolio] . . . it led me to think about many questions that I never think of.

The learning portfolio will be discussed in Chapter 10 as an example of aligned teaching. My point here is simply that the TLAs associated with the portfolio accessed the higher cognitive processes of students despite assumed 'cultural' impediments. Using groups and particularly learning partners provided culturally acceptable ways of allowing the portfolio to do its work, just as the speech therapy students worked out their fruitful ways for the unpleasant business of handling conflict among friends. That is the key to teaching across cultures; the cultural differences become instrumental in engaging in appropriate learning.

If Ah Hung, with his alleged propensity for rote learning, can be encouraged to behave more like Susan, I don't see why Robert can't.

Approaches to teaching ISs

Two methods of dealing with ISs have emerged: the deficit and the contextual models. As noted, level 1, and level 2 in practice, refer to a deficit that lies in the students: their lack of knowledge of and skill in handling learning in the One Right Way; that is, the Western way. Level 3 produces the contextual approach to teaching.

The deficit approach

In the deficit approach to teaching, the strategy is to identify the skills and procedural knowledge that the target students lack and that mainstream students are presumed to have already. The target students are then given separate out-of-class remediation, after which, their deficit duly repaired, they rejoin the mainstream. This model is common in special education and in dealing with ISs (Ballard and Clanchy 1997).

A recent and successful example of an apparent deficit programme is reported by Pearson and Beasley (1996). These writers searched the literature for ways in which South East Asian and Australian students might differ, and then devised an 'integrative learning strategy' taught in six classes halfway through the semester. The intervention comprised communication-based strategies: planning and writing essays and reports, reading critically, oral reporting, exam strategy and so on, using 'collectivist' (group) techniques, and content from the course (management). Attendance at the intervention classes was voluntary, and available to both locals and ISs. It worked very well for all students who attended. In fact, the Australian/IS differences were irrelevant.

Deficit models proceed along the following lines, here specified for ISs:

1 Asian students memorize and are therefore 'surface learners'.
2 Hence, the way Asian students learn is inferior to that used by mainstream local students.
3 Therefore Asian students have a 'deficit' to be remedied.

All three assumptions are incorrect. Memorizing is not surface learning. The evidence for both 1 and 2 is strongly the other way; Asians are likely to be deeper learners than Westerners. In 3, we have students with learning-related deficits performing better than those without them. Do local students show similar 'deficits'? That we don't know; that question is not asked. The deficit approach to teaching is thus methodologically and perhaps even ethically hard to justify (Volet and Renshaw 1996).

The contextual approach

The Volet and Renshaw study (1996) redefines the issue as a matter of *learning in context*, not as one of deficit. Thus, in Singapore you learn one set of adaptive strategies, in Australia you learn another set, but there will be some overlap (searching-for-main-ideas is adaptive in both contexts). The teacher's task is to make it *clear* what is required for the immediate context, not just to assume it as the tacit Right Way that any decent student instinctively knows. This requires level 3 thinking: using a model of teaching to decide specifically what students are required to do, and how they are supposed to go about doing it.

Learning in context is thus another way of describing aligned teaching: the TLAs encourage students to engage those cognitive processes most likely to achieve the objectives. And just to make sure, you use assessment tasks that will give them a healthy reminder that you mean business, as we see in Chapters 8 and 9.

If the level 3 position means anything at all, it is that all students benefit from good teaching. Conversely, under poor teaching, both local and international students face similar problems. In a comprehensive study across three universities, both local and international students nominated the following difficulties (Mullins *et al.* 1995):

- poor teaching;
- mismatch between student and staff expectations;
- lack of access to staff;
- workload.

Differences between the two groups of students were not in the nature of the problems they experienced, although international students often experienced more difficulty in handling some of them. You can't solve these problems by nominating one group of students as being unable to adapt to our teaching, when other students already have the same problems! The problem lies in the teaching, not in the students.

Summary and conclusions

Who are international students? What kinds of problem do they present?

In this chapter we address the problems perceived by many teachers, particularly pertinent in these days of selling our academic wares to overseas 'consumers', in teaching students of non-Anglo-Celtic ethnic backgrounds. Of course, they experience problems of adjustment, homesickness and language. But these raise different questions from that of teaching method itself, which is our concern here. Non-Anglo-Celtic students are perceived as not fitting well into our established ways of teaching. But how you perceive that depends on your vantage point; each of our three levels of teaching presents a different perspective on the teaching of ISs.

We have tended to concentrate here on ISs from East Asian countries. That is because the relevant research has been done on these students. The present argument, and the remedy, is precisely the same whether the students are African, Asian or European.

Level 1: teaching as assimilation

A level 1 view belongs in the pre-multicultural days of enforced assimilation. The more ISs are seen to differ from local students, the greater the expected problems in teaching them. So they must become more like local students. Teachers with this view look for differences between ISs and locals, and find them. Many differences are real enough in themselves, but they lead to stereotyping, which in turn leads to self-fulfilling prophecies: 'They will only rote learn, so all I can do is lecture them and give recall tests. I'd prefer not to, of course!' Of course.

Level 2: teaching as accommodation

Level 2 thinking asks that teachers accommodate to student differences. The extreme view of this is that we learn several packages of 'alien teaching technologies', as one writer suggested, so we can teach each alien group in its own alien-specific way – which is quite absurd. What we can do is to accommodate in our normal teaching by speaking more slowly, less colloquially, backing up verbal with non-verbal content; as Ballard and Clanchy say, 'Address the problems presented by ISs, and you'll teach better.'

Level 3: teaching as educating

I say, 'Teach better, and you'll address the problems presented by ISs.' You teach better by focusing not on how students differ, not even on what you are doing, but on what your students are doing. The level 1 view that Asians, for example, find difficulty with 'active' teaching methods is dangerously wrong. Active methods are the basis of good teaching with any students. Examples are given where Asian students do as well as Westerners under innovative teaching methods, any differences lying in the tactics of implementation, not in the strategy of teaching.

Approaches to teaching ISs

Levels 1 and 2 lead to deficit approaches to teaching, which cannot be justified empirically or in principle. Level 3 leads to a contextual approach, which uses the context established to extract the appropriate learning behaviour from students – all students, whether Anglo-Celtic or not. Contextual teaching is inclusive, and it rests on three propositions:

1 It is useful to assume that persistent teaching problems lie not in the student but in the teaching.
2 The focus in teaching should be on the similarities between students rather than on the differences. This is not to deny that the latter exist.
3 Allowing for the needs of special groups, such as international students, is best done within the whole teaching system, not as a separate exercise.

Level 3 teaching is inclusive, addressing the needs of all students: Robert, Susan, Nirmala and Ah Hung.

Further reading

Allen, A. and Higgins, T. (1994) *Higher Education: the International Student Experience*, London: Heist Publications.

Ballard, B. and Clanchy, J. (1997) *Teaching International Students*, Deakin, ACT: IDP Education Australia.

McNamara, D. (ed.) (1997) *Overseas Students in Higher Education*, London: Routledge.

Watkins, D. and Biggs, J. (eds) (1996) *The Chinese Learner: Cultural, Psychological and Contextual Influences*, Hong Kong: Centre for Comparative Research in Education/Camberwell, Vic.: Australian Council for Educational Research.

The first three books give background on ISs in Britain and in Australia. While the issues are the same – naturally given the message of this chapter – the specifics are different, in particular the cultural backgrounds of ISs in these two countries.

The last book focuses on students in the Chinese diaspora, and particularly on the so-called 'paradox of the Chinese learner': given that the classroom teaching conditions seem by Western criteria to be sub-standard, how is it that Chinese students do so very well in international comparisons? Addressing that 'paradox' raises many of the issues addressed in the present chapter.

8

Assessing for learning quality: I. Principles

What and how students learn depends to a major extent on how they think they will be assessed. Assessment practices must send the right signals, but current practice is distorted because two quite different models of summative assessment have for historical reasons been unwittingly confused. In this chapter, these problems are clarified. We examine the purposes of assessment, the relation between assessment and the assumed nature of what is being assessed, who might usefully be involved in the assessing process, and assessing for desirable but unexpected learning outcomes. The underlying principle is that the assessment tasks comprise a genuine representation of the objectives of the course or unit.

Backwash: the effects of assessment on learning

We teachers might see the curriculum objectives as the central pillar of teaching in an aligned system, but our students think otherwise: 'From our students' point of view, assessment always defines the actual curriculum' (Ramsden 1992: 187). Students learn what they think they will be tested on. In a poorly aligned system, where the test does not reflect the objectives, this will result in inappropriate surface learning. Students' understandings take the form they think will suffice to meet the assessment requirements. This is *backwash*, when the assessment determines student learning, rather than the official curriculum.

While backwash is almost invariably seen as negative (Crooks 1988a; Frederiksen and Collins 1989), learning for the test is bad learning only if the test is bad. Students' learning may also be as good as the assessment tasks they are given, in which case backwash becomes positive. The basic principle of good assessment, then, is to ensure that the assessment is aligned to the curriculum (Figure 8.1).

To the teacher, assessment is at the end of the teaching–learning sequence of events, but to the student it is at the beginning. If the curriculum is reflected in the assessment, as indicated by the downward

Figure 8.1: Teacher's and student's perspectives on assessment

arrow, the teaching activities of the teacher and the learning activities of the learner are both directed towards the same goal. Backwash works positively when assessment tasks are deliberately and firmly referenced to learning standards contained in the curriculum. In preparing for the assessments, students will then be learning the curriculum.

It sounds easy, but there is a long tradition of thinking about assessment, and some time-honoured assessment practices, that complicate matters. In this chapter, we clarify some of the conceptual issues involved; in the next, we look at assessment practices that more readily tell us what we want to know, which is how well our students are learning what we have taught them.

Why assess?

Formative and summative assessment

There are many good reasons why we should assess students, but two are outstandingly important:

1 *Formative* assessment, the results of which are used for *feedback*. Students and teachers both need to know how learning is proceeding. Feedback may operate both to improve the learning of individual students, and to improve teaching.
2 *Summative* assessment, the results of which are used to grade students at the end of a unit, or to accredit at the end of a programme.

Other reasons would include selecting students, controlling or motivating students (the existence of assessment keeps class attendance high and set references read) and to satisfy public expectations as to standards and accountability. These and other aspects of assessment will be addressed as necessary.

Formative assessment is inseparable from teaching. Indeed, the effectiveness of different teaching methods is directly related to their ability to provide formative feedback. The lecture itself provides little. You might now see that the improvements to the lecture mentioned in Chapter 6 were almost all formative in function, in particular checking ongoing under-standings. In a good learning system, the students learn to take over the formative role for themselves, monitoring themselves as they learn.

Summative evaluation is carried out after the teaching episode has concluded. Its purpose is to see how well students have learned what they were supposed to have learned. That result, the grade, is final. Students fear this outcome, as futures hinge on it. They will be singularly unwilling to admit their mistakes. Error no longer is there to instruct, as in formative assessment; error now signals punishment.

The difference between summative and formative assessment is well summed up in the following: 'When the chef tastes the sauce it is formative assessment; when the customer tastes, it is summative' (Anon).

Progressive assessment

Progressive, or continuous, assessment uses results taken during the course, while learning is proceeding, for grading purposes. While this seems to take the heat off a final summative assessment, it must not conflate the formative and summative roles. For formative to work, students should feel free to reveal their ignorance and the errors in their thinking, but if the results are to be used for grading, they will be highly motivated to conceal possible weaknesses.

Formative assessment, as a vital function of teaching, should always be present, but the results should be not 'counted', unless the student agrees. For example, a trial go at the final assessment tasks can be used both formatively – that is, the mistakes used to improve next time – and summatively, if individuals are happy with the result. If they are not happy, they can be allowed another go at the task later on. This is not to say that summative assessments should not be collected while a unit is ongoing, as long as the formative and summative functions are separated. For example, working on the kinds of problems that will make up the final exam throughout the semester is an excellent formative experience. But if some are to 'count' in the final grade, students should know which ones.

For the rest of this chapter, we focus on the most problematic form of assessment, summative. It arouses passion, resistance and subterfuge.

Two models of summative assessment

Part of the reason for all this unpleasantness is that, over the years, two models of summative assessment have emerged, with different uses and different conceptual roots. They tend to fight each other.

1 The *measurement* model is designed to assess the stable characteristics of individuals, for the purpose of comparing them with each other or with general population norms. Such assessment is *norm-referenced* (NRA). This model was originally developed by psychologists to study individual differences (Taylor 1994).

2 The *standards* model is designed to assess changes in performance as a result of learning, for the purpose of seeing what, and how well, something has been learned. Such assessment is *criterion-referenced* (CRA). This model is the relevant one for summative assessment at university (Taylor 1994).

The measurement model of assessment (based on NRA)

The measurement model is designed to measure characteristics of people, so that they may be compared to each other with reference to that characteristic, so that a decision can be made: to refer for some treatment, or to be admitted to university. The measurement model requires the following (Nicholls 1994; Taylor 1994):

1 Performances must be reduced to numbers along a scale, so that comparisons can be made. If statistical treatments are to be carried out, certain mathematical conditions should be met, such as scores being normally distributed.

2 The characteristic being measured should remain stable over time.

3 When the test result is used for selection purposes, it must be a valid predictor of the performance to be predicted.

4 The test needs to spread students out, sorting high performers from low performers.

5 Students need to be tested under conditions that are standardized for everyone.

When university places are in short supply, this model is an excellent way of sorting out the most promising from the least promising students. Students need to be placed in rank order on the basis of their scholastic ability, which must be assumed: (a) to relate to future success at university; and (b) to remain relatively stable over the next few years. If neither applied, the predictions will be unreliable, and the selection unfair.

A convenient estimate of scholastic ability is obtained by summing a student's best three, or best five, HSC or A-level subjects. In attempting to arrive at a common scale, percentages are usually used, which is theoretically questionable but works. Refinements could include penalties for second attempt, using school means on one common subject to weight scores so that school effects can be 'moderated' and so on. It is complex actuarially, but the general principles are clear. What you get is a measure of scholastic ability which is robust enough to allow direct comparisons between students in different subject areas.

The measurement model and teaching

When the students have been sorted and are at university, the game changes. We no longer want to identify *students* in terms of some characteristic, but to identify *performances* that tell us what has been learned, and how well. The purpose of assessment is now so different that none of the following measurement model assumptions apply to teaching:

1 *Quantifying performances gives little indication of the quality of performance, or of what has been learned.* The effect of the measurement model is to rank order students, which tells us who is better than who at learning, but nothing about what has been learned. Knowledge is not suitably represented as marks accrued. Students don't learn 'marks'; they learn structures, concepts, theories, narratives, procedures, performances of understanding and so on. 'Marking' is only a secondary device necessitated by NRA in order to make comparisons more precise.

2 *Teaching assumes change, not stability.* Teaching is an intervention that is meant to encourage learning. Learning means that something has changed; students now understand or can do something they couldn't do before. Measuring stable traits has nothing to do with the changes brought about by learning and teaching. Tests constructed to maximize stability of scores will in fact hide the effects of teaching on learning.

3 *As teachers, we don't want a 'good spread' in our grade distributions.* We have long been told by measurement experts that a good attainment test yields 'a good spread' that follows the bell curve. But why should that be so? That only applies if ability is the sole determinant of academic attainment, and if ability is normally distributed. But the ability of our students is not likely to be normally distributed, because students are not randomly selected (not quite yet, anyway). There is not only no reason to expect a bell curve distribution of ability in our classes, there is every reason *not* to expect such a distribution.

In any event, ability is not the sole determinant of students' learning outcomes. Another factor is called 'teaching'. As argued in Chapter 1, good teaching tends to override individual differences, producing a *smaller* spread of final results than that predicted by the initial spread of ability, more students now attaining the higher-level objectives, reflected in higher grades. The gap between Robert and Susan is narrower. The resulting distribution of results is not bell-shaped, but skewed, with higher scorers more frequent than lower scorers. Forcing attainment scores to follow the curve prevents us from seeing the real picture of what standards are being achieved.

Requiring results to conform to a predetermined curve is just one example of the hangover from measurement model thinking in current practice. A common examining system, which separates assessment from teaching, is another. Teaching occupies the greater part of the academic year, assessment a frantic couple of weeks at the end. I can recall, now with shame, not even thinking about the final examination until the papers were due to be sent to the central examinations section.

Examination sections conducted this autonomous exercise of examining under their own university-wide jurisdiction and procedures, in just the same way as the public examination boards at school level have responsibility over assessment. The job of these boards is to assess students under standardized conditions so that they can be directly compared with each other for selection purposes. As most students, teachers and administrators, and many parents, have had first-hand experience with the procedures and the philosophy adopted by these public examination boards, the latter's norm-referenced framework spills over into the tertiary sector, exerting a strong influence on how people think about assessment.

The application is straightforward. You teach as it comes, you set an examination, the examination centre invigilates it for you, you allocate marks. The purpose of the examination is to provide a basis for rank-ordering the students. If you grade on the curve (for example, 10 per cent HDs, 15 per cent Ds, 25 per cent Cs, 45 per cent Ps) the results will be stable from year to year, and from department to department. All looks impeccable, no questions asked. If there is the odd query from a student about the final grade, you can point to an unarguable figure: all objective, very precise. You didn't earn enough marks. Sorry. It simply does not occur to many teachers to query this. Yet when you think about it, there is no *structural* requirement that the exam should even look in the direction of the curriculum. Alignment is all over the place.

There are numerous other examples where current practice is muddied with norm-referenced assumptions. For example, some academics see the purpose of the undergraduate years as one of weeding out the 'pass' level students from the potential postgraduate research students. This is a legitimate concern. But if it overrides the main purpose of the undergraduate years, which is to teach the mainstream undergraduates, it can distort the assessment methods, by focusing on the traits and abilities students possess, not on the performances that demonstrate student learning.

Likewise with the terminology of grading. One common term, 'high distinction', carries the strong suggestion that it should be limited to those who are highly distinguished. It becomes a person-term, referring to rare qualities that people carry around with them, not a performance-term, referring to standards of performance in a particular context. Defining who is highly distinguished begs to be norm-referenced: the HDs are the top 5 or at most 10 per cent of the class. Entrance to postgraduate work is then limited to those who have consistently shown such distinction. This sounds very reasonable, except that it is irrelevant.

Surely entry to postgraduate work should be restricted to those students who display the characteristics needed for doing research: content mastery, ability to generate original ideas, mastery of the appropriate research methods and so on. That is a criterion- not a norm-referenced question. However, the norm-referenced cast of mind sees distinction not in what people can do, but in the exclusivity of what they are. Paradoxically, those who would cultivate excellence through exclusivity see 30 per cent of a class obtaining high distinctions as a contemptible fall in standards, not as a cause for congratulation. Grade categories with loaded names such as 'high distinction' invite this sort of cross-think. A more neutral 'A' for the top grade makes it easier for a high proportion of genuinely criterion-referenced 'As' to be seen as a cause more for celebration than for scorn.

Following are some other contaminants from the measurement model.

- Expressing assessment results as 'marks' along a continuous scale, such as a percentage scale (a practice so common as to be almost universal).
- Using assessment results to produce a rank order of students.
- Inserting trick questions that aren't in the curriculum 'to identify the high fliers'. The aim is clearly to search for an ability or quality inherent in the student, not to see how well the curriculum has been learned.
- Allocating grades on a comparative basis, the top z per cent receiving A or high distinction, the next y per cent B or distinction and so on.

Now let us turn to what we should be doing.

The standards model of assessment (based on CRA)

The standards model of assessment is designed to tell us directly what, and how well, the students have learned, as in CRA. CRA is stunningly obvious: say what you want students to be able to do, teach them to do it and then see if they can in fact do it; if they cannot, try again until they can (Keller 1968; Bloom *et al.* 1971).

The CRA teaching strategy is used universally outside formal education, from parents to driving instructors. With CRA you have to match a performance with an objective. With complex objectives that are defined qualitatively (see Chapter 3), that requires judgement, which traditionalists say makes assessment 'subjective': imprecise, open to bias. The issue of using judgement, and the criticisms of it, involve a detailed argument to which we return below. One CRA strategy that in the past had some success in universities is the Keller Plan (Keller 1968), which allows students as many tries at the assessment as they (reasonably) need in order to pass the preset standard. Some students pass in short order, others take much longer, and that requires flexible organizing. But the main problem with the Keller Plan historically was that the preset standards tended to be very quantitatively defined. In Chapter 3 we saw how these criteria could be defined qualitatively.

Despite the prevailing norm-referenced cast of mind in universities, the sheer logic of CRA already prevails in some aspects. Assessing theses and dissertations is almost always criterion-referenced, however vague or inconsistently applied the criteria might be in practice. We expect a dissertation to display certain characteristics: coverage of the literature, definition of a clear and original research question, mastery of research methods and so on. The categories of honours (first class, upper second, lower second) originally suggested qualities that students' work manifested: a first was qualitatively *different* from an upper second, it was not simply that the first got more sums right. Today, this approach might be in jeopardy, as these categories seem increasingly to be defined in terms of ranges of marks, which is unfortunate, as will unfold.

To summarize, then, our function as teachers is to establish how well our students have learned what they are supposed to have learned. To find this out, we first need to be clear about what our students *should* be learning, in terms of qualities or performances that define the grading categories (HD, D, Cr, P; or A, B, C, D), and then to devise assessment tasks that tell us how well they have done so. The first task is a matter of setting objectives, which was the subject of Chapter 3; the second is the major task for this chapter and Chapter 9.

Differences between NRA and CRA: summary

Because of the universality of many NRA practices in teaching, and the educational logic of CRA, we should be quite clear about the differences.

1 NRA results are expressed in terms of comparisons between students after the teaching episode. CRA results are expressed in terms of how well a given student's performance matches set criteria, and are independent of any other student's result.
2 CRA standards are usually set before teaching has taken place. Exceptionally, you might find after teaching that the criteria for CRA were inappropriately high or low, and need changing before reporting the final grades. But any student's grade is still in terms of the final criteria, point 1 above, not relative to other students' performances, which of course are known only after the event.
3 NRA is concerned with making judgements about *people*, CRA with judgements about *performance*.

Task 8.1 presents a quick, criterion-referenced, test to sort the sheep from the goats (joke). Answers can be found at the end of this chapter.

Task 8.1: NRA or CRA?

Two common queries. I am assessing two students in a CRA system, and note that I have awarded Robert a B and Susan an A. I then take a second look and decide that Robert's paper is as good as Susan's, so I give both an A. Is this now NRA (comparing students) or CRA (judging on standards)? Why?

_____

_____

I am intending to operate a CRA system, and in deciding what standards are reasonable to set for the grading categories, I look at last year's distributions of As, Bs, Cs, Ds and Fs, and adjust the difficulty of the tasks so that I am likely to obtain a similar result this year. NRA or CRA? Why?

_____

_____

_____

_____

What is being assessed?

We assess to see what students know, and in doing that we are making assumptions about the nature of what has been learned. These assumptions tend to be either quantitative or qualitative in nature (Cole 1990; Marton *et al.* 1993).

The level 1 view of teaching makes essentially quantitative assumptions, as we noted briefly in Chapter 2: teaching involves transmitting the main points, assessment involves marking students on their ability to report them back accurately. The early, uni- and multistructural, stages of SOLO are quantitative, learning at those levels being a matter of finding more and more about the topic.

The level 3 view makes qualitative assumptions: teaching involves helping the learner to construct more effective ways of viewing a section of the world. The relational and extended abstract SOLO levels are qualitative, involving the way data have been structured rather than the amount of data present.

Let us see how these conceptions apply to assessment.

Quantitative ways of looking at knowledge

A quantitative view of learning has the following implications for assessment:

1 Learning performances are unitized: for example, a word, an idea, a point. If the performance to be assessed is not already a quantifiable unit, it is made so by allocating ratings or 'marks' in a subjective if not arbitrary way.
2 These units are either correct or incorrect.
3 The correct units, or their arbitrary transformations into marks, may be treated additively, their sum becoming an index of learning that lies along a single scale.
4 Any one correct unit must therefore be 'worth' the same as any other. It doesn't then matter *what* is correct, as long as there are enough (usually 50).

Multiple-choice tests enact these assumptions exactly. Learning is represented as the total of all items correct. Students quickly see that the score is the important thing, not how it is comprised, and that the ideas contained in any one item are of the same value as those in any other item (Lohman 1993). We return to a more detailed consideration of this assessment format in the next chapter.

The essay format, technically open-ended, does not, however, preclude quantitative means of assessment. When multiple markers use marking schemes, they give a mark as each 'correct' or 'acceptable' point is made, possibly with bonus points for argument, or style. This too sends misleading messages to students about the structure of knowledge, and also about how to exploit its assessment (Biggs 1973; Crooks 1988a).

In timed examinations, the law of diminishing returns states that time spent on the first half of an essay nets more marks than the same time spent on the second half. Some teachers thus instruct their students to attempt all five questions, rather than writing a properly structured answer to only four. The message couldn't be clearer: the more facts the better, never mind the structure they make. It is like examining architects on the number of bricks their designs use, never mind the structure, function or aesthetics of the building itself.

In other words, tests constructed and used within quantitative assumptions about learning simply do not reflect the nature or the diversity of what students have learned. Such assumptions underlie both norm-referenced testing in the traditional measurement model and criterion-referenced testing in the mastery learning models (Keller 1968; Bloom *et al.* 1971). In line with the backwash argument, classical mastery learning works very well with surface-oriented students. Lai and Biggs (1994) found that surface-oriented biology students got better and better under mastery learning, but deep-oriented, initially better, students ended performing much lower than the surface students: a rare finding in the student learning literature.

Assessing for learning quality is thus a matter not only of using CRA rather than NRA, but of the nature of the learning to be assessed. CRA can be either quantitatively or qualitatively conceived, but NRA can only be quantitative.

Qualitative ways of looking at knowledge

A qualitative view of learning has different implications for assessment:

1 As learning occurs, it builds upon previous knowledge and its structure becomes more complex. Assessment should therefore inform on the present state of complexity, and how that matches the objectives, not how it compares across students. The assessment grade is not therefore a quantitative sum, but a statement or category describing how good the match is for any given student.
2 A learning outcome should therefore be assessed holistically, not analytically. A structure can only be assessed as a whole, not in terms of the sum of its parts. Oscars aren't awarded by marking each frame in a movie, and adding to see which movie got most marks. Just so do reductive marking scales lose the academic plot.
3 Each student's assessment is independent of any other student's.

The point of qualitative assessment is not *how much* the final score is, but whether the final grade tells us *how well* the performance matches the objectives. If you have arranged your objectives in a letter-grade hierarchy, your assessment tasks then tell you the level in the hierarchy at which a given student can perform: that level becomes the grade.

Authentic or performance assessment

Closely related to the quantitative/qualitative issue is what has become known in the literature as 'authentic' assessment (Wiggins 1989; Torrance 1994). This says that the context of testing should genuinely reflect the goals of learning, which is remarkable only because it needed to be said. We teach students in order that they will think, decide and act in the real world in a more informed and effective manner: performatively, in other words. The assessment tasks should at some point require an *active demonstration* of the knowledge in question, as opposed to talking or writing about it. For this reason, we now speak of 'performance', rather than of 'authentic', assessment (Moss 1992).

Contextualized and decontextualized assessments

Whether the assessment should be performative or not depends on the objectives. Where the objectives target declarative knowledge, it is quite appropriate to assess it using declarative methods such as conventional pencil-and-paper tests. We thus arrive at an important distinction in assessment formats:

- decontextualized assessments such as a written exam, or a term paper, which are suitable for assessing declarative knowledge;
- contextualized assessments, such as a practicum, problem-solving or diagnosing a case study, which are suitable for assessing functioning knowledge.

However, while both decontextualized and contextualized learning and assessment have a place, in practice decontextualized assessment has been greatly over-emphasized in proportion to its place in the curriculum. As we saw in Figure 3.1, functioning knowledge is underwritten by declarative knowledge, and we need to assess both: the general understanding prior to how students use what they know, in real-world applications. A common mistake is to assess only the lead-in declarative knowledge, not the functioning knowledge that emerges from it.

For example, take the following SOLO hierarchy of assessment, from declarative to functioning, in rehabilitation science:

1 Test knowledge of the bones and the muscles of the hand (multi-structural, declarative).
2 Explain how the bone and muscle systems interact to produce functional movement of the hand: for example, in picking up a small coin from the floor (relational, but still declarative).
3 Given a trauma to one muscle group rendering it out of action, design a functional prosthesis to allow the hand to be used for picking up a coin (relational, functioning).

Holistic and analytic assessment

As mentioned, a valid assessment must be of the total performance, not just aspects of it. Example 3 above refers to a total performance. Consider this example from surgery. You want to be sure that the student can carry out the whole operation with high and reliable competence. An analytic assessment would test and 'mark' knowledge of anatomy, anaesthesia, asepsis and the performance skills needed for making clean incisions, and then add the marks to see if they reach the requisite 50 (or in this case perhaps 80) per cent. The student could do extremely well in everything but anatomy, and remove the wrong part, but accrue more than the number of marks needed to pass. So a pass it must be.

Absurd this example may be, but exactly this process is involved in an analytic marking scheme. Some aspects of knowledge are traded off against others. The solution is not to blur the issue by spreading marks around to fill the cracks, but to require different levels of understanding or performance, according to the importance of the subtopic. Here, knowledge of anatomy was insufficient to allow the correct performance: hence, fail.

Holistic assessment recognizes the intrinsic meaning of the target performance. A decision made, a problem solved, a case presented, a literary criticism made; all are whole acts with their own integrity and should be assessed as such. Analytic marking destroys their essential meaning. This is not to say that mastery of components cannot be undertaken as a partial learning, but in every major topic taught, whether declarative or functioning, at the end of the road, assessment should address the whole.

The role of judgement

In the making of holistic assessments, however, the details are not ignored. The question is whether, like the bricks of a building or the characters in a novel, the specifics are tuned to create an overall structure or impact. That is a matter of judging how well the performance matches the appropriate criteria of learning. Such judgement is called 'hermeneutic': that is, we arrive at a judgement by understanding the whole in light of the parts. For example, an essay requiring reasoned argument involves making a case, just as a barrister has to make a case that stands or falls on its inherent plausibility. The judge does not rate individual aspects of the barrister's case – uses legal terms correctly (+10 marks), eye-contacts the jury (+5 marks), for too long (− 3 marks) . . . – and then aggregate, the counsel with most marks winning the suit. The argument as a whole has to be judged.

Critics argue that, because holistic assessment involves judgement, it is 'subjective'. But awarding marks is a matter of judgement too. The difference is that in analytic marking you make a whole series of mini-judgements, each one small enough to be handled without qualm, and then you let the numbers make the big ones: if the numbers add up to 50 per cent, then it is a pass, if to 76 per cent then it is a distinction (or whatever). At no point does one have to consider *what the nature* of a 'distinction' level of performance is. One of the major dangers of quantitative assessment schemes is that teachers can shelter under them and avoid the responsibility of making the judgements that really matter: what is a good assessment task; why is this a good performance (Moss 1992)?

The strategy of reducing a complex issue to isolated segments, rating each independently and then aggregating to get a final score in order to make decisions seems peculiar to schools and universities. It not only oversimplifies the complexity of the reality, but actually distorts judgements made about it. It is not the way things work in real life. Moss (1994) gives the example of a journal editor judging whether to accept or reject a manuscript on the basis of informed advice from referees. The referees don't give marks, but argue on the intrinsic merits of the paper as a whole, and the editor has to incorporate their advice, resolve conflicting advice, and make a judgement about the whole paper: reject it, revise it, accept it. Moss reports that one of her own papers, which argued for a hermeneutic approach to educational assessment, was rejected by the editor of an educational journal on the grounds that a hermeneutic approach was not the model of assessment accepted in the educational fraternity. When she pointed out that *he* had used a hermeneutic approach to arrive at that conclusion, he had the grace to admit the silliness of his position. Her paper was accepted.

In order to assess learning outcomes holistically, it is necessary to have a conceptual framework that enables you to see the relationship between the parts and the whole. Teachers need to develop their own framework, but the SOLO taxonomy can be useful in assisting that process (see Figure 3.2; Dart and Boulton-Lewis 1998).

In sum, it is the whole dissertation that passes, the complete argument that persuades, the comprehensive but concise proposal that gets funded, the individual applicant that wins promotion. Holistic assessment addresses that integral act.

Convergent and divergent assessment

We used the terms 'convergent' and 'divergent' in Chapter 5 in connection with student questioning. These terms were used originally by Guilford (1967) to describe two different forms of ability, but it is more productive to think of them as processes.

- *Convergent*: solving problems that have a particular, unique answer, as in most intelligence and ability test items. Convergent thinking is focused, or 'closed'.
- *Divergent*: generating alternatives, where the notion of being 'correct' gives way to broader assessments of value, such as aesthetic appeal, originality, usefulness, self-expression, creativity and so on. Divergent thinking is 'open'.

Sciences are seen as requiring convergent thinking, with bodies of knowledge to be mastered, and literary criticism as requiring divergent thinking, to generate a point of view. Hudson (1966) showed that undergraduate students with a convergent 'bias' in their thinking did better at science, while those with a divergent 'bias' did better in arts. However, scientific research requires a dose of divergent thinking; researchers and research students need to think generatively: 'What is wrong with this experiment?' 'How can I test this hypothesis?'

In fact, both processes are involved in most higher-level thinking, and in professional work. Although the extended abstract end of the SOLO taxonomy is replete with open-ended verbs, such as 'generate', 'hypothesize', 'theorize', 'reflect', they cannot be effectively activated without prior content mastery. Creativity and originality need a solid knowledge base.

Teaching and assessment should therefore address both convergent and divergent processes, but for various reasons convergent ones receive far more emphasis. It is much easier to teach, and especially to assess, convergently. A right answer is easy to tell from a wrong answer. A creative answer is much more challenging:

> *Teacher.* Can anyone tell me what infinity means? (*silence*) What is infinity?
> *Billy.* Uh. I think it's like a box of Creamed Wheat.
> *Teacher.* Don't be silly!
>
> (Jones 1968: 72)

Creamed Wheat boxes had a picture of a man holding up a box of Creamed Wheat which had a picture of a man . . .

A homely little example, but you can see why highly divergent students, even those who achieve well, tend to be disliked by teachers (Getzels and Jackson 1962). This applies at tertiary level too. In our convergent focus, we can too easily dismiss an insight that at first glance seems irrelevant. But that flexibility of perspective is what sparks research ideas: what would happen if? Fortunately, divergent thinking can be encouraged by the appropriate teaching environment; I found plenty of divergent surprises in my student portfolios that conventional assessment would have missed, as reported in Chapter 10.

As to processes of assessment, a level 1 view of teaching sees all assessment as convergent: get right what I have just taught you. When essays are 'marked' (I use the term advisedly) with a checklist, there are only marks for matching the prescribed points, no marks for scoring bullseyes on others just as good or better. For obvious reasons, convergent assessment is particularly likely in large classes where tutors are used as markers. This is not what assessment should be about. Virtually all university-level subjects require at least some divergent assessment. Setting only closed questions is like trying to shoot fish in murky water. We look at open- and closed-ended assessment tasks in the next chapter.

Unintended outcomes

Now consider another metaphor for assessment, provided by a student teacher: 'When I stand in front of a class, I don't see stupid or unteachable learners, but boxes of treasures waiting for us to open' (An in-service teacher education student, University of Hong Kong). What 'treasure' students find in their educational experience is something that can surprise, delight and disappoint. In the traditional or convergent assessment format something like this occurs:

Teacher. How many diamonds have you got?
Student. I don't have any diamonds.
Teacher. Then you fail!
Student. But you didn't ask me about my jade.

Learners can construct treasure of all kinds, not just in diamonds. If you only ask a limited range of questions, then you will probably miss the jade: the treasure that you didn't know existed because you didn't ask.

Any rich teaching context is likely to produce learning that is productive and relevant, but unanticipated. The value of many formal activities lies in the surprises: excursions, practica and lab sessions are cases in point. Informal activities bring about unanticipated learning in infinite ways. The student talks to someone, reads a book not on the reading list, watches a television programme, browses the Net, does a host of things that spark a train of thought, a new construction. Such learnings probably will not fit the questions being asked in the exam, but could nevertheless be highly relevant to the unit objectives. Probably most scientific discoveries came about as a result of paying attention to unintended outcomes. Assessment practices should allow for such rich learning experiences.

Two questions then arise:

1 What modes of assessment would pick up unintended learning outcomes?
2 How can the results be incorporated into standard assessment procedures?

Traditional assessment procedures do not easily allow the student to display such learning, apart from extremely open-ended exam questions, or assignment topics. In my undergraduate days, my psychology professor occasionally included the following in the final exam paper: 'Based on the first year syllabus, set and answer your own question on a topic not addressed in this paper.' Another was: 'Psychology. Discuss.' You had to answer these questions extremely well.

The portfolio is ideal for assessing unintended outcomes. In this mode of assessment, students choose examples of their work carried out during the semester or year that they consider matches the objectives, or that they consider best illustrates the quality of their learning. The operational details of portfolio assessment are discussed in more detail in Chapter 9, an in-use example in Chapter 10.

In assessing unintended outcomes, some may see a problem of 'fairness'. Shouldn't all students be assessed on the same criteria? This complaint has weight only in a norm-referenced context, when you are comparing students with each other. Then, yes, you have to standardize so that all have a fair crack at however many As or HDs have been allocated. In a criterion-referenced system, however, the complaint is irrelevant. The aim is to see what people have learned; if student A has learned X, and student B has learned Y, and X and Y are both interesting and valuable things to learn, where is the problem? Where the top level of objectives specifies creativity and originality, it is unfair if the system doesn't allow for their assessment.

Who takes part in the assessing?

Three processes are involved in assessment:

1 *Setting the criteria* for assessing the work.
2 *Selecting the evidence* that would be relevant to submit to judgement against those criteria.
3 *Making a judgement* about the extent to which these criteria have been met.

Traditionally, the teacher is the agent in all three assessment issues. As just noted, level 1 teaching sees assessment through convergent eyes. The teacher decides in advance that the evidence for learning comprises correct answers to a set of questions that again in the teacher's opinion address and represent the essential core content of the course.

Self- and peer-assessment

Self-assessment (SA) and peer-assessment (PA) usually refer to student involvement in stage 3, but students can and often should be involved in stages 1 and 2 as well. Arguments can be made for all or any of these combination (Harris and Bell 1986; Boud 1995). Students can be involved in discussing with the teacher what the criteria might be, and in that case they need not be the same for all students, as happens in a contract system. Students can also be involved in 2: that is, as the ones responsible for selecting the evidence to be put up against the criteria, as happens with assessment by portfolio.

The most conservative kind of SA and PA is on teacher-set criteria, in response to teacher-set tasks. Boud (1986) describes a conventional mid-session examination, where students in an electrical engineering course were, after the examination, provided with a paper of an unnamed fellow student and a detailed model answer, and asked to mark it. They then did the same to their own paper, without knowing what marks someone else might have given it. The self- and other-marks were then compared: if the mark was within 10 per cent of what the other student had awarded, the higher mark was given. If the discrepancy was greater than 10 per cent, the lecturer remarked the script. Spot checking is needed to discourage collusion ('Let's all agree to mark high!').

More radical is self-assessment on student-generated criteria, on student-selected tasks (Boud 1986). The teacher can brainstorm the class for points to be included in the assignment, which are written up on the board and regrouped into smaller categories. The teacher avoids suggesting criteria, so that the students feel 'ownership' over what constitutes a good essay, project etc. The class decides which categories to use, with what emphasis. A marking sheet is prepared and distributed. The students then do the assignment, mark their own work in terms of the criteria and place that marking and its justification in a sealed envelope, which is returned to the teacher, with the assignment itself. The teacher then decides whether the mark is used formatively, as teaching feedback, or summatively, as part or all of the final grade. In either case the students have gone through an important learning experience: they have *decided* the important features of the assignment, and have *evaluated* their own work in terms of those criteria. As Boud describes this, however, it uses the averaging procedures that could result in passing the anatomically challenged surgeon.

Falchikov and Boud (1989) reviewed 57 studies to determine the factors that lead to good agreement between teacher and self-assessment. Agreement was greatest with advanced students, least in introductory courses; and in convergent content, science, medicine and engineering, rather than divergent, arts and social science. Good agreement requires explicit criteria of assessment, and discussion and training in using them (Fox 1989).

Self-assessment considerably sharpens content learning. In Boud's conservative example, the students not only learn the curriculum content to the extent usual for sitting exams, they then study three versions: a model paper, another student's and their own. The content is processed several times and from different perspectives. The main disadvantage is that it works best in convergent formats.

Other uses of SA and PA are given in Chapter 9, and a case study of PA as a teaching device in Chapter 10.

Reliability and validity

Any discussion of assessment, particularly of new forms of assessment, would not be complete without reference to reliability and validity. These questions, respectively, are: Can we rely on the assessment results? Are they assessing what they should be assessing?

Traditionally, reliability meant *stability*: a test needed to come up with the same result on different occasions, independently of who was giving and marking it. Hence the use of multiple items to measure the same characteristic, and the measures of reliability: test–retest, split-half and internal consistency. But this is all measurement model stuff; learning assumes change, not stability. To construct tests that are measurement-model reliable is to ensure that they are insensitive to what has been taught.

The kind of reliability that is educationally relevant is *inter-* and *intra-judge* reliability:

1 The same person would make the same judgement about the same performance on two different occasions.
2 Different judges would make the same judgement about the same performance on the same occasion.

This form of reliability then becomes a matter of making sure that judges know clearly what their framework of judgement is, and how to use it. It is not a matter of sophisticated statistical operations, but of being very clear about what you are doing, what learning outcomes you want and why. In other words, reliable assessments are part and parcel of good teaching. We have been explicating the framework and the specific criteria for making informed and reliable judgements about students' learning from Chapter 3 onwards.

Likewise with validity. Traditionally, the validity of a test 'is its ability to measure what it is supposed to measure' (Biggs and Moore 1993: 409). Such a definition sees validity as a property of the test, rather than of the *interpretations and uses* to which test scores are put (Messick 1989). For example, backwash is part of the validity of a test; if an exam results in students rote-learning model answers, then that is a consequence that invalidates the test. An aligned, or properly criterion-referenced, assessment task is valid, a non-aligned one is invalid.

There is now quite a good deal of agreement about reliability and validity in qualitative assessment (Frederiksen and Collins, 1989; Moss 1992, 1994; Shepard 1993; Taylor 1994). It all comes back to the question we have been discussing at length: *judgement*, a matter of judging how well the assessment tasks address the teaching objectives. That being so, Ramsden's stern words are a good way of summarizing and concluding:

> Be suspicious of the objectivity and accuracy of all measures of student ability and conscious that human judgement is the most important element in every indicator of achievement.
>
> (Ramsden 1992: 212)

Summary and conclusions

Backwash: the effects of assessment on learning

The effects of assessment on learning are usually deleterious. This is largely because assessment is treated as a necessary evil, the bad news of teaching and learning, to be conducted at the end of all the good stuff. Students second-guess the assessment and make that their syllabus; they will under-estimate requirements if the assessments tasks let them. In aligned teaching, on the other hand, the assessment reinforces learning. Assessment is the senior partner in learning and teaching. Get it wrong, and the rest collapses. This chapter and Chapter 9 aim to help you get it right.

Why assess?

The first thing to get right is the reason for assessing. There are two paramount reasons why we should assess: formative, to provide feedback during learning; and summative, to provide an index of how successfully the student has learned when teaching has been completed. Formative assessment is basic to good teaching, and has been addressed in earlier chapters. Our main concern in this chapter is with summative.

Two models of summative assessment

Summative assessment has recently undergone a major rethink. For years the thinking and the methodology of educational assessment was based on the assumption that what we are measuring is a stable characteristic, and the measurement is expressed numerically so that individuals can be compared (NRA). Teachers should, however, be more interested in comparing individual progress with a criterion for learning based on what we want students to learn (CRA). The backwash from NRA tells students that they need to grub for marks, which requires them to atomize academic tasks rather than see the meaning of the whole. The backwash from CRA tells students they need to match the target performances as well as they are able, to learn properly what they are supposed to learn.

In theory, NRA should be used for selecting students for university, but when teaching begins, CRA should be used to assess and report the progress of students in terms of the standards of performance reached. In practice, the thinking and practices of NRA have muddied the waters, in undergraduate education particularly.

What is being assessed?

The curriculum is divided into declarative and functioning knowledge.

Both have their place in higher education, but when it comes to assessment, functioning knowledge is frequently assessed as if it were declarative. Students *say* what they have learned rather than show it performatively.

We need a conceptual framework to guide assessment-related decisions. The most common framework is quantitative: we reduce performances to the aggregation of units, or of marks on a rating or percentage scale. Such a framework does violence to the structure of knowledge at the tertiary level, and sends misleading messages to students about what needs doing in order to demonstrate competence.

The alternative framework is qualitative, which deals with forms of knowledge to be reached at the end of teaching, expressed as various levels of acceptability in the objectives and grading system. This framework requires higher levels of judgement on the part of the teacher as to how well the students' performances match the objectives than does quantitative assessment.

Authentic or performance assessment

The assessment tasks need to be 'authentic' to the objectives; they need to stipulate a quality of performance that the assessment task then demands. Authenticity leads us to consider contextualized or decontextualized assessment, holistic or analytic assessment and divergent or convergent assessment.

Declarative knowledge may validly be assessed out of context, but functioning knowledge is always in a context. Authenticity requires the whole act to be assessed, not various parts of it which are then summed. Analytic assessment does not do justice to the integrity of what is being learned, and it blurs the differential importance of topics, which can lead to silly consequences. Assessment is usually heavily biased towards convergent processes, but many important complex skills are open-ended or divergent.

Who takes part in the assessing?

Traditionally, the teacher is the one who sets the tasks, selects the evidence and makes the summative judgements. There are, however, many reasons why students might be brought into some or all of these assessment processes. Students will always learn relevant content in ways or forms that the teacher cannot anticipate, and cannot discover, if only closed questions are asked. Allowing students to set their own questions, or to select their own evidence for their learning, allows assessment of these unintended outcomes. Self- and peer-assessment not only sharpen content learning, they provide opportunities for students to learn the metacognitive processes of self-monitoring, which they will be required to perform in professional and academic life.

Task 8.2: Choose your assessment package

Assessment Package 1 (Source: the measurement model)

Norm-referenced:

- knowledge is conceived as aggregated from units
- assessment tasks are decontextualized
- assessed analytically; processed and reported in quantitative terms
- the teacher controls all aspects of assessment.

This model has a sophisticated technology, very effective for comparing students and for making actuarial decisions about students. While it does violence to the structure of knowledge, it is not about knowledge, but about measuring characteristics of people.

Assessment Package 2 (Source: the standards model)

Criterion-referenced:

- knowledge conceived as expressed in the objectives
- usually assessed qualitatively (but the criteria could be quantitative where that is appropriate)
- assessment tasks are contextualized for assessing functioning knowledge and decontextualized for assessing declarative knowledge
- assessment is essentially holistic but could be analytic for determining ongoing progress
- reporting in qualitative categories (perhaps later convertible to quantitative scales)
- aspects of assessment can be teacher-controlled, peer-controlled or self-controlled as suits the task to be learned.

In this model, assessment is integral to teaching, the intention being to represent the objectives authentically.

Choose your package!

Reliability and validity

Most of the prevailing wisdom about the reliability and validity of assessment is based on the measurement model. As that model goes out the window, so too do many of our assumptions about what is a 'good' test. As the quantitative scaffolding is dismantled, we find that notions as to reliability and validity depend more and more upon the teacher's basic professional responsibility, which is to make judgements about the quality of learning.

Conclusions

To this point, we have been looking at a variety of concepts and issues, but in fact they cluster to form two distinct models of assessment. To conclude this rather complex chapter, I summarize these assessment packages. We need to understand what each is about, and then make a commitment to one or the other (Task 8.2). It is counter-productive to select aspects from each, as they are designed to perform different functions, they speak different languages. Much common practice suffers from confusion between the two models. We must be clear about what we are doing.

Having made our choice between package 1 and package 2, there is the practical matter of actually carrying out summative assessment in line with the chosen package. We need to decide what particular modes of assessment might best suit our objectives, how to evaluate using these tasks and to form summative statements of performance, and then to report the results. These practical matters are the concern of the next chapter.

Further reading

Astin, A. W. (1985) *Achieving Educational Excellence: a Critical Assessment of Priorities and Practices in Higher Education*, San Francisco: Jossey-Bass.

Crooks, T. J. (1988) *Assessing Student Performance*, Green Guide No. 8, Sydney: Higher Education Research and Development Society of Australasia.

Dart, B. and Boulton-Lewis, G. (1998) *Teaching and Learning in Higher Education*, Camberwell, Vic.: Australian Council for Educational Research.

Moss, P. A. (1994) Can there be validity without reliability?, *Educational Researcher*, 23(2), 5–12.

Taylor, C. (1994) Assessment for measurement or standards: the peril and promise of large scale assessment reform, *American Educational Research Journal*, 31, 231–62.

Torrance, H. (ed.) (1994) *Evaluating Authentic Assessment: Problems and Possibilities in New Approaches to Assessment*, Buckingham: Open University Press.

Astin's book focuses on formative assessment and its role in teaching, but I include it here, where our focus is mostly on summative assessment, because there are relatively few books that deal with *principles*. Most address practical issues, the focus of the next chapter. I have included two of the seminal review articles that outline the principles of the rethink on assessment, where the criteria are qualitatively defined. Taylor traces the historical and conceptual roots of NRA and CRA, clearly outlining where the confusions in current practice have crept in. Moss brings this up to date conceptually, while Torrance's book contains some commentaries on the new approach. Crooks gives a useful outline of some basic principles as they apply to tertiary education. Dart and Boulton-Lewis contains chapters by Boulton-Lewis, Dart, and Hattie and Purdie, which specifically deal with SOLO as a conceptual structure for assessing holistically.

Answers to Task 8.1

Both are examples of CRA. Despite the fact that Susan's and Robert's performances were compared, the purpose was not to award the grades but to check the consistency of making the judgement. Essentially, in CRA, a student's performance is matched with the predetermined standards to see which grading category applies. What happened here was that my initial judgement of Robert's performance was inaccurate, very possibly because of a halo effect. ('Ah, here's Robert's little effort. That won't be an A,' I very possibly murmured to myself, and promptly fulfilled my own prophecy.) It took a direct comparison with Susan's effort to see the mistake. The standards themselves were unaltered.

In the second case the standards were set up before grading began. The fact that they were in part defined from norm-referenced data is irrelevant. At the end of teaching each student's performance would be compared to those preset standards, not with each other: hence, CRA.

9

Assessing for learning quality: II. Practice

In this chapter we look at implementing assessment package 2. What assessment tasks are available, and for what purpose is each best used? How can large classes be assessed effectively? How can students be quickly provided with feedback, particularly in large classes? When, and how, should self/peer-assessment be used? How can qualitative assessments be combined across several tasks, or across units, to yield a single final grade? How can students' performance be graded qualitatively when the results have to be reported in percentages? These are the bread-and-butter questions we address in this chapter.

What are the best formats for summative assessment?

Let us say you chose assessment package 2 (if you didn't, you might as well skip the rest of this chapter). You are now faced with assessing a large class. I will put it to you in the form of a multiple-choice test item:

My question: What format will you use to assess your class of 400 first-year (biology) students?

1 An individual research project (maximum 5000 words).
2 A multiple-choice test.
3 A 2000 word assignment during the term, and a final three-hour examination.
4 A contextualized problem-based portfolio.

Your reply. Not 1, it takes too long to mark; same for 3. In 4 is Biggs trying to be funny, or is he serious but hopelessly unrealistic? Should be 2, which is what most people use, but it's clear what the prejudices of He Who Set the Question are. But I'll risk it and say 2.

Well, you could be right, but the question is unanswerable as it stands. A crucial consideration has been omitted: *what are your objectives?* The 'best' assessment method is the one that best realizes your objectives. In your first-year class, are you targeting declarative knowledge, or functioning knowledge, or both? What levels of understanding do you require, and for what topics: knowledge of terminology, description, application to new problems . . .? As you rightly said in response to our multiple-choice question, multiple-choice *is* widely used, and yes, it is convenient. But will it assess what you are after?

We need to clarify further. Although you chose package 2, some issues are not entirely clear-cut. Let me again think aloud on your behalf:

- *NRA or CRA?* CRA. I want the grades to reflect learning, not relativities between students. (However, there's no room in second year for all of them, we may have to cull somehow . . .)
- *Quantitative or qualitative?* Qualitative, I hope, but aren't there certain basic facts and skills I want students to get correct?
- *Holistic or analytic?* Holistic, but how do I combine holistic assessments of several tasks to make one final grade?
- *Convergent or divergent?* Do I want students to get it right, or to show some lateral thinking? Probably both.
- *Contextualized or decontextualized?* Both. Students must understand the literature, but they need to solve problems in context.
- *Teacher assessed or self/peer assessed?* I intend to be the final arbiter, but self/peer assessment has educational and workload advantages.
- *Backwash?* What effect will my assessment tasks have on students' learning?
- *Time-constrained? Invigilated?* Does my institution require me to impose formal examinations conditions?

There are no right answers, only better or worse ones, and the range of assessment formats to choose from is large. We have to strike a balance between practicality and validity. Chapter 8 set a stern example to live up to, but we have to be realistic. There are 400 students to assess, and their results have to be sent to the board of examiners the week following the examination.

Throughout this chapter, we will be reviewing many different modes of assessment. You should read reflectively as before, with a particular problem class in mind. Ask yourself: how might this help in developing my own assessment practices? At the end of the chapter, we return to the problem posed by the first-year class.

How important is the format of assessment?

First, let us see if it matters, apart from convenience, whether you use multiple-choice, or essay exam, or assignment. This depends on the

---

Box 9.1: Learning activities reported by students in preparing for (a) short essay question examination, and (b) assignment

(a) Short essay examination

rote learning, question spotting, going through past papers, underlining, organizing study time and materials, memorizing in meaningful context, relating information, visualizing patients' conditions, discussing with other students.

(b) Assignment

choosing easy questions/interesting questions/what lecturers expect, copying sources, reading widely/searching for information sources, relating question to own knowledge, relating to patients' conditions and clinical application, organizing, revising text to improve relevance, discussing with other students.

Source: from Tang 1991.

---

activities an assessment format usually elicits. Are they ones that match your teaching objectives? If they do match your objectives, the backwash is positive, but if they do not, the backwash will encourage students to use surface approaches to learning.

The evidence is very clear that different formats do produce typical forms of backwash. They get students doing different things in preparing for them, some being much more aligned to the unit objectives than others. Tang (1991) used questionnaire and interview to determine how physiotherapy students typically prepared for short essay examinations and for assignments (see Box 9.1).

In essence, exams tended to elicit memorization-related activities, assignments application-related activities. The assignment required deep learning from the students with respect to one topic, the exam required acquaintance with a range of topics. The teachers concerned realized that the assignment better addressed the desired course objectives, but only with respect to one topic. They accordingly adopted a policy to use both: short answer exams to ensure coverage, the assignment to ensure depth. A not unusual compromise.

Scouller (1996, 1998) found that students were likely to employ surface strategies in the multiple-choice (MC) format; they saw MC tests as requiring low cognitive level processes. Indeed, Scouller found that using deep approaches was *negatively* related to MC test performance. The opposite occurred with essays. Students saw essays as requiring higher level processes, and were more likely to use them, and those who didn't, using surface approaches instead, did poorly. Students who preferred MC to essay assignment gave surface-type reasons: you can rely on memory, you can 'play the game' (see Box 9.2). Yet these were the same reasons why

---

Box 9.2: Two examples of students' views on multiple choice tests

I preferred MCQ . . . It was just a matter of learning facts . . . and no real analysis or critique was required which I find tedious if I am not wrapped in the topic. I also dislike structuring and writing and would prefer to have the answer to a question there in front of me somewhere.

. . . A multiple choice exam tends to examine too briefly a topic, or provide overly complex situations which leave a student confused and faced with 'eenie, meenie, minie, mo' situation. It is cheap, and in my opinion ineffectual in assessing a student's academic abilities in the related subject area.

Source: from Scouller 1997.

---

other students disliked the MC; these students were angry at being assessed in a way that they felt did not do justice to their learning. When doing assignments, they felt they were able to show higher levels of learning. Short answer examinations did not attract their anger, but the level of cognitive activities assessed was no better than with MC.

Assessment by portfolio leads students to see it as 'a powerful learning tool . . .', and as requiring them to be divergent: 'it led me to think about many questions that I never think of' (see p. 136). Wong (1994) used SOLO to structure a secondary 5 (Year 10) mathematics test in the ordered outcome format (see below), and compared students' problem-solving methods on that with those they used on the traditional format. The difference was not on items correct, but on how they went about the problems. They behaved like 'experts' on the SOLO test, solving items from first principles, while on the traditional test they behaved like 'novices', applying the standard algorithms.

In sum then, MCs and short answers tend to elicit low-level verbs, leaving students feeling that MCs and short answers do not reveal what they have learned, while portfolios and SOLO encourage high-level verbs. Unfortunately, there appears to be little further research on backwash from other assessment modes. Tang's study suggests how one might go about this, matching verbs denoted as desirable in the objectives with the verbs students say the assessment tasks encouraged them to use.

We now review particular assessment formats in detail, under four headings: extended prose, objective, performance and rapid assessments, which are particularly suitable for large classes.

Extended prose (essay type) formats of assessment

The essay, as a continuous piece of prose written in response to a question or problem, is commonly intended for assessing higher cognitive levels. There are many variants:

- the timed examination, students having no prior knowledge of the question;
- the open-book examination, students usually having some prior knowledge and being allowed to bring reference material into the exam room;
- the take-home, where students are given notice of the questions and several days to prepare their answers in their own time;
- the assignment, which is an extended version of the take-home, and comprises the most common of all methods of evaluating by essay;
- the dissertation, which is an extended report of independent research.

Let us discuss these.

Essay examinations

Essay exams are best suited for assessing declarative knowledge. They are usually decontextualized, students writing under time pressure to demonstrate the level of their understanding of core content. The format is open-ended, so theoretically students can express their own constructions and views, supporting them with evidence and original arguments. The reality is often different.

The time constraint for writing exams may have several reasons:

1 *Convenience.* A time and a place is nominated for the final assessment, which teachers, students and administration can work around. We all know where we stand.
2 *Invigilation.* Having a specified time and place makes it more easy for the time-keeper to prevent cheating. This enables the institution to guarantee the authenticity of the results.
3 *Conditions are standardized.* No one has an 'unfair advantage'. But do you allow question choice in a formal examination? If you do, you violate the standardization condition, because all candidates are not then sitting the 'same' examination (Brown and Knight 1994). Standardization is in fact a hangover from the measurement model; it is irrelevant in a criterion-referenced situation.
4 *Models real life.* The time constraint reflects 'the need in life to work swiftly, under pressure and well' (Brown and Knight 1994: 69). This is unconvincing. In real-life situations where functioning knowledge is time-stressed – the operating theatre, the bar (in the courts, that is) or the classroom – this point is better accommodated by performance assessment, rather than by pressurizing the assessment of declarative knowledge in the exam room. Alignment suggests that time constraints be applied only when the target performance is itself time-constrained.

Time constraint creates its own backwash. Positively, it creates a target for students to work towards. They are forced to review what they have learned throughout the unit, and possibly for the first time see it as a whole: a tendency greatly enhanced if they think the exam will require them to demonstrate their holistic view. Students' views of examinations suggest that this rarely happens.

The more likely backwash is negative; students memorize specific points to be recalled at speed (Tang 1991). Students go about memorization differently. Learners who prefer a deep approach to learning create a structure first, then memorize the key access words ('deep-memorizing'), while surface learners simply memorize unconnected facts (Tang 1991). So while timed exams encourage *memorizing*, this is not necessarily *rote* memorizing or surface learning. Whether it is or not depends on the students' typical approaches to learning, and on what they expect the exam questions to require.

Does the time constraint impede divergent responses? Originality is a temperamental horse, unlikely to gallop under the stopwatch. However, if students can guess likely questions, they can prepare their original answers at leisure, and with a little massaging of the exam question, express their prepared creation. You as teacher can encourage this high-level off-track preparation, by making it known you intend asking very open questions ('What is the most important topic discussed in the unit this semester? Why?'), or by telling the students at the beginning of the semester what the exam questions will be. Assessing divergent responses must be done holistically. The use of a model answer checklist does not allow for the well argued surprise. Students should be told how the papers are to be marked; then they can calculate their own risks.

In sum, time constraints in the exam room cannot easily be justified educationally. The most probable effect is to encourage memorization, with or without higher-level processing. In fact, time constraints exist for administrative not educational reasons. They are convenient, and they make cheating more difficult. Whether these gains are worth the educational costs is a good question.

Open-book examinations remove the premium on memorization of detail, but retain the time constraint. Theoretically, students should be able to think about higher-level things than getting the facts down. Practically, they need to be very well organized; otherwise they waste time tracking down too many sources.

Exams are almost always teacher assessed, but need not be. The questions can be set in consultation with students, while the assessing and award of grades can be done by the students themselves, and/or their peers, as we saw in Chapter 8. The backwash, and range of activities being assessed, change dramatically with self/peer assessment.

The assignment, the term-paper, the take-home

The assignment, or term paper, deals with declarative knowledge, the project (see below) with 'hands-on' research-type activities. The assignment is not distorted by immediate time limitations, or by the need to rely on memory. In principle, it allows for deeper learning; the student can consult more sources and, with that deeper knowledge base, synthesize more effectively. However, plagiarism is easier, which is why some universities require that a proportion of the assessments in a unit are invigilated. The take-home with shorter time limits, often overnight, makes plagiarism a little more difficult.

Self/peer-assessment can be used to assess assignments. Given the criteria, the students award a grade (to themselves, to a peer's paper or both), and justify the grade awarded. That in itself is a useful learning experience. But whether the self/peer grading(s) stand as the official result, or part of it, are matters that can be negotiated. In my experience, students like the self-assessing process, but tend to be coy about its being a significant part of the final result.

Assessing extended prose

Years ago, Starch and Elliott (1912; Starch 1913a, b) originated a devastating series of investigations into the reliability of assessing essays. Marks for the same essay ranged from bare pass to nearly full marks. Sixty years later, Diederich (1974) found things just as bad. Out of the 300 papers he received in one project, 101 received every grade from 1 to 9 on his nine-point marking scale.

Judges were using different criteria. Diederich isolated four families of criteria, with much disagreement as to their relative importance:

- *Ideas*: originality, relevance, logic.
- *Skills*: the mechanics of writing, spelling, punctuation, grammar.
- *Organization*: format, presentation, literature review.
- *Personal style*: flair.

Each contains a family of items, according to subject. 'Skills' to Diederich meant writing skills, but they could be 'skills' in mathematics, chemistry or fine arts. Likewise for the other components: ideas, organization and personal style. It would be very valuable if staff in a department collectively clarified what they really are looking for under these, or other, headings.

Back to the holistic/analytic question

When reading an essay, do you rate separately for particular qualities, such as those mentioned by Diederich, and then combine the ratings in some kind of weighted fashion? Or do you read and rate the essay as a whole, and give an overall rating?

We dealt with the general argument in Chapter 8. The analytic method of rating the essay on components, and adding the marks up, is appealing. It leads to better agreement between markers. But it is slow. Worse, it does not address the essay as a whole. The unique benefit of the essay is to see if students can construct their response to a question or issue within the framework set by the question. They create a 'discourse structure', which is the point of the essay. Analytic marking is ill-attuned to appraise discourse structure.

Assessing discourse structure requires a framework within which that holistic judgement can be made. SOLO helps you to judge if the required structure is present or not. Listing, describing and narrating are multistructural structures. Compare-and-contrast, causal explanation, interpretation and so on are relational. Inventive students create their own structures, which when they work can make original contributions: these are extended abstract.

The facts and details play their role in these structures in like manner to the characters in a play. And the play's the thing. You do not ignore details, but ask of them:

- Do they make a coherent structure (not necessarily the one you had in mind)? If yes, the essay is at least relational.
- Is the structure the writer uses appropriate or not? If yes, then the question has been properly addressed (relational). If no, you will have to decide how far short of satisfactory it is.
- Does the writer's structure open out new ways of looking at the issue? If yes, the essay is extended abstract.

If the answer is consistently 'no' to all of the above, the essay is multistructural or less, and should not be given good marks, because that is not the point of the essay proper. If you do want students to list points, the short answer, or even the MC, is the appropriate format. These are easier for the student to complete, and for you to assess.

This distinction recalls that between 'knowledge-telling' and 'reflective writing' (Bereiter and Scardamalia 1987). Knowledge-telling is a multistructural strategy that can all too easily mislead assessors. Students focus only on the topic content, and tell all they know about it, often in a listing or point-by-point form. Using an analytic marking scheme, it is very hard not to award high marks, when in fact the student hasn't even addressed the question. Take this example of an ancient history compare-and-contrast question: 'In what ways were the reigns of Tutankhamen and Akhnaton alike, and in what ways were they different?' The highest scoring student gave the life histories of both pharaohs, and was commended on her effort and depth of research, yet her discourse structure was entirely inappropriate (Biggs 1987b).

Reflective writing transforms the writer's thinking. E. M. Forster put it thus: 'How can I know what I think until I see what I say?' The act of writing externalizes thought, making it a learning process. By reflecting on what you see, you can revise it in so many ways, creating something quite new, even to yourself. That is what the best academic writing should be doing.

The essay is obviously the medium for reflective writing, not knowledge-telling. Tynjala (1998) suggests that writing tasks should require students;

- actively to transform their knowledge, not simply to repeat it;
- to undertake open-ended activities that make use of existing knowledge and beliefs, but that lead to questioning and reflecting on that knowledge;
- to theorize about their experiences;
- to apply theory to practical situations, and/or to solve practical problems or problems of understanding.

Put otherwise, the question should seek to elicit higher relational and extended abstract verbs. Tynjala gave students such writing tasks, which they discussed in groups. They were later found to have the same level of knowledge as a control group, but greatly exceeded the latter in the *use* to which they could put their thinking. The difference was in their functioning, not in their declarative, knowledge.

Maximizing stable essay assessment

The horrendous results reported by Starch and Elliott and by Diederich occurred because the criteria were unclear, were applied differently by different assessors and were often unrecognized. The criteria must be aligned to the objectives from the outset, and be consciously applied.

Halo effects are a common source of unreliability. Regrettable it may be, but we tend to judge the performance of students we like more favourably than those we don't like. Attractive female students receive significantly higher grades than unattractive ones (Hore 1971). Halo effects also occur in the order in which essays are assessed. The first half-dozen scripts tend to set the standard for the next half-dozen, which in turn reset the standard for the next. A moderately good essay following a run of poor ones tends to be assessed higher than it deserves, but if it follows a run of very good ones, it is marked down (Hales and Tokar 1975).

Halo and other distortions can be greatly minimized by discussion; judgements are social constructions (Moss 1994; see pp. 81, 99 above). There is some really strange thinking on this. A common belief is that it is more 'objective' if judges rate students' work without discussing it. In one fine arts department, a panel of judges independently award grades without discussion; the student's final grade is the undiscussed average. The rationale for this bizarre procedure is that works of an artist cannot be judged against outside standards. Where this leaves any examining process I was unable to discover.

Out of the dozens of universities where I have acted as an external examiner for research dissertations, only one invites examiners to resolve disagreement by discussion before the higher degrees committee adjudicates. Consensus is usually the result. Disagreements between examiners are more commonly resolved quantitatively: for example, by counting heads, or by hauling in additional examiners until the required majority is obtained. In another university I could mention, such conflicts are resolved by a vote in senate. The fact that the great majority of senate members haven't seen the thesis aids detachment. Their objectivity remains unclouded by mere knowledge.

Given all the above, the following precautions suggest themselves:

- All assessment should be 'blind', with the identity of the student concealed.
- All rechecking should likewise be blind, with the original mark concealed.
- Each question should be marked across students, so that a standard for each *question* is set. Marking by the student rather than by the question allows more room for halo effects, a high or low mark on one question influencing your judgement on the student's answers to other questions.
- Between questions, the papers should be shuffled to prevent systematic order effects.
- Grade coarsely (qualitatively) at first, say into 'excellent', 'pass' and 'fail', or directly into the grading categories. It is then much easier to discriminate more finely within these categories.
- Departments should discuss standards, to seek agreement on what constitutes excellent performances, pass performances and so on, with respect to commonly used assessment tasks.
- Spot-check, particularly borderline cases, using an independent assessor. Agree on criteria first.
- The wording of the questions should be checked for ambiguities by a colleague.

Objective formats of assessment

The objective test is a closed or convergent format requiring one correct answer. It is said, misleadingly, to relieve the marker of 'subjectivity' in judgement. But judgement is ubiquitous. In this case, it is simply shifted from scoring items to choosing items, and to designating which alternatives are correct. Objective testing is not more 'scientific', or less prone to error. The potential for error is pushed to the front end, where the hard work is designing and constructing a good test. The advantage is that the cost-benefits rapidly increase the more students you test at a time. With machine scoring, it is as easy to test one thousand and twenty students as it is to test twenty: a seductive option.

The following forms of the objective test are in common use:

- Two alternatives are provided (true–false).
- Several, usually four or five, alternatives are provided (the MC).
- Items are placed in two lists, and an item from list A has to be matched with an item from list B (matching).
- Various, such as filling in blank diagrams, completing sentences. One version, the cloze test, is used as a test of comprehension.
- Sub-items are 'stepped' according to difficulty or structure, the student being required to respond as 'high' as possible (the ordered outcome).

Of these, we now consider the MC, and the ordered outcome. The cloze is considered later, under 'rapid' assessment.

Multiple-choice tests

The MC is the most widely used objective test. Theoretically, MCs can assess high-level verbs. Practically, they rarely do, and some students, the Susans rather than the Roberts, look back in anger at the MC for not doing so (Scouller 1997). MCs assess declarative knowledge, usually in terms of the least demanding process, recognition. But probably the worst feature of MCs is that they encourage the use of game-playing strategies, by both student and teacher. Some examples:

Student strategies
- In a four-alternative MC format, never choose the facetious or the jargon-ridden alternatives.
- By elimination, you can create a binary choice, with the pig-ignorant having a 50 per cent chance of being correct.
- Does one alternative stimulate a faint glow of recognition in an otherwise unrelieved darkness? Go for it.
- Longer alternatives are not a bad bet.

Teacher strategies
- Student strategies are discouraged by a guessing penalty: that is, deducting wrong responses from the total score. (Question: why should this be counter-productive?)
- The use of facetious alternatives is patronizing if not offensive (I can play games with you but you can't with me). Not nice.

- Rewording existing items when you run out of ideas. Anyway, it increases reliability.

MC tests have great coverage, that 'enemy of understanding' (Gardner 1993). One hundred items can cover an enormous number of topics. But if there is exclusive use of the MC, it greatly misleads as to the nature of knowledge, because the method of scoring makes the idea contained in any one item the same value as that in any other item. But consider Lohman's (1993) instance, where an MC test was given to fifth-grade children on the two hundredth anniversary of the signing of the US Constitution. The only item on the test referring to Thomas Jefferson was: 'Who was the signer of the Constitution who had six children?' A year later, Lohman asked a child in this class what she remembered of Thomas Jefferson. Of course, she remembered that he was the one with six children, nothing of his role in the Constitution. Students, including tertiary students, quickly learn that: 'There is no need to separate main ideas from details; all are worth one point. And there is no need to assemble these ideas into a coherent summary or to integrate them with anything else because that is not required' (Lohman 1993: 19). The message is clear. Get a nodding acquaintance with as many details as you can, but do not be so foolish as to attempt to learn anything in depth.

MC tests can be useful if they supplement other forms of assessment, but when used exclusively, they send all the wrong signals. Unfortunately, they *are* convenient.

Ordered outcome items

An ordered outcome item looks like an MC, but instead of opting for the one correct alternative out of the four or so provided, the student is required to attempt all sub-items (Masters 1987). The sub-items are ordered into a hierarchy of complexity that reflects successive stages of learning that concept or skill. The students ascend the sequence as far as they can, thus indicating their level of competence in that topic.

All that is required is that the stem provide sufficient information for a range of questions of increasing complexity to be asked. How those questions are derived depends on your working theory of learning. SOLO can be used as a guide for working a sequence out. A SOLO sequence would look like this:

1 *Unistructural*: use one obvious piece of information coming directly from the stem.
2 *Multistructural*: use two or more discrete and separate pieces of information contained in the stem.
3 *Relational*: use two or more pieces of information each directly related to an integrated understanding of the information in the stem.

Box 9.3: An ordered outcome item for physiotherapy students

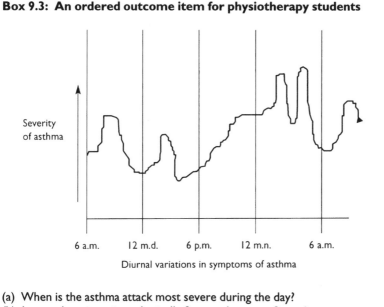

Severity
of asthma

6 a.m.   12 m.d.   6 p.m.   12 m.n.   6 a.m.

Diurnal variations in symptoms of asthma

(a) When is the asthma attack most severe during the day?
(b) Is an asthmatic patient physically fitter at 1 p.m. or 8 p.m.?
(c) Do you expect an asthmatic patient to sleep well at night? Give your reasons.
(d) Advise an asthmatic patient how to cope with diurnal variation in symptoms.

Source: Tang, private communication.

4 *Extended abstract:* use an abstract general principle or hypothesis which can be derived from, or suggested by, the information in the stem.

The student's score is the highest correct level. If the response to the first question is inadequate, the student's understanding is assumed to be prestructural.

The levels do not, however, need to correspond to each SOLO level, or to SOLO levels at all. In a physiotherapy course (C. Tang, private communication), an extended abstract option was inappropriate for the first year, and so two levels of relational were used, as in (c) and (d) in Box 9.3, where (c) refers to conceptual integration (declarative) and (d) to application (functioning). Sub-item (a) is unistructural because it only requires a correct reading of the diagram: a simple but essential first skill. Sub-item (b) is a multistructural response, requiring the comparison of two different readings. Sub-item (c) requires interpretation at a simple relational level response, while (d) is relational but more complex, requiring a complete interpretation integrated with functioning knowledge of caring skills.

Key situations can be displayed in this format, and a (d) or (c) level of performance required (in this case, anything less would not be of much help to patients). It is sometimes possible to use a one-correct-answer format for extended abstract items: 'Formulate the general case of which the preceding (relational) item is an instance.' Often, however, extended abstract items use open-ended verbs, so we have in effect a divergent short-answer sub-item: 'Give an example where (c) – the preceding item – does *not* occur. Why doesn't it?'

The ordered outcome format sends a strong message to students that higher is better: recognition and simple algorithms won't do. This was the format in which Wong (1994) found students to behave theoretically, like experts do (see p. 168).

Constructing ordered outcome items is the difficult part. The items need to form a staircase: unistructural items must be easier than multistructural, and multistructural than relational, and relational than extended abstract. This can be tested with trial runs, preferably using the Guttman (1941) scalogram model, or software is available (Masters 1988). Hattie and Purdie (1998) discuss a range of measurement issues involved in the construction and interpretation of ordered outcome SOLO items. Basically, it is as always a matter of judgement.

Scoring ordered outcome items makes most sense on a profile basis. That is, you have nominated key situations or concepts, about which the students need to achieve a minimal level of understanding. In the physio item, (c) is possibly adequate in first year, but by the second year students really should be responding at an applied treatment (d) level. The profile sets minimum standards for each skill or component.

It is tempting to say (a) gets 1 mark, (b) 2 marks, (c) 3 marks, and (d) (let's be generous) 5 marks. We then throw the marks into the pot with all the other test results. However, this destroys the very thing we are trying to assess, a level of understanding. If the score is less than perfect, a nominal understanding of one topic could be averaged with a performative under-standing of another, yielding 'moderate' understanding across all topics, which wasn't the case at all.

Performance assessment

Performance assessment requires students to perform tasks that mirror the objectives of the unit. Students should be required to demonstrate that they *see and do things differently* as a result of their understanding.

The problems or tasks set are, as in real life, often divergent or ill-formed, in the sense that there are no single correct answers. For example, there are many acceptable ways a software program could be written for use in an estate agency office. What is important is that the student shows how the problem may reasonably be approached, how resources and data are used, how previously taught material is used, how effectively the solutions meets likely contingencies and so on. Clearly, this needs an open-ended assessment format and assessment process. Almost any scenario from the professions can be used: designing a structure, teaching a new topic, dealing with a patient with a strange combination of symptoms.

Various formats reflect this authentic intention with varying fidelity.

The practicum

The practicum, if properly designed, should call out all the important verbs needed to demonstrate competence in a real-life situation, such as practice teaching, interviewing a patient, any clinical session, handling an experiment in the laboratory, producing an artistic product. It goes without saying that CRA is the most appropriate way of evaluation. An assessment checklist should *not* look like this:

A: Definitely superior, among the best in the year
B: Above average
C: Average
D: Below average, but meets minimal standards
E: Not up to standard.

It should be quite clear that the student has to perform certain behaviours to a specified standard. It then remains to find if the learner can perform them, and if not, why not. Video-taping is useful, as then students can rate their own performance against the checklist of desired behaviours before discussing the supervisor's rating.

The closer the practicum is to the real thing, the greater its validity. The one feature that distorts reality is that it *is* an assessment situation, so that some students are likely to behave differently from the way they would if they were not being observed and assessed. This may be minimized by making observation of performance a continuing fact of life. With plenty of formative assessment before the final summative assessment, the student might nominate when he or she is 'ready' for final assessment. This might seem labour intensive, but recording devices can stand in for *in vivo* observation, as can other students.

In fact, the situation is ideal for peer assessment. Students become accustomed to being observed by each other, and they can receive peer feedback. Whether student evaluations are then used, in whole or in part, in the summative assessment is worth considering. In surgery possibly not; in the expressive arts possibly so.

Presentations and interviews

The class presentation is evaluated in terms of what content is conveyed, and how well. Where the focus is on declarative understanding, the students declaring to their peers, we have the traditional *seminar*, which is not necessarily meant to reproduce a situation in which students will later find themselves. The seminar, if used carefully, offers good opportunities for formative discussion, and peer assessment both formative and summative. However, as we have seen (pp. 86–7 above), it can easily become a poor substitute for proper teaching.

Student presentations are best for functioning rather than declarative knowledge. Peer input can be highly appropriate in this case. The Fine Arts Department at the University of Newcastle (NSW) (not the department mentioned earlier) has an examining panel comprising teachers, a prominent local artist and a student (rotating), who view all the student productions, have a plenary discussion with all staff and students about each, and then submit a final, public, examiners' report. This is not only a very close approximation to real life in the gallery world, but actively involves staff and students in a way that it is rich with learning opportunities.

The *poster presentation* follows the well known conference format. A student or group of students display their work according to an arranged format during a poster session. This provides excellent opportunities for peer-assessment, and for fast feedback of results. However, Brown and Knight (1994: 78) warn that the poster 'must be meticulously prepared'. The specifications need to be very clear, down to the size of the display, and how to use back-up materials: diagrams, flow-charts, photographs. Text needs to be clear and highly condensed. Assessment criteria can be placed on an assessment sheet, which all students receive to rate all other posters. Criteria would include substance, originality, impact and so on.

The *interview* is used most commonly in the examination of dissertations and theses. In the last case, the student constructs a 'thesis' that has to be 'defended' against expert criticism. Almost always, these oral defences are evaluated qualitatively. The student makes a case, and is successful, conditionally successful, unsuccessful but is given another try (with or without formal re-examination) or irredeemably unsuccessful. Here again the criteria are usually clearly spelt out: the structure of the dissertation, what constitutes good procedure, what is acceptable and what unacceptable evidence, clarity of writing, format and so on. These criteria are seen as 'hurdles' – they have to be got right eventually – while the assessment itself is on the *substance* and *originality* of the thesis itself.

In undergraduate teaching, the interview is seen as 'subjective' (which it is, but see above), and it 'takes too long'. However, a properly constructed interview schedule could see a fruitful interview through in 20 minutes, possible 30. How long does it take to assess properly each written product of a three-hour examination, or a 2500 word assignment? Thirty minutes? Gobbets (see below) could be a useful way of structuring and focusing an assessment interview. Unstructured interviews can be unreliable, but bear in mind that the point of interviewing is lost if the interview is too tightly structured.

That point is that the interview is interactive. Teachers have a chance to follow up and probe, and students have a chance to display their jade: their unanticipated but valuable learning treasures. Certainly, the interview might be supplemented with a written MC or short answer (to cover the basics), but the most interesting learnings could be brought to light and assessed within 20 minutes or so. Oral assessments should be tape recorded, both in case of dispute (when student and an adjudicator can hear the replay) and so that you may assess under less pressure, or subsequently check your original assessment.

Self-assessment is an interesting option here, with the teacher- and self-assessments themselves being the subject of the interview.

Critical incidents

Students can be asked to report on 'critical incidents' that seem to them powerful examples of unit content, or that stimulate them to think deeply about the content. They then explain why these incidents are critical, how they arose and what might be done about it. This gives rich information about how students (a) have interpreted what they have been taught, and (b) can make use of the information.

Such incidents might be a focus in a reflective journal, or be used as portfolio items (see below).

Project

Whereas an assignment usually focuses on declarative knowledge, the project focuses on functioning knowledge applied to a hands-on piece of research. Projects can vary from simple to sophisticated, and often in the latter case will be best carried out by a group of students. The teacher can allot their respective tasks, or they can work them out among themselves.

There are several ways of awarding grades for a group project. The simplest is to give an overall grade for the project, which each student receives. The difficulty is that it does not allow for passengers, and some of the harder workers will feel aggrieved. Various forms of peer-assessment may be used to modify this procedure, most of which rely on quantification:

• The project is awarded 60 per cent; there are four participants, so there are 240 marks to be allocated. You find out as best you can who did what, and you grade the sections accordingly.

- The project is awarded 60 per cent; there are four participants, so there are 240 marks to be allocated. The students decide who is to get how many marks, with criteria and evidence of effort. One problem is that they may be uncontroversial and divide them equally – some hating themselves as they do so.
- The project is awarded 60 per cent; there are four participants. Each receives a basic 40 per cent. There are now 20 × 4 marks to be allocated. Again, they decide the allocation. The most blatant passenger gets no more, and ends up with 40 per cent; the best contributor gets half of the remainder, by agreement, and ends up with 80 per cent, and so on. This mitigates, slightly, egalitarian pressures.

Some qualitative alternatives:

- Where there is a category system of grading, all receive the same grade.
- The students grade each other, building extent of contribution into the grading system.
- The students grade each other according to contribution, but you decide the categories to be allocated.

A problem with collaborative projects is that individual students too easily focus only on their own specific task, not really understanding the other components, or how they contribute to the project as a whole. The idea of a group project is that a complex and worthwhile task can be made manageable, each student taking a section he or she can handle. However, the tasks are divided all too readily according to what students are already good at: Mario will prepare the literature review, Sheila will do the stats. In that case, little *learning* may take place. We want students to learn things other than what they already know, so the allocation might better be decided so that Sheila does the literature review, and Mario the stats. This is likely to end up with each helping the other, and everyone learns a lot more.

Most importantly, we want them to know what the whole project is about, and how each contribution fits in, so an additional holistic assessment is necessary. For that a concept map would be suitable, or a short answer. And perhaps that is the answer to the group-sharing problem. If a student fails the holistic part, that student fails the project. The backwash is this: make sure you know what your colleagues are doing and why.

Contracts

Contracts replicate a common everyday situation. A contract would take into account where an individual is at the beginning of the course, what relevant attainments are possessed already, what work or other experience, and then, within the context of the course objectives, he or she is to produce a needs analysis from which a programme is negotiated: what is to be done and how it is proposed to do it, and within what time-scale. Individuals, or homogeneous groups of students, would have a tutor to consult throughout, with whom they would have to agree that the contract is met in due course. The assessment problem hasn't gone away, but the advantage is that the assessments are tied down very firmly from the start and the students know where they stand (Stephenson and Laycock 1993).

A more conventional and less complicated contract is little different from clear criterion-referencing: 'This is what an A requires. If you can prove to me that you can demonstrate those qualities in your learning, then an A is what you will get.' This is basically what is involved in portfolio assessment (see below).

Reflective journal

In professional programmes, it is useful if students keep a reflective journal, in which they record any incidents, thoughts or reflections that are relevant to the unit. Journals are valuable in capturing the students' judgement as to relevance, and their ability to reflect upon experience using the content taught. Such reflection is basic to proper professional functioning. The reflective journal, then, is especially useful for assessing content knowledge, reflection, professional judgement and application.

Assessment can be delicate, as journals are often very personal; and boring, as they are often very lengthy. It is a good idea to ask students to submit selections, possibly focusing on critical incidents. Journals should not be 'marked', but taken as evidence of quality in thinking.

Case study

In some disciplines, a case study is an ideal way of seeing how students can apply their knowledge and professional skills. It could be written up as a project, or as an item for a portfolio. Case studies might need to be highly formal and carried out under supervision, or be carried out independently by the student. Possibilities are endless.

Assessing the case study is essentially holistic, but aspects can be used both for formative feedback and for summative assessment. For example, there are essential skills in some cases that must be got right: otherwise the patient dies, the bridge collapses or other mayhem ensues. The component skills here could be pass–fail; fail one, fail the lot (with latitude according to the skill and case study in question). Having passed the components, however, the student then has to handle the case itself appropriately, and that should be assessed holistically.

There are some excellent software options for clinical decision-making for medical case studies, which fit the authentic format extremely well. However, this is a rapidly expanding area and no doubt other disciplines will have their own versions in due course.

Portfolio assessment

In a portfolio, the student presents and explains his or her best 'learning treasures' (p. 155) *vis-à-vis* the objectives. Students have to reflect and use judgement in assessing their own work, and explain its match with the unit objectives. When students give their creativity free reign, portfolios are full of complex and divergent surprises, aligned to the unit aims in ways that are simply not anticipated by the teacher.

In their explanations for their selection of items, students explain how the evidence they have in their portfolios addresses their own or the official unit aims. One danger with portfolios is that students may go overboard, creating excessive workload both for themselves and for the teacher. Limits must be set (see below).

Assessing portfolio items can be deeply interesting. It may be time-consuming, but that depends on the nature and number of items. Many items, such as concept maps, can be assessed in a minute or so. In any event, a morning spent assessing portfolios feels like 30 minutes assessing look-alike assignments. Following are some suggestions for implementing portfolio assessment.

1 *Make it quite clear in the teaching objectives what the evidence for good learning may be.* The objectives should be available to students at the beginning of the semester.
2 *State the requirements for the portfolio.* These need to be made very clear:

- *Number of items.* In a semester-long unit, four items is about the limit.
- *Approximate size of each item.* The total portfolio should not be much longer than a project or assignment you would normally set. I suggest no more than 1500 words for any one item, but that depends on the nature of the item. Some items, such as concept maps or other diagrams, require less than a page.
- *A list of sample items;* but emphasize that students should show some creativity by going outside that list, as long as the items are relevant. Items should not be repetitive, making the same point in different ways.
- *Any compulsory items?* In my courses (in teacher education) I usually prescribe a journal, leaving the other items to student choice.
- *Source of items.* Items may be specific to a unit, or drawn from other units in the case of evaluating at the end of a course/programme. In some problem-based courses, students will be continually providing inputs, often on a pass/fail basis, over a year, or two years. The final evaluation

could then comprise – *in toto* or in part – samples of the best work students think they have done to date.

● *What are the items supposed to be getting at?* Are your teaching objectives best addressed as a package, or as a list of separate items?

3 *Decide how the portfolio is to be graded.* There are two alternatives:

(a) assessing individual items, and then combining;
(b) assessing the portfolio as a whole (the 'package').

If (a), the situation is the same as combining several assessments within a unit to arrive at a final grade (see pp. 190–4 below). It is tempting to mark each item separately, and then total, but that misses the point of the portfolio, which is embedded in (b). Each item should address some aspect of learning, so that the whole addresses the thrust of the unit. This really gets back to *your* conception of your unit: do you see yourself teaching a collection of topics, or do those topics constitute a *thrust*? If the latter, the students' portfolios should address that thrust. In the last case, the student is in effect saying: '*This* is what I got out of your class. I have learned these things, and as a result my *thinking* is changed.' If their package can show that they have learned well indeed.

You might include other assessment tasks apart from the portfolio: for example, a conventional assessment to establish 'coverage' of basics. You will then need to decide how to combine the two sets of results.

Portfolios have been used for years in the fine arts, but they can be used to assess almost any course content. A case study of portfolio assessment is given in Chapter 10.

Assessing in large classes

If lecturing is the default for large-class teaching, MCs and timed exams are the default for large-class assessment. Exams take a lot of time to assess, but with tutor assistance and the clear time slots in which things have to be done and reported, we can come to terms with them. Unfortunately, as we have seen, exams are not the best modes of assessment. We now look at alternatives for large-class assessment that:

(a) are rapidly administered, completed and assessed;
(b) get at higher order learnings than is usually the case with the two default modes.

First, some strategic decisions need to be made.

1 You may be able to justify postponing time-consuming qualitative assessments in the first year, such as individual practica or portfolios, to the, it

is hoped, sparer second and third years. At least students will have had the experience of these assessments before they do graduate.

2 Cut down on massive, mind-numbing single-mode assessments such as the final exam. Assess more often, with more varying assessments (Brown and Knight 1994; Davis and McLeod 1996b).

Let us then see what further assessment tasks we might use.

Concept maps

Concept maps, introduced as a TLA (see pp. 82–3), can also be used for assessment. They enable us to tell at a glance if a student has an impoverished knowledge structure relating to the topic, or a rich one (see Task 5.1). While they are to be assessed holistically, you could rate the structure on a 10-point scale, say, just in order to derive a figure for reporting.

Venn diagrams

Venn diagrams are a simple form of concept map, where the boundary of a concept is expressed in a circle or ellipse, and interrelations between concepts are expressed by the intersection or overlap of the circles. Venn diagrams, like concept maps, are very economical ways of expressing relationships. They can be used for teaching purposes, in conveying relationships to learners, and for assessment purposes, so that learners may convey their ways of seeing relationships between concepts. Getting students to draw and briefly explain their own Venns, or to interpret those presented, can be done quickly, where the target of understanding is relationships between ideas. Venns make good gobbets (see below).

Three-minute essay

We met the three-minute essay in Chapter 6, as a method of introducing reflective activity into large-class teaching, by asking such questions as:

- What do I most want to find out in the next class?
- What is the main point I learned today?

These questions may provide very useful information for the teacher in two respects: formatively, in finding out how the content is being interpreted by students; and summatively, in finding out if students have made appropriate interpretations, which can be used for grading purposes. Such questions can be answered in minutes in a large class.

Short answer examinations

In short answers, the student answers in note form. This format is useful for getting at factual material, e.g. addressing or interpreting diagrams, charts and tables, but is limited in addressing main ideas and themes. The examination is usually after something quite specific, and operates in practice more like the objective format than the essay (Biggs 1973; Scouller 1996). However, it has advantages over the standard MC, in that it is less susceptible to test-taking strategies (you can't work out the answer by elimination), it requires active recall rather than just recognition and it is easier for you to construct, but not as easy to score.

Gobbets

Gobbets are significant chunks of content with which the student should be familiar and to which the student has to respond (Brown and Knight 1994). They could be a paragraph from a novel or of a standard text, a brief passage of music, a Venn diagram, an archaeological artefact, a photograph (a building, an engine part) and so on. The students' task is to identify the gobbet, explain its context, say why it is important, what it reminds them of, or whatever else you would like them to comment on.

Gobbets should access a bigger picture, unlike short answers, which are sufficient unto themselves. That big picture is the target, not the gobbet itself. Brown and Knight point out that three gobbets can be completed in the time it takes to do one essay exam question, so that to an extent you can assess both coverage and depth.

Letter to a friend

In the 'letter to a friend', the student tells an imaginary or real friend, who is thinking of enrolling in the unit next year, about his or her own experience of the unit (Trigwell and Prosser 1990). These letters are about a page in length and are written and assessed in a few minutes. The students should reflect on the unit and report on it as it affects them. Letters tend to be either multistructural or relational, occasionally extended abstract. Multistructural letters are simply lists of unit content, a rehash of the course outline. Good responses provide integrated accounts of how the topics fit together and form a useful whole, while the best describe a change in personal perspective as a result of doing the unit. They also provide a useful source of feedback to the teacher on aspects of the unit.

Like the concept map, letters supplement more fine-grained tasks with an overview of the unit, and they make good portfolio items.

Cloze tests

Cloze tests were originally designed to assess reading comprehension. Every seventh (or so) word in a passage is eliminated, and the reader has to fill in the space with the correct word (more flexible versions allow a synonym). A text is chosen that can only be understood if the topic under discussion is understood, rather like the gobbet. The omitted words are essential for making sense of the passage.

The simplest way of scoring is to count the number of acceptable words completed. You could try to assess the quality of thinking underlying each substitution, but this diminishes its main advantage, speed.

Procedures for rapid assessing

We should now look at some procedures that speed up assessment.

Self/peer-assessment
This can fractionate the teacher's assessment load in large classes, even when you use conventional assessments such as exam or assignment. Using posters, the assessment is over in one class session. But of course the criteria have to be absolutely clear, which makes it less dependable for complex, open-end responses.

If self/peer-assessments agree within a specified range, whether expressed as a qualitative grade or as a number of marks, award the higher grade. The possibility of collusion can be mitigated by spot-checking. Boud (1986) estimates that self/peer-assessment can cut the teacher's load by at least 30 per cent.

Group assessment
Carrying out a large project suggests teamwork and group assessment. Teaching large classes also suggests group assessment, but here the logic is more basic. With four students per assessment task (whether assignment, project or whatever), you get to assess a quarter the number you would otherwise, while the students get to learn about teamwork, and assessing others, not to mention the content of what was being assessed. Considerations about allocation of assessment results apply as before (pp. 181–2).

Random assessment
Gibbs (1998) cites the Case of the Mechanical Engineer, who initially required 25 reports through the year, but as each was worth only a trivial 1 per cent, the quality was poor. He then changed the requirements: students still submitted 25 reports, but in a portfolio by the end of the semester, as a condition for sitting the final exam, but only four reports, marked at random, comprised 25 per cent of the final grade. Two huge benefits

resulted: the students worked consistently throughout the term and submitted 25 good reports, and the teacher's marking load was a sixth of what it had previously been.

Feedback, open information

Make sure the students know exactly what is expected of them. Following are some things that cut time considerably.

Get assessment criteria down on a pro-forma, which is returned to the students. You don't have to keep writing basically the same comments.

Assess the work globally, but provide a quick rating along such dimensions as may be seen as desirable. You could rate them on a quantified scale, but that encourages averaging. It is better to put an X along each line, which just as clearly lets the students know where they are:

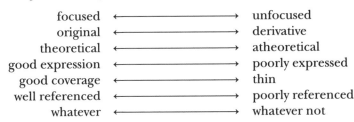

You are letting the student know that these individual qualities are important, whether or not they make a quantifiable difference to the final grade. You could do as is done in dissertations and treat them as hurdles, which have to be cleared satisfactorily before the real assessment begins.

Keep a library of comments on computer for each typical assignment you set. They can be placed in a hierarchy corresponding to the grade or performance level in which they occur. New comments can of course be added, while it saves you having to keep rewriting the common ones ('this point does not follow . . .'). R. G. Dromey (private communication) is developing a program that takes this much further, making assessment of lengthy papers highly reliable, feed-back rich and done in one-third the usual time.

Put multiple copies in the library of previous student assignments (anonymous, but you had nevertheless better get permission), representing all grades, and annotated with comments. Students can then see exactly what you want, that you mean it, and what the difference between different grades is (which is also likely to save time on *post mortems*).

Deadlines

Part of the felt pressure on both staff and students in large-class assessment is due to the pile-up of work, as much as to the amount of work itself. One value of multiple assessments is of course that some can be collected earlier in the seminar if the topics have been completed, but be careful not to confuse the formative and summative roles of assessment (pp. 142–3). In large classes, you have to be ruthless about deadlines. It is important to discuss your deadlines with colleagues to make sure they are evened out for the students.

Final grades and reporting assessment results

The final stage of assessing involves converting one's judgements of the student's performance into a final summative statement, in the form required by administration. This raises several issues:

1 Combining results in several assessment tasks to arrive at a final grade
2 Reporting in categories, or along a continuous scale.
3 Is there any distribution characteristic to be imposed on the results?

Combining several assessments within a unit to arrive at a final grade

As the grade awarded for a unit usually depends on performances assessed in a number of topics, and those topics will be passed at various levels of understanding, we need to decide how to combine these separate estimates to yield one final grade. Our commitment to holistic assessment makes this an important issue.

Say we have four assessment tasks: AT1, AT2, AT3 and AT4. (These could be separate tasks, or portfolio items.) Determining the final grade from these components is conventionally achieved by *weighting* important tasks so that they count more. But on what basis can you calculate that AT3 is 'worth *twice* as much' (or however much) as AT1? Expected time taken is the only logical currency I can think of, but that is more a matter of the nature of the task than of its educational value. In holistic and qualitative assessment, we must 'weight' tasks in other ways.

In selecting these tasks, presumably we wanted each to assess a particular quality. Let us say AT1 is to assess basic knowledge, the task being main ideas taken throughout the course; AT2 problem-solving (a case study, group assessed); AT3 an overview of the unit (a concept map); AT4 the quality of the student's reflections on course content (a journal). Now we have a logical package, which makes a statement about what we want students to learn, and how well. The logic is that all aspects being assessed are important, and must all be passed, at *some* level of competence (otherwise why teach them?).

There are two main strategies for handling the problem of weighting and combining assessment results: working qualitatively throughout, and using numerical conversions for achieving the combinations.

Work qualitatively all the way
There are several ways of preserving your holistic purity:

1 *The dissertation model.* Pass/fail on subtasks, grading on the key task only. As long as minor tasks are satisfactory, the level of pass of the whole depends on the central task, as is the case in a dissertation. In our example, you might decide that the case study AT2 is the key task, so the qualitative grading of AT2 sets the final grade for the whole unit, as long as all the other tasks are satisfactory. If they are not, they should be redone and resubmitted (with due care about the submission and resubmission deadlines).
2 *The profile.* Where all tasks are of equal importance, each is graded qualitatively, then the pattern is looked at. Is the modal (most typical) response distinction? If so, the student is mostly working at distinction level, so distinction it is. In the case of an uneven profile, you might take the highest level as the student's final grade, on the grounds that the student has demonstrated this level of performance in at least one task. A student who got the same grade on all tasks would, however, see this as 'unfair'. Alternatively, you can devise a conversion: high distinction = maximum performance on all tasks; distinction = maximum on two tasks, very good on remaining ones; credit = one maximum, two very good, rest pass . . . and so on.
3 *Implied contract.* Different tasks are tied to different grades. If students want only a pass, they do AT1 alone, say, which will show they have attended classes, done the reading and got the general drift of the main ideas dealt with. To obtain a credit, they add AT3 to AT1, showing they can hang all the ideas together. Distinction requires all for the credit plus AT4, to show in addition they have some reflective insights into how it all works. High distinction needs all the rest plus AT2, the key test of high-level functioning, the case study.
4 *Weighted profile.* Require different levels of performance in different tasks. Some require a high level of understanding (e.g. relational in SOLO terms), others might require only 'knowledge about' (multistructural), others only knowledge of terms (unistructural). All have to be passed at the specified level. This is a form of pass/fail, but the standards of pass vary for different tasks. 'Weighting' in this case is not an arbitrary juggling of numbers, but a profile determined by the structure of the curriculum objectives. The only problem is in the event of one or more fails. Logically, you should require a resubmission until the task is passed. Practically, you might have to allow some failure, and adjust the final grade accordingly.

Convert categories into numbers

First, let us distinguish absolutely clearly between assessing the perform-ance, which may be done qualitatively, and dealing with the results of that assessment, which may be done quantitatively. Quantifying performances that have been assessed holistically is simply an administrative device; there is no educational problem as long as it follows *after* the assessment process itself has been completed.

Quantifying can be used for two related tasks:

(a) combining results of different tasks in the same unit to obtain a final grade;
(b) combining the results of different units to obtain a year result, as, for example, does the familiar grade-point average (GPA).

The GPA is the simplest way of quantifying the results of a qualitative assessment: A = 4, B = 3, C = 2 and D = 1. You weight and combine the results as you like.

You may, however, want finer discrimination within categories. There are two issues to decide:

1 Qualitative: what *sort* of performance the student's product is.
2 Relative: how *well* it represents that sort of performance.

Issue 2 is often addressed in three levels: really excellent As (A+), solid middle-of-the-road As and As but only just (A–). Here, the original assess-ment of each task is first done qualitatively, then quantitatively. The final result using a four-category system is a number on a 13-point scale (A+ = 12 . . . D– = 1, F = 0). (Note, however, that this is not really a linear 13-point scale (12 + F), but a two dimensional structure (4 × 3 + F) that we have opened out for practical reasons.)

The results can now be combined in the usual way, but the conceptual difficulty is that we are back to assigning numerical weights arbitrarily: even taking an average is using a weighting system of one, which is just as arbitrary as saying that a task should be given a weighting of 2, or 5.7. Nevertheless, it is what is usually done, and it is at least convenient. When the results of different subjects have been combined, the final report can be either along the same scale, or converted to the nearest category grade. For example, if the weighted outcome score is 9.7, the nearest grade equivalent is 10, which becomes A–.

Reporting in categories or along a continuous scale

Having combined the results from several assessment tasks, we now have the job of reporting the results. This is a matter of institutional procedure, and obviously we need to fit in with that. There is no problem for us level 3 teachers where the policy is to report in categories (HD, D . . . or A, B,

Per cent   Grading category

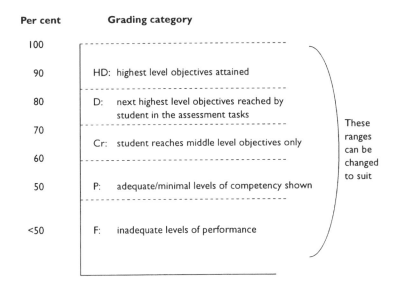

Figure 9.1: Assessing qualitatively and reporting as a percentage

C . . .). But what if your institution requires you to report in percentages? Or, as some do, report in percentages so that they can then convert back to categories: HD = 85+, D = 75–84, credit = 65–74, pass = 50–64? (This last case is exasperating. Why not report in categories in the first place?)

All is not lost. We simply extend the principle of the 13-point scale.

1 The first step is the same. The assessment tasks are criterion-referenced to the objectives, which tells you whether the performance is high distinction (or A) quality, distinction (or B) quality, and so on through the category system you use.
2 Allocate percentage ranges within each category according to your institutionally endorsed procedures (see Figure 9.1).
3 Locate the individual student's performance along that within-category scale.

Step 3 now uses a much finer scale than the previous three-level scale, something like 15 points within each category, and the student performance is quantified accordingly. You can do that by using a global or holistic rating scale, or, if you must, by awarding so many marks for this, so many for that. But at least the *major* classification into high distinction or A, or whatever system is used, has been done holistically. The rest is only a matter of fine-tuning.

Of course, this is a compromise. We have conceded defeat over the question of weighting, but the *backwash* for students is still positive. Students are likely to shoot for quality, because a category shift means a disproportionately large increase in their final score. That score also tells them something about the quality of their performance, because it falls within a range that is tied to a category. So they know the quality of their performance, and how well they did within the quality of performance. They will also be clearer about what they would need to do to obtain a better score in future.

In sum, then, qualitative and holistic assessment can meet the logistic and administrative demands of: (a) combining assessment tasks to achieve a final grade for the unit; and (b) reporting in percentages, or any other quantitative scale, if that is what is required.

Is there any distribution characteristic to be imposed on the results?

If the answer to the above is 'yes', we cannot be so accommodating. Requiring results to fit some predetermined distribution, normal, rectangular or whatever, *cannot be justified on educational grounds.*

I am often surprised in discussing this issue at staff workshops at how many people think that CRA is pie in the sky because they *must* grade on the curve. Few institutions are in the event rigid on this point. Many 'suggest' that grades follow a distribution – 'It would usually be expected that in large classes no more than 10 per cent of high distinctions be awarded . . .' – but I have found that the operative word is 'usually'. In most cases, it is accepted that in 'special' circumstances – for example, a criterion-referenced system – the grades of a particular class might depart from the suggested guidelines. Mind you, calling CRA 'a special circumstance' is galling, but if a special circumstance is the Trojan horse that makes aligned teaching possible, so be it.

If a teacher is employed in an institution where summative results really are required to adhere closely to some predetermined curve, there is a problem. The solution then can only be political: lobby to get the policy changed.

Implementing assessment package 2

Let us now return to the problem we faced at the beginning of the chapter: implementing assessment package 2 in a class of 400 first-year students in a laboratory-based science course, say biology. You might remember that practicalities suggested MC as the preferred mode of assessment. We now know that there are many better alternatives. How might we now address that problem?

First, let us make the scene, a common one, more specific.

- *Class*: 400 first-year students.
- *Teaching structure*: two plenary lectures, one tutorial of 20 groups of 20 students, and one 2–3 hour lab a week, again 20 groups of 20 students. There are eight major topics introduced and variously elaborated in the lectures and tutorials over the 12-week semester.
- *Staff*: one lecturer in charge, who delivers all the lectures and takes a couple of tutorials. Three teaching assistants between them take the remaining tutorials and help with the assessment. Twenty student demonstrators conduct the labs and assess the lab reports for their own groups.
- *Assessment* (existing):

		Per cent of final
Mid-semester:	1 hour MC	30
Final exam 2 hours:	1 hour MC	30
	2 essay questions	30
Lab reports		10

Institutional regulations require that at least 60 per cent of the final grade is determined by invigilated exam. The mid-semester is used to alleviate the pressure at the end of the semester, and to provide feedback to students. The MCs are all machine scored, so the main assessment load is provided by the two essay questions, which are marked by checklist by the lecturer and three tutors, and by spot-checking the lab reports. Say that the final occurs at the end of the examination weeks, and there is only a weekend and five working days in which to mark, collate and report the assessment results.

In previous years, there was pressure to cull the first years by about 50 per cent, in order to ease pressures in the second year, and to focus on promising research students. This pressure led to grading on a curve designed so that the bottom half received no more than a pass; credit and above thus became the *de facto* prerequisite for the second year. However, with the current realization that more students means more money, that pressure has largely disappeared, and with it the pressure for norm-referencing using predetermined grade proportions.

Problems with existing assessment

The major problem is that the assessment tasks are overwhelmingly quantitative, and address declarative knowledge. An attempt was made to offset the MCs with the essay questions, but the gesture is nullified by checklist marking. Students are not in practice encouraged to look for relating ideas, broad principles or functioning knowledge. The only non-declarative knowledge is assessed in the lab reports, but they contribute 10 per cent

Table 9.1: Required levels and kinds of understanding, and suitable assessment tasks

Objectives	Kinds and levels of understanding	Suitable assessment tasks
1 Basic facts, terminology	recall, recognition	MC or short answer
2 Topic knowledge	individual topics, relational, some multistructural relations between topics	gobbets, critical incidents
3 Discipline knowledge	conception of unit as a whole	letter to a friend, concept map
4 Functioning knowledge	topic or discipline knowledge put to work	problem-solving, research project
5 Laboratory skills	procedural knowledge	laboratory behaviour, lab reports
6 Monitoring and evaluation skills	metacognitive knowledge, self-directed learning	self- and peer-assessment

only and are in the event assessed by student demonstrators, not content experts. An attempt is made to provide formative feedback, apart from informal feedback in tutorials and labs, with the mid-semester, but it is in the form of marks only.

A suggested rescue package

Our present task is to design a package that would work for the given teaching structure. Let us say that resource and other limitations prevent any drastic change in the number of plenaries, labs and tutorials, and that the average assessment time per student for the final exam cannot exceed much more than 15 minutes per student (which rules out portfolios and other extended qualitative assessment tasks).

We do not immediately consult Table 9.2 under 'rapid assessment' and start throwing in concept maps, cloze tests, gobbets and so on. We first should specify what we *want* to assess, what our objectives are; then we might look at the most practical ways of assessing that, given the present constraints. Given the number of component assessments, the need to weight and combine them, and traditional practice, one advisable constraint would be to collate and report the assessment results quantitatively, even though we shall be using qualitative tasks for the assessments proper (see pp. 191–2).

Table 9.1 suggests some of the levels or kinds of understanding that we should want from the students, and what kinds of assessment tasks, practical within our constraints, might be used.

1 Basic factual knowledge and terminology is suitably assessed by MC or short answer, as long as we are clear that that is all they are doing, and that these modes do not dominate the assessment package. Let us use short answer for the mid-term, which being open-ended might also show more revealing misunderstandings than an MC, and when marking time is not so pressing. MC will then be used in the final exam when time is more pressing.

2 Topics ideally should be understood at least at relational level, but 'knowing about' will do as long as the most important topics are understood relationally, and as functioning knowledge. The topics could then be embedded in gobbets, at the individual topic level in the mid-semester, and gobbets requiring integration of topics in the final. A critical incident or case study in the final would also be useful; for example, the student selects a newspaper clipping of an eco-problem and relates it to topics dealt with.

3 By 'discipline knowledge' I mean the picture of the whole: having studied a list of topics that make up a first-year biology course, what is the student's view of biology itself? Letter to a friend is a good way of ascertaining this (Trigwell and Prosser 1990). A description or list of topics studied (multistructural) is not good enough, a working view of an integrated subject called biology is very good (relational), a changed perspective of the biological world would be marvellous (extended abstract), if rather unlikely at this level.

4 Functioning knowledge. It is reasonable to expect that students can solve real-world problems. It is suggested that six such problems are given throughout the semester as the subject of peer-assessment, much as described by Gibbs (1998), two such problems being self- and peer-assessed for inclusion in the final grade (Boud 1995).

5 Laboratory skills are mainly assessed *in situ* by student demonstrators, and probably do not go much further than the procedural level, i.e. correct performance of laboratory procedures and writing them up appropriately. Laboratory work ultimately involves functioning knowledge, but it is doubtful if it would be validly assessable in the first year under these conditions. This can be better addressed in labs in higher years.

6 Monitoring and evaluation skills, as argued elsewhere (pp. 92–3), are essential learnings for students if they are to become autonomous and self-directed in their tertiary learning, and later in their professional lives. Internalized standards of competence, which enable reflective thinking and self-direction, can be developed by self- and peer-assessment (Boud 1995; Gibbs 1998). Essentially, four of the six problems are assessed by a peer according to a marking sheet, and then each is returned to the owner. The last two problems become part of the final grade: students first self-assess on a separate sheet of paper, which is

handed in, then the peer-assessment is made. If these agree within specified limits, the higher grade is taken; if they disagree, the lecturer adjudicates, and also spot-checks some of the others at random.

A range of assessment tasks has emerged here: quantitative (MC and short answer), qualitative (three gobbets, critical incident, letter to a friend, problem-solving) and procedural (lab report). For logistic reasons, we need to turn all these into numbers, while retaining the qualitative nature of the majority of the assessment tasks. The qualitative tasks, with the possible exception of the problems (see below), may be assessed with SOLO, using a five-point scale within each:

SOLO level	Range
unistructural	1–5
multistructural	6–10
relational	11–15
extended abstract	16–20

In other words, top of the multistructural range is in conventional terms a bare pass (10 out of a possible 20) in six of the main assessment tasks. This sends a strong message to the students that 'knowing more' just will not do; you have to structure and use your knowledge.

How this applies to the problems is held in abeyance at this stage. It depends on each individual problem, but as we are also using these problems for self- and peer-assessment, the assessment procedures need to be especially clear. In short, the lecturer needs to devise a 20-point marking scheme that students can use, but there is no reason why it too shouldn't be structured along similar lines: four categories (SOLO or other), five points within each.

The SOLO scale arbitrarily but conveniently yields a maximum of 20 'marks' per task, which can be combined with the results from other tasks, including the MC. This may sound complicated but in fact it is not, as may be seen from the following assessment schedule:

Mid-semester exam	Max. points	Final exam	Max. points
2 gobbets, 20 each	40	1 gobbet	20
Short answer	20	1 critical incident	20
		1 letter to a friend	20
		2 problems (SA/PA)	40
		MC	20
Total	60	Total	120

With 20 points for the lab report, the total number of points becomes 200: divide by two if you want to report in 'percentages'.

The weightings here for mid-semester, final and labs are identical to those for the previous, traditional, assessment. However, these can easily be changed, if you think, say, the lab reports ought to get more and the problems less (being self- and peer-assessed); perhaps you would prefer to leave the self- and peer-assessments out of the final grade.

Let us now take a look at the marking load. Let us say that each of the qualitative assessments, problems aside, is written on no more than one page. You read this, first decide on its category (multistructural, relational) and then you rate how well it exemplifies that category on a five-point scale. This takes no more than five minutes, with practice rather less. (It will, however, be necessary for the lecturer and the TAs to have a training session, and to reach a criterion of at least 90 per cent agreement allowing one category difference, which is better than the usual agreement on essay ratings using the Bloom taxonomy (Hattie and Purdie 1998).)

The time needed for assessing individual students now becomes:

For the mid-term

the short answer test	5 mins
2 gobbets	10 mins
Total	15 mins

For the final

MC	minimal, clerical work
3 qualitative assessments	15 mins max.
spot-checking problems	5 mins?
Total	20 mins maximum

In addition, you will probably want to spot-check the demonstrators' marking of the lab reports. If this is too much, perhaps you could cut out the critical incident, or a gobbet.

As to formative assessment, that synonym for good teaching (pp. 142–3), the previous scheme did very little apart from reporting relative progress in marks. The changes suggested here for the summative assessment tasks also suggest ways in which the plenary and tutorials can be used more effectively (see Chapters 5 and 6). One would be to use the pauses in the lecture (see pp. 106–9) and the 'three-minute essay' to provide feedback: what students thought to be the main point of a particular lecture could become the focus of tutorial discussion. Like the four peer-assessed problems, also carried out in the plenaries, these essays could be required but not formally assessed before the student is allowed to sit the final exam.

We now have an assessment package that takes only a little more time, but it is manageable within the resources allowed. The assessments specifically address the higher-level objectives of the unit, so that they will

Table 9.2: Some different assessment tasks and the kinds of learning assessed

Assessment mode	Most likely kind of learning assessed
Extended prose, essay-type	
essay exam	rote, question spotting, speed structuring
open book	as for exam, but less memory, coverage
assignment, take home	read widely, interrelate, organize, apply, copy
Objective test	
multiple choice	recognition, strategy, comprehension, coverage
ordered outcome	hierarchies of understanding
Performance assessment	
practicum	skills needed in real life
seminar, presentation	communication skills
posters	concentrating on relevance, application
interviewing	responding interactively
critical incidents	reflection, application, sense of relevance
project	application, research skills
reflective journal	reflection, application, sense of relevance
case study, problems	application, professional skills
portfolio	reflection, creativity, unintended outcomes
Rapid assessments (large class)	
concept maps	coverage, relationships
Venn diagrams	relationships
three-minute essay	level of understanding, sense of relevance
gobbets	realizing the importance of significant detail
short answer	recall units of information, coverage
letter to a friend	holistic understanding, application, reflection
cloze	comprehension of main ideas

encourage better quality learning from the students, will equally certainly be more interesting for both you and the students and will provide much more effective formative feedback to students.

None of these suggestions is cast in stone, however. You might prefer fewer gobbets. If we didn't operate with the restriction of 60 per cent final exam, we might have had fewer plenaries (lectures) and more out-of-class group tasks that would save assessment time. The important thing is the intention and conceptualization, not the specific techniques you use. Note that when you do rethink what you are doing to one aspect, assessment, adaptive changes occur throughout the system: objectives become clearer, teaching methods themselves improve, and of course the assessment tasks get at what they should be assessing.

Summary and conclusions

This has been an encyclopaedic chapter. Table 9.2 is a better way of summarizing the major points on assessment tasks than section summaries.

Expressing and reporting the results of assessment

We then addressed administrative issues: how to combine results to give a single summative statement, how to report in numerical form such as percentages when assessing holistically and how to avoid grading on the curve.

When the final grade depends on performances assessed in a number of topics, passed at various levels of understanding, the different results need to be combined. Two general ways of combining results were described: consistently holistic, and doing the major assessments holistically, then converting into numbers for ease of administrative handling. The latter is a compromise but the important point is that grades are defined qualitatively in the first instance, and the result tells students something meaningful. The one problem we couldn't solve was an uncompromising insistence on reporting grades along a curve, which makes criterion-referencing imposs- ible.

The major thrust of both chapters on assessment is really quite simple. You can't beat backwash, so join it. Students will always second guess the assessment task, and then learn what they think will meet those require- ments. But if those assessment requirements mirror the curriculum, there is no problem. Students will be learning what they are supposed to be learning.

Implementing assessment package 2

Finally, we returned to the difficulty facing first-year teachers in particular: how to assess qualitatively under the usual conditions of large numbers of students and poor resources.

Has this helped you with your own assessment problems? Turn to Task 9.1.

Further reading

Boud, D. (1995) *Enhancing Learning through Self-assessment,* London: Kogan Page.

Brown, S. and Knight, P. (1994) *Assessing Learners in Higher Education,* London: Kogan Page.

Task 9.1: Choosing appropriate modes of assessment

What key topics do you want to assess? Turn to your objectives (Chapter 3, Task 3.1):

- What less important topics do you want to assess?
- What levels of understanding of each? Use the appropriate verbs to operationalize this.
- Do the topics refer to declarative, functioning knowledge, both?
- Are there any basic facts, skills, you want to check?
- What physical constraints do you have to accommodate:
   Large-class assessment methods?
   Final exam? If so, is it invigilated?

Now choose from Table 9.3 those assessment modes that seem most suitable:

_____

_____

How do you propose to combine the results from each assessment task to produce a student's final grade for the unit?

Holistic throughout?_____

Holistic then convert to numbers?_____

Other?_____

Comments_____

_____

_____

Erwin, T. D. (1991) *Assessing Student Learning and Development*, San Francisco: Jossey-Bass.

Gibbs, G., Habeshaw, S. and Habeshaw, T. (1989) *53 Interesting Ways to Assess Your Students*, Bristol: Technical and Educational Services.

Gibbs, G., Jenkins, A. and Wisker, G. (1992) *Assessing More Students*, Oxford: PCFC/Rewley Press.

Harris, D. and Bell, C. (1986) *Evaluating and Assessing for Learning*, London: Kogan Page.

Nightingale, P., Te Wiata, I., Toohey, S., Ryan, G., Hughes, C. and Magin, D. (eds) (1996) *Assessing Learning in Universities*, Kensington, NSW:

Committee for the Advancement of University Teaching/Professional Development Centre, UNSW.

Stephenson, J. and Laycock, M. (1993) *Using Contracts in Higher Education,* London: Kogan Page.

The list of practical suggestions on assessment is formidable; the above is a good sample. Some are obviously one-topic: Boud on self-assessment, Stephenson on contracts. Nightingale *et al.* collate 'best practice' from 100 university teachers, grouped under 'verb' headings: thinking critically, solving problems, performing skills, reflecting, demonstrating knowledge and understanding, designing, creating, performing, communicating. The other books are good sources for ideas.

10

Some examples of aligned teaching

In this chapter we look at some examples of teaching that illustrate how alignment may work. The first embodies an apparently minor and low-cost change in an otherwise conventional teaching programme, in which peer assessment became the major TLA. The second is problem-based learning (PBL), which is becoming increasingly popular, particularly in professional education. In essence, the objectives are compiled from professional problems, the major TLAs involve solving them and the assessment is concerned with how well. The final example uses the learning portfolio, the alignment here arising bottom-up as the students negotiated how they could provide examples of their learning that would meet the objectives.

Peer assessment as a TLA

Gibbs (1998) reports a case study of a compulsory second-year engineering programme where what seemed to be a fairly minor change in assessment procedures produced a dramatic change in performance. Teaching and assessment had been quite traditional: two lectures and one problem-solving tutorial session a week, and an end of session final examination. In the problem tutorials, students worked on problem sheets handed out at the lectures, similar to the problems in the final exam. Initially, when the problem classes comprised only ten students, the system worked reasonably well.

Difficulties arose when the problem tutorials became drastically larger. In classes of 20, instead of the original ten, students could 'hide' – not ask questions, avoid eye contact – thereby getting away with little preparation. Marking the weekly problem sheets created a crippling workload on the tutors, and was dropped. The failure rate increased, the average mark 45 per cent.

To improve matters, an innovation was adapted from Boud's (1986) work on peer assessment. Everything remained as before, except that six times during the unit the students met in a plenary session in a lecture theatre, bringing problem sheets they had completed since the previous plenary. They handed these in, with their names written clearly on them, and the sheets were redistributed at random, with a how-to-mark sheet. They then marked the problem sheets they were given, with written comments, in the knowledge of whose work they were marking. No further instruction in marking was given, and no monitoring of their marking took place. The sheets were then handed back to their owners, who could not tell who had marked and commented on their work. The marks were not recorded, and did not contribute to the final grade, but students had to complete a specified number of problem sheets; otherwise they were failed.

Although the work done for the peer-assessment sessions did not count, and all other aspects of the unit (lectures, problem sessions and exam) remained unchanged, the average in the final exam increased from 45 to 75 per cent, with no failures.

In accounting for these dramatic results, associated with an apparently minor and low-cost change (the six plenary peer assessment sessions), Gibbs refers to five principles of learning that were invoked by the peer assessments:

1 Not only did the students have to spend more time (out of class) on problem-solving, their time was distributed evenly rather than concentrated on the last week or so in preparation for the final exam.
2 The activities generated were those required by the course. Students didn't spend out-of-class time on instrumental activities such as reading lecture notes. 'The best way to learn how to tackle problems is to tackle lots of problems', as Gibbs puts it. Marking other students' problem-solving is itself a rich learning experience; students see how others might do the task, some using better problem-solving strategies than they themselves used, some using worse strategies and thus signalling to the assessor errors to avoid. The model answers provided them with standards to monitor their own future problem-solving.
3 Students received feedback on their own work by the end of each session, not weeks later when the tutor had managed to mark them all.
4 The feedback they received was socially amplified. Bad work was marked and commented on by their own peers, which Gibbs claims hits home much more effectively than negative feedback from a tutor they hardly knew.
5 A fundamental principle of any quality performance is knowing when a performance is good or not. This requires internalizing appropriate standards of quality control. Traditionally, students expect teachers to tell them if their work is up to scratch; they often do not even check work they hand in. According to Gibbs, this is basically why many students object to self- and peer-assessment: this is the job teachers are paid to do.

However, not to play the role of assessor means that the very standards one needs in order to become an autonomous learner will not be internalized. Hence, it is a vital part of learning to assess learning performances.

The 'motivation' for handing in good work on a constant basis comes here from the social dimension, so that the problems are willingly attempted although they do not form part of the final assessment, except in so far as they must be handed in. Gibbs comments that it hardly matters if the feedback is unfair or inexpert, the important thing is that it focuses the students' attention on appropriate learning activities.

In sum, what has happened here is that the six peer-assessment sessions produced alignment in a system that was thrown out of alignment by the increased student numbers. The course objectives addressed problem-solving, and the final exam likewise, but the problem sessions, which were the main TLA after the lecture, had become ineffectual. The peer-assessments became TLAs that directly addressed the final assessment (the final exam comprised similar problems). Peer-assessment was not so much an assessment device, but a teaching-learning device.

This strategy of using peer-assessment as a TLA may not work in all subjects. It would probably require conditions where peer-assessment itself works best: that is, where the assessment tasks are clearly defined, and mirror the course objectives (see p. 158). Under those conditions, alignment can be achieved at little extra cost (the supervision of the six extra plenary sessions), while the academic gains are considerable.

Problem-based learning (PBL)

PBL started out in the 1960s at Case Western Reserve and at McMaster Medical Schools, in the USA and Canada respectively, and was adopted by several medical schools during the 1970s, before being applied to other areas of educating for the professions. It is a total approach to teaching that has many variations, and could embody several possible TLAs and assessment methods. It can be implemented in a single unit, or across a whole course or programme, and applied to basic academic subjects as well as to professional education (Poliquin and Maufette 1997). It is, however, particularly common in medical and paramedical education. It is estimated that, by the end of the 1990s, over 40 per cent of Australian medical education programmes will be problem-based (Hendry and Murphy 1995).

All PBL approaches agree that 'the starting point for learning should be a problem, query or a puzzle that the learner wishes to solve' (Boud 1985:

13). That means what it says: the problem, or a series of problems, is where learning starts. PBL is not an ordinary curriculum with problems added, the problems *are* the curriculum, and in going about solving those problems the learner seeks the knowledge of disciplines, facts and procedures that are needed to solve the problems. The traditional disciplines do not define what is to be learned, the problems do. However, the aim is not only to solve those particular problems, but in the course of doing so, the learner will acquire knowledge, content-related skills, self-management skills, attitudes, know-how: in a word, professional wisdom.

In sum, if the aim is to become a doctor, then the best way of doing so is being a doctor – under appropriate guidance and safeguards. If the aim is to apply biology to solving biological problems, then solving biological problems is the main TLA. PBL is alignment itself. The objectives stipulate the problems to be solved, the main TLA is solving them, and the assessment is seeing how well they have been solved. It is our first example (Gibbs 1998) on a much more radical scale, dealing with functioning knowledge rather than pencil-and-paper problems.

PBL reflects the way people learn in real life; they simply get on with solving the problems life puts before them with whatever resources are to hand. They do not stop to wonder at the 'relevance' of what they are doing, or at their 'motivation' for doing it. Formal schooling, on the other hand, operates on a fill-up-the-tanks model of knowledge acquisition. Young people are taught the sorts of things they are likely to need to know one day, and some skills for finding out more, before they are let loose on the world.

Education for the professions for years followed this proactive model, and much of it still does. The disciplines are taught first, independently of each other, and armed with all that declarative knowledge, and with some skills, the student is accredited as ready to practise as a professional. However, many students acquire knowledge in traditional programmes specifically for the purpose of passing examinations (Entwistle and Entwistle 1997), and often only incidentally acquire the skill of putting knowledge to practical use. Professional practice requires functioning knowledge that can be put to work immediately, not just declarative knowledge (see Chapter 3). If the objectives nominate professional competence on graduation, but declarative knowledge is the output, something has been missed. Curriculum, teaching and assessment are not aligned.

PBL in effect simulates everyday learning and problem-solving. The problems are, however, carefully selected, so that by the end of the programme, the learner is expected to cover perhaps less content than is covered in a traditional programme, but the *nature* of the knowledge so gained is different. It is acquired in a working context and is put back to use in that context. Coverage, so dominant in discipline-centred teaching, is considered less important. Instead of trying to cover everything they might need to know, students learn the *skills* for seeking out the required knowledge when the occasion arises.

A typical PBL sequence goes like this:

- The *motivational context* is pressing. In a typical medical programme, students in their first week of the first year are faced with the responsibility of a real patient with, say, a broken leg. The felt need to learn is strong.
- Learners become *active* very quickly. They are assigned to small problem-solving groups and begin *interacting* with teachers, peers and clients (who present the problem).
- Learners *build up a knowledge base* of relevant material; they learn where to go to check it and to seek out more. They are variously guided towards resource materials, including films, videos, the library and the lecture room. Knowledge is *elaborated and consolidated*. Students meet a tutor and discuss the case in relation to the knowledge they have obtained.
- The knowledge is *applied*: the case is treated.
- The case is reviewed, and learners develop *self-management and self-monitoring skills* which they review throughout the programme.

The italicized words may remind you of the characteristics of a rich learning context described in Chapter 5. PBL makes use of them all.

Varieties of PBL

There are several modifications and versions of what is called 'PBL', but all should address the four goals distinguished by Barrows (1986):

1 *Structuring knowledge for use in clinical contexts.* Professional education is concerned with functioning knowledge. That is the target of PBL; it is concerned with constructing knowledge that is to be put to work.
2 *Developing effective clinical reasoning processes.* Although stated in medical terms, this refers to the cognitive activities required in the professional area concerned. General processes include problem-solving, decision-making, hypothesizing etc., but each area has its own specific processes, to be developed as relevant problems are solved.
3 *Developing self-directed learning skills.* Included here are the three levels of skills mentioned in Chapter 5: generic study skills, content specific study skills and especially the metacognitive or self-management skills focused on what the learner does in new contexts. The latter should be the ultimate aim of all university teaching, but are normally not specifically addressed outside PBL.
4 *Increased motivation for learning.* As already described, students are placed in a context that requires their immediate and committed involvement:

the value is high, likewise the expectation of success, as problems and cases are selected to be soluble.

To these four may be added a fifth:

5 *Developing group skills, working with colleagues.* Medical and paramedical practice often require that professionals work in a team. Teamwork is also basic to the application of PBL.

Various forms of PBL address these goals more or less effectively. Two major variables determine different kinds of PBL (Barrows 1986):

(a) *The degree the problem is structured.* Some problems are tightly structured, and the case study is given in detail, with all the needed information to solve it. Others have some facts provided, the student having to find the rest. Open or ill-defined problems present no data, it being entirely up to the student to research the case.
(b) *The extent of teacher direction.* The most conservative case is where the teacher controls the amount and flow of information, problems being discussed by the teacher in a lecture. Case-based methods present case studies to students before the lecture; it then depends what they are required to do prior to, and then during, the following class that determines the kind of PBL. Variations revolve around how free students are to utilize and develop effective information handling skills.

The form of PBL that best addresses all four objectives is what Barrows calls 'reiterative' PBL. Here, problems are minimally structured, and teacher guidance is low, and when the case has been resolved, students are required to reflect back and evaluate their previous reasoning and knowledge. This form of PBL is basically action learning.

What is the best form of PBL to introduce? Practically, it has to be manageable with available resources, and consistent at least initially with the educational philosophy of the teachers and tutors participating (Ryan 1997). In the ongoing study at the Polytechnic University of Hong Kong mentioned earlier (Tang *et al.* 1997), modifications were introduced to fit the aims of the six departments, and the different expectations of full- and part-time students. The full-time students found most difficulty with assessment, not surprisingly given their exam-dominated school background. As one student put it, 'it is difficult to guess what is the marking scheme of the lecturer' (Tang *et al.* 1997: 586). Part-time students, on the other hand, took to PBL straightaway: 'when I encounter a problem, I will have a solution, like that in my workplace' (*ibid.*).

Accordingly, a 'basic template' of PBL was designed, with rather more lectures and teacher guidance in the first stages than might be ideal, and variations made as suiting each department's needs. Most departments started with a lecture, which provided much of the information needed and some structuring, followed by group discussions, at which the problem was introduced; one department (design) started with the problem. The distinction is whether the problem is provided first, then the information needed to solve it, or the information first, then the problem. The first case is classical PBL, the second a modification to help ease conservative students into the programme.

Assessment in PBL

The complaint of the full-time student quoted above signals that assessment is a particularly sensitive issue in PBL. The sensitivity is due to the fact that PBL is an essentially divergent or open-end mode of teaching that is not aligned to the more common convergent formats of assessment.

Implementing successful assessment in PBL is no different in principle from any other teaching system. The questions at the beginning of Chapter 9 can be used, and the answers are actually very clear: CRA, qualitative, holistic, divergent (some convergent), decontextualized and a lot of peer- and self-assessment, an aspect appearing in many PBL designs (Tang *et al.* 1997; Wetherell and Mullins 1997). The essential feature of a teaching system designed to emulate professional practice is that the crucial assessments should be performance-based, holistic, allowing plenty of scope for students to input their own decisions and solutions (Kingsland 1995). Some version of the portfolio, as open-ended, may be useful in many programmes, but essentially the assessment has to be suitable for the profession concerned.

Medical PBL developed the 'triple jump' (Feletti 1997), a three-step exercise, with the student evaluated at each step:

1 *Dealing with the problem or case*: diagnosing, hypothesizing, checking with the clinical database, use made of information, reformulating.
2 *Review of independent study*: knowledge gained, level of understanding, evaluating information gained.
3 *Final problem formulation*: synthesis of key concepts, application to patient's problem, self-monitoring, response to feedback.

These steps emulate real life, but there are some problems still. Do all steps have to be passed or can you average? Is there an underlying 'problem-solving ability'? Should performance at the various steps correlate together or not? (Feletti 1997). Interestingly, all are hangovers from the measurement model.

The structure of the triple jump could be applied to any area.

Does PBL work?

The goals of PBL are usually accepted as structuring knowledge for clinical use, developing effective clinical reasoning processes, developing self-directed learning skills, increased motivation for learning and effective teamwork. How effectively does it attain these goals?

If you attend the PBL sections of higher education conferences, or the specifically PBL conferences (e.g. PROBLARC in Australia, see end of chapter), you will get a strong impression of enthusiasm and commitment. Yes, people who use it say, PBL works extremely well, and student response is highly positive. That is nice to know, but harder evidence would be even nicer. Several evaluations have gone beyond single case anecdote.

Albanese and Mitchell (1993) conducted a major meta-analysis of all studies published between 1972 and 1992. The results are complex, not least because 'PBL' was not utilized in the same way in all studies, but the following conclusions emerge:

1 Both staff and students rate PBL higher in their evaluations, and enjoy PBL more than traditional teaching.
2 PBL graduates perform as well and sometimes better on clinical performance. More PBL (medical) graduates go into family practice.
3 PBL students use higher-level strategies for understanding and for self-directed study.
4 PBL students do worse on examinations of basic science declarative knowledge.

Newble and Clarke (1986) compared the approaches to learning, as measured in the Study Process Questionnaire, of students from first to final years in a PBL and in a traditional medical school, and the results were very clear. PBL students scored lower on surface and higher on deep as they progressed through the programme, whereas traditional students did what we have noticed most students do: score higher on surface and lower on deep as they progress. Likewise, McKay and Kember (1997) describe the introduction of PBL to a paramedical course in Hong Kong: performance significantly improved, as did approaches to learning; the students changed from fairly extreme alienation to high enthusiasm. In other words, PBL beats the system.

Hmelo *et al.* (1997) argue that PBL by its nature requires a *different way* of using knowledge to solve problems. Their argument takes over from our distinction between acquiring functioning knowledge, and acquiring declarative knowledge which has then to be integrated and converted to be applied. They distinguish two strategies in clinical decision-making:

• Bottom-up or data-driven: 'This patient has elevated blood sugar, therefore he has diabetes.'
• Top-down or hypothesis-driven: 'This patient has diabetes, therefore

blood sugar should be up, and rapid respiration, 'fruity' breath odour . . .'

Experienced and expert doctors use the data-driven strategy, except for unfamiliar or complex problems. Novice doctors, such as students in training, lack that experience and should therefore work top-down from first principles, with longer reasoning chains: 'If this, then because of that, it would follow that we should find symptoms X, Y and Z . . .' The traditionally taught students tried to follow the experts – and couldn't, they didn't have the background. PBL taught students increasingly used hypothesis-driven reasoning, with longer and clearer reasoning chains. PBL students also used a wider variety of knowledge resources, whereas traditionally taught stuck with the textbook. Anyone familiar with PBL would not be at all surprised by these findings, because they are completely in line with what PBL is trying to do, but it is nice to have it confirmed.

An important aspect of evaluating PBL is its implementation, particularly cost-benefits. The economies of large lectures are offset by the economies of self-directed learning, and the size and number of tutorial groups complementing the lectures. Albanese and Mitchell (1993) estimate that for fewer than 40, and up to around 100, students, PBL once set up can be equivalent in cost to traditional teaching.

Problem-based problems

PBL is particularly sensitive to context and climate. Remember (p. 75) the disastrous effect a know-it-all tutor had on the questioning strategy needed for the problem-solving process ('That's for me to know and you to find out'). An equally devastating effect was achieved in another case when the course coordinator decided to retain the traditional final-year examination, leaving the students unsure whether their conclusions drawn from case study work would be relevant to the final exam. They weren't. Not surprisingly, performance was low, and the course evaluation of PBL was unfavourable (Lai *et al.* 1997). The bloody-minded tutor achieved affective non-alignment, in that the climate created was incompatible with the spirit of PBL. The bloody-minded course coordinator achieved instructional non-alignment, in that the assessment matched neither the objectives nor the TLAs used.

Albanese and Mitchell (1993) say that PBL students cover only 80 per cent of the traditional syllabus, and then do not perform as well in standard examinations. That worries traditional critics more than PBL teachers, who would prefer the PBL graduate to know less declaratively, but put what is known to work more readily; and where that knowledge is insufficient, they have the self-directed skills to know where to go and how to acquire what is required.

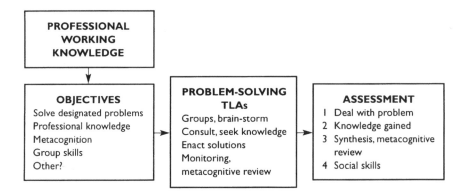

Figure 10.1: Alignment in problem-based learning

The reasons why PBL is not used more widely are not educational but organizational. It requires not only a different epistemology from teachers – seeing professional education as something more than the acquisition of separate bodies of knowledge, in one of which the teacher is professed expert – but also considerable institutional flexibility. It is much easier for experts to give lectures on their speciality, leaving integration and application as the students' problem to solve. Most will, eventually, but it will be years down the track for some. It is more effective and more responsible if integration and application are seen as targets before the professional has begun to practise rather than after.

Conclusions

PBL is undoubtedly a really effective approach to teaching. I would argue that its effectiveness is due to the fact that it exemplifies a high degree of alignment. That alignment is evident (Figure 10.1).

To practise as a particular professional requires solving problems that belong to that profession. Thus, professional skill is the goal, professional practise comprises the TLAs, professional skill is what is assessed (among other things). It is distinguished from apprenticeship in that it is theory-based; it is not just a matter of performing the skills in an uninformed manner. If you look at the triple jump, for example, the student is required to base decisions in knowledge, to hypothesize, to justify, to evaluate and to reformulate, all of which are the kinds of cognitive activities that are required in professional practice.

The learning portfolio

My last example of aligned teaching is the use of the learning portfolio.

This started simply as portfolio assessment in a unit in a professional programme, but the backwash took over, and in effect dictated the TLAs. In this case, alignment was created bottom-up.

The nature of teaching and learning was a compulsory semester-long unit in the third year of a four-year part-time evening Bachelor of Education programme at the University of Hong Kong, which I taught with the help of a teaching assistant. The 82 students (technically a 'large' class) were primary and secondary teachers in government schools, in a conservative educational system. The general aim of the unit was not to teach students about psychology (they had already completed a first-year unit in educational psychology), but to get them to demonstrate that they could drive their classroom decision-making with their psychological knowledge, based on reflective practice. Such an aim would be applicable to advanced units in most professional programmes.

Formulating and clarifying curriculum objectives

The objectives were formulated as outlined in Chapter 3. It is necessary to decide on the topics to be addressed and the level, and to put them together in a grading system that can be directly addressed by the assessment tasks.

Topics

These had been taught as declarative knowledge in a first-year unit: the nature of learning and constructivist learning theory, the growth of learning (SOLO), approaches to learning, expectancy-value theory of motivation, principles of assessment. The aim was to turn all that into functioning knowledge. There was some expository teaching, to revise, update and profile the content, but basically the students were required to put this knowledge to work, by using it for reflecting on their own classroom experiences, and make better professional decisions. (During the day they were all practising teachers, which provided them with plenty of first-hand experience and critical incidents.)

Levels of understanding

These topics became the knowledge base upon which students could demonstrate extended abstract and relational levels of functioning knowledge. Deriving the criterion-referenced objectives expressed as grading categories was then quite easy, the level of activity defining the category (these verbs are italicized). Students are to:

A *Reflect* on their own teaching, *evaluate* their classroom decisions in terms of theory, and thereby *improve* their teaching, *formulate* a theory of teaching that demonstrably drives decision-making and practice, *generate* new approaches to teaching on that basis.

B *Apply* course content, *recognize* good and poor applications of principles. 'Missed A': that is, had a good try at reflecting but didn't quite make it.

C *Understand* declarative; *discuss* content meaningfully, *know about* a reasonable amount of content. Also include 'missed B'.

D *Understand* in a minimally acceptable way: essentially 'missed C' or 'badly missed B'.

F 'Miss D'; plagiarize; not participate satisfactorily; not hand in work.

If students could unequivocally demonstrate in their portfolios the level of performance indicated by the verbs in the category, that category grade would be awarded, given that the other performance tasks were all satisfactory. As an aside, I might comment that category A is what university teachers should be able to do; it is an educational version of the reflective practitioner (Schön 1983; Cowan 1998). How it applies to readers of this book is described in Chapter 9.

In this example, we can see that formulating the actual objectives was not at all complicated. The ensuing assessment procedures were also straight-forward.

Learning portfolio

The next step was not in fact to choose the TLAs. I wanted to use learning partnerships and a reflective journal, but was thereafter open to nego-tiation with the students when they realized what they had to do. The crucial step was the choice of the learning portfolio.

In the first class of the semester, I circulated the above objectives and discussed them, making sure the students knew the standards they would have to meet. They were told that they had to convince me that their learning in the unit met the objectives. They were to decide on the evidence for their learning in the form of items for their portfolio, and to explain where they thought the portfolio as a whole met the objectives. Specifically, the requirements were:

1 Four pieces of evidence selected by the student.

2 A reflective journal, including answers to the main idea questions for each plenary session.

3 A justification for selecting the items, and the overall case they were supposed to make as a learning package. This provided very good evidence of students' metacognitive awareness of their learning.

A list of suggested items was provided, but original items were encouraged.

The portfolio was a completely new task to them, to which most initially reacted very negatively. They demanded guidelines and examples of possible items, and complained bitterly about the perceived workload. In the event, I have to admit that their initial complaints about the workload were justified. Four items, in addition to the journal and the justifications, were too many. Three would have been better.

They were invited to submit a sample item for feedback. This was very successful in bringing them round, particularly as they could include that item in their end-of-semester portfolio if they were satisfied with my comments on it. It was at this stage that negotiations on the TLAs began.

Choosing the TLAs

The verbs I wanted students to enact are italicized above in the grading scheme. Below are the TLAs (italicized) that were eventually used to elicit those desired learnings. How they came to be chosen was a matter of negotiation, described below.

1 To understand the psychological concepts mentioned above. These were reiterated in *notes* and *readings* to be read before each class. *Self-addressed questions* were responded to in note form in a *journal*. Before the class: 'What do I most want to find out in the next class?' After the class: 'What is the main point I learned today?' and 'What was the main point left unanswered in today's session?' Class time was used for clarification and elaboration, sometimes by *mass lecture*. Each student chose a *learning partner* to help in clarifying and elaborating, and interacting in whatever ways they thought might be helpful.
2 To see how these concepts might be applied to their own teaching. Partners were helpful, but to extend the range of exposure to different views and professional experiences, *groups* of around ten students, teaching in the same general content area, were arranged. The groups had a question to address, but were basically self-directed, and students had to draw their own conclusions.
3 To reflect on their own teaching, in the light of the psychological content current for that week. Reflection was intended to be encouraged by the *journal*, which contained the self-addressed questions for each day. They were asked to record learning related incidents, particularly critical incidents, and to reflect upon them.

Occasionally, the class remained in plenary session for a mass lecture, but usually it split, half remaining for discussion with me and with learning partners (more manageable with 40 than with 80), the other half moving to an adjoining room, which could accommodate four discussion groups of ten each. The medium for group discussion was invariably Cantonese, and the teaching assistant rotated among groups. Her feedback from group discussions was most important in designing future activities. In practice, the groups were student-led.

Initially, the students expected and wanted straight lecturing, but they quickly saw that lecturing would not be much use in compiling their portfolios. The backwash from the portfolio made it evident that different TLAs were needed. These emerged from negotiation. The following dialogue, condensed from several sessions, illustrates how this happened (*S* are students, *T* is teacher):

S: What sort of items do we select?

T: That's up to you. Think hard about the objectives. Here's a list of sample items you might include. [I take a few and explain how they might work.]

S: Can we have a trial run?

T: Yes, and if you're happy with my assessment of it you can submit it as an item.

S: How do we show we can reflect?

T: Use your journal.

S: What do we put in it?

T: What you think are critical incidents in your teaching? Talk it over with your colleagues. Form a learning partnership. Sit next to your partner in class, get their phone number. You can help each other.

S: Wouldn't it be better if we had discussion groups of students teaching the same subjects as we do? Then we can share experiences on similar problems.

T: Certainly. You can form groups in the room next door.

S: We need direct teaching on the topics. Will you lecture us?

T: Here's the schedule; there's a topic for each session. You have some pre-reading to do, just a few pages, before each session. Then answer the first of these questions [the self-addressed question in 1 above]. I'll then meet half the class at a time, while the others are having discussion groups, and we can clarify each topic . . .

And so on.

In short, the assessment task drove the students' learning activities, which had to address the objectives, and the TLAs evolved around that. Student reactions confirmed that this was so. One student referred to the portfolio as 'a learning tool'. In fact, it was difficult to separate what was a TLA and what an assessment task. The journal, for example, was both. Students used it to learn how to reflect, and it was used later as evidence of reflection. Likewise, the self-addressed questions ('What was the most important idea . . .') is both a learning activity and evidence of the quality of learning. We noted the same thing with PBL and the Gibbs example. It is in fact a necessary consequence of alignment. Grappling with the task you want students to learn is automatically both a learning process and a learning outcome. When you are learning to drive a car, is the act of driving a learning process or an outcome of learning? The negotiated teaching activities stimulated the students to respond in the way required.

- 'What (we are expected) to prepare for the portfolio undoubtedly provides me a chance to reflect on my daily teaching. This would never happen if this module proceeded in the same way as the other modules. I would not be as alert about my own teaching and eager to make changes and improvements.'
- 'Instead of bombing us with lengthy lectures and lecture notes, we have to reflect on our own learning experiences and to respond critically . . . I feel quite excited as this course is gradually leading me to do something positive to my teaching career and to experience real growth.'

The assessment results

Individual excellence of particular portfolio items was not sought as much as how the objectives were addressed overall. For example, a balanced portfolio could include a concept map and a letter to a friend (to show how the unit overall is perceived), a lesson plan or an account of a lesson taught (application), a review (critical analysis of related declarative knowledge); and, most important, the reflective journal (reflection, application, analysing critical incidents). All items had to be satisfactory, and the grade was awarded corresponding to the level of activity unequivocally displayed. Thirty-seven per cent achieved an A (able to develop a personal theory and teach in terms of that); 40 per cent a B (able to discuss and/or change various teaching and assessment practices in terms of theory); 22 per cent a C (able only to provide evidence that they comprehended the basic taught content); 1 per cent D, and no failures.

Student reactions (drawn from journals and other portfolio items) were as follows. To the *journal*:

Doing the reflective journal is tough work. However, I like the reflection part in it because it really helps me to stretch my mind to think about each topic deeply. Moreover, by reflecting on my own teaching and learning, I do make a lot of improvements in my teaching . . . [usually] we are so familiar with the daily routine . . . the same old way every year. So reflection really gives me the time to stop and think about my teaching and how my pupils view it.

The reflective journal is no longer a threat to me. Every time that I write it, I'm pouring out the ideas that I've got.

I see the idea of keeping a 'reflective journal' as very helpful because as we know more about the nature of learning, our understanding will change as we reflect on our own experiences. When we read back the reflective journal, we can see the changes taking place as we move along the course.

To the *portfolio*: initially highly negative, as mentioned in Chapter 7. Others:

> How about the assessment? Aiyaa! *Anxiety! Anxiety! Anxiety!* I was so puzzled and worried about it when I received the handout on the first meeting.

And a backhanded one:

> This [the portfolio] is going to be a nightmare! At least, if it had been an essay, I would have known what is expected of me . . . Have I ever caused the same kind of fear among my students? *I must bear in mind to be more reasonable and careful when giving my students assignments from now on* . . . Only give them assignments that are well designed and really necessary to help them in their learning . . . make sure they understand what is expected of them . . . make sure sufficient time is given for completing . . .

Others:

> You will be willing to do more than what the lecturers want you to do. The circumstance is like a little kid who has learnt something new in school and can't wait to tell his/her parents.

> I learn more from the portfolio than in the lesson.

And finally:

> All [the teacher] said was 'show me the evidence of your learning that has taken place' and we have to ponder, reflect and project the theories we have learnt into our own teaching . . . How brilliant! If it had only been an exam or an essay, we would have probably just repeated his ideas to him and continued to teach the same way as we always do!

Conclusions

I have called this case study of using a learning portfolio 'bottom-up' alignment, or alignment that evolved in the course of negotiating with students struggling to cope with a new form of assessment. I contrasted this with the 'top-down' alignment of formally structured PBL. The important thing is that, however it came about, alignment with qualitatively and holistically defined objectives brought about quality learning in both cases (see Figure 10.2).

It could easily be argued that the portfolio is an example of PBL. The central problem for each student is to select an item of relevant learning,

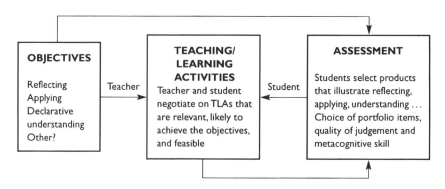

Figure 10.2: Alignment in learning portfolio

and demonstrate that it manifests the qualities nominated in the objectives. In the course of this, students have to demonstrate:

1 Sufficient mastery of content to show that it can be used in their everyday professional decision-making.
2 Professional skills relevant to dealing with classroom problems, setting assessments, designing curricula or whatever comes up.
3 Metacognitive and self-management skills, such as reflection, independence and so on.
4 Motivation and involvement with the task.
5 Usually, examples of teamwork and cooperative learning.

This is in fact very close to Barrows' (1986) list of goals for PBL (see pp. 208–9).

PBL and learning portfolios thus have much in common. Both require the conditions of good learning contexts described in Chapter 5: they construct and then make use of a sound knowledge base, require high levels of learner activity, both cognitive and metacognitive, and interaction with others.

Second, the objectives are clear in both cases, they refer to performances of high cognitive quality, and they then determine all subsequent TLAs. A portfolio is a neat way of throwing the responsibility of matching the assessment tasks to the objectives on to the student. Alignment is then clinched when the learning activities are themselves the assessment tasks. Other TLAs might need more formal structuring by the teacher, such as plenary sessions, to address other aspects: to provide guidance, to present new material and different information and interpretations, to coordinate contacts between students and so on.

Finally, what is important is not the particular techniques of teaching or assessing, but the framework in which decisions are made. Had the portfolio class been 282 instead of 82, then many of the particular decisions would have been different. We would have had more plenary sessions, but more self-directed tasks involving learning partners outside the classroom; possibly more peer- and self-assessment, possibly even an MC test if I couldn't be sure of the baseline declarative knowledge (not an issue here, as I had taught the same students in first year). Again, had these students not been part-time, they would not have had the rich database provided every day in their own professional activities. In that case, the tasks would have to have been defined differently. Obviously, these 'technique level' decisions are all relative to the context, and cannot be prescribed in advance.

The real point is how you will make those decisions yourself, to fit your context. We shall have a final word about that in the next and last chapter.

Summary and conclusions

Three examples of effective teaching were discussed in this chapter, all embodying a high degree of alignment.

Peer assessment as a TLA

Gibbs reports a case of an otherwise quite traditional lecture, problem session/tutorial and final examination structure, where conventional assessment tasks, similar to those used in the final examination, were peer-assessed but the results were not used summatively. The effect was sharply to increase appropriate student learning activity, to convey to students the criteria of good problem-solving and dramatically to increase the students' examination performance.

Problem-based learning (PBL)

There are many varieties of PBL, depending principally on the amount of teacher direction, but in all forms, *problems* define the curriculum, not topics. In solving these selected problems, the necessary knowledge and skills are acquired, plus skills for acquiring new knowledge, and the metacognitive skills for evaluating the knowledge and the effectiveness of problem solutions.

PBL taught students think differently from traditionally taught students: they have less declarative knowledge, but use what they have more effectively with richer reasoning chains; they have greater self-awareness and self-direction, and manifest more enjoyment, as do teachers. However, PBL is as good as those who implement it; it is sensitive to insensitive teaching. An institutional problem is that the infrastructure for PBL is not discipline-based, whereas most universities are organized on disciplinary lines. Teachers tend to identify themselves as scholars in their home discipline, and PBL might seem to threaten their academic identity.

The learning portfolio

The learning portfolio turned out to be a version of PBL. The problem is: what shall I put in my portfolio to convince the teacher that I have learned in the way nominated in the objectives? That question dominated the dynamics of teaching and assessing.

The last two examples illustrate the two demands of constructive alignment:

1 A theory of learning that enables the teacher to focus on the high level cognitive activities that determine quality performance in their teaching subjects.
2 An aligned system of teaching and learning, where the objectives are clear, and the TLAs and the assessment tasks address those objectives.

Figures 10.1 and 10.2 define two approaches to alignment, one driven by the TLAs flowing from the objectives, the other by student reaction to the assessment tasks, which themselves flow from the objectives: the first produces the alignment by tuning *teaching* to the objectives, the second by tuning the *assessment* tasks to the objectives.

What that means in the teaching of any given subject is entirely dependent on the context and the resources available. The most important resource of all is human: a teacher who teaches from a level 3 perspective.

Further reading

On using peer assessment for teaching

Boud, D. (1986) *Implementing Student Self-assessment*, Green Guide No. 5, Sydney: Higher Education Research and Development Society of Australasia.
Gibbs, G. (1998) Using assessment strategically to change the way students learn, in S. Brown and A. Glasner (eds) *Assessment Matters in Higher Education: Choosing and Using Diverse Approaches*, Buckingham: Society for Research into Higher Education/Open University Press.

Boud describes many ways of using peer-assessment; Gibbs describes in more detail the example quoted here.

On problem-based learning

Boud, D. (1985) *Problem-based Learning in Education for the Professions*, Sydney: Higher Education Research and Development Society of Australasia.

Boud, D. and Feletti, G. (eds) (1991/7) *The Challenge of Problem Based Learning*, London: Kogan Page.

Research and Development in Problem Based Learning. Volumes 1–4 (1997) The Australian Problem Based Learning Network, c/o PROBLARC, CALT, the University of Newcastle, NSW 2308.

The first describes the principles of PBL from the beginning; Boud and Feletti contains contributions by users in many different areas. Both are basic reading for anyone interested in this area. The last is a serial publication of the Australian Problem Based Learning Network, which holds biennial conferences, of which these volumes are the proceedings.

On the learning portfolio

There is nothing written on the case study that is not already included in the present volume.

11

On implementation

So far, this book may simply have provided you with some declarative knowledge about aligned teaching. To achieve its purpose, however, its contents must be put to work as functioning knowledge. The meta-Susans among you will have been doing this already, but to be consistent, I should be providing a TLA or two to help everyone do so. The chief TLA in effecting that transformation is reflection, action learning its main support structure. But it would be blaming the teacher if we thought that all would be well once individual teachers did some action research on their teaching. Teachers do not work as isolated individuals. They work in departments, with colleagues. Their units contribute to programmes; they need resources for their teaching, and support and time to reflect on it – and they need to be rewarded for doing so. Teaching is a system, of which individuals, departments, faculties and institutional policies are all part. But this raises a new book of issues, and we can only look at its table of contents here.

Researching your teaching

Let us now systematically explore your own teaching. Turn back to Task 1.1, where you were asked to nominate the three most worrying problems in your teaching. Are you any further down the track towards solving any of them? Decide now which one you would most like to follow up for the present; you can go back to the others later as you like. Or you might like to take a problem nominated by the students in Task 4.1.

I will now suggest some further steps. Keep a note of your thinking as you proceed. We will use an action learning structure to define and then attack your problem.

Defining the problem

The first step is to define the problem in a way that tells you how you might go about finding a possible solution. However, the search should not be just for a technique that will fix things. That is the level 2, cookbook approach, focusing on what *you* do. The issue is what the *students* are doing that you don't want them to do, or not doing that you do want them to do.

The source of the problem student behaviour could lie in the objectives, the climate, your rapport with them, inappropriate TLAs, poor large-class management skills, unaligned assessment tasks or any combination of these. You need a working theory of teaching to guide you through the possibilities. Finding a solution is a matter of conceptualizing the problem, which is where I hope this book might be most useful.

So the first step is to reflect on the problem, using the constructive alignment theory in Chapter 2, which addresses both students' learning behaviour and the design of your teaching. Examine your problem in these terms, hypothesize as to the possible reasons for it, and possible solutions. The process can be made much easier with the help of a 'critical friend' (see below).

Implementing a change

The next step is to find out more about the problem, and possible solutions, from whatever chapters might be appropriate. If there is not enough relevant material there, you might find it in the further reading in each chapter, or in the particular references in the text. This additional knowledge should suggest possible ways of handling the problem. These then need to be translated into specific action in your context.

Monitoring the change

Before putting the change into effect, you need to decide how you are going to make sure that what you are proposing to do will be effective. It is necessary to observe systematically what is going on, to know where you and/or the student behaviour started from, and where it ends up after the change has been implemented.

The next step is to obtain a baseline, recording where you are before the problem is addressed. This could involve pre- and post-measures of the troubling student behaviour, such as measures of poor learning outcomes, observations of repetitive material in exams or assignments, keeping track of complaints about time stress . . . The possibilities are of course as numerous as the problems themselves. Suggestions for pre- and post-instruments could include questionnaires, student ratings, performance tests, your own controlled observations, keeping a diary yourself of what is happening and your own reflections on progress. This diary should be kept whatever other data are collected.

Fine-tuning

Action learning recycles: you try something, see if it works, then try again with a slight variation. You will be unlikely to get something as complex as teaching right first time round. So it is a matter of looking back over your observations, after you have implemented the change you had decided to make, and seeing how things are going. Did matters improve? If not, or if not enough, what might have been the problem? This requires reflecting again, back to step 1, but with the extra knowledge of what has happened in the meantime.

The role of 'critical friend'

Reflection is often not best carried out alone. You have been living with the problem possibly for some time. So as the fish is the last to discover water, it is very helpful to have someone on dry land, a 'critical friend'. This is a complex role, part partner, part consultant, but essentially a mirror to facilitate reflection (Stenhouse 1975). On the one hand, your reflections are sharpened with a different perspective and some technical advice. On the other hand, you as action researcher need to retain 'ownership' over the definition and control of the problem; it is your own teaching we are talking about. The critical friend should not tell you what to do, because that shuts down the reflection process, and makes your teaching their problem not yours.

Different people can take this role: a friend in the same department (but not the head of department, even if he or she is a friend), a staff developer or someone from outside. It is often convenient for a colleague in the same department to act as critical friend, particularly one with some educational expertise, who could at the right time gently feed in suggestions to be reflected upon. Staff developers are ideal, but the staff development unit may not have the resources to deal with many action learning projects in the one institution.

In one action learning project, comprising 50 independent projects over six separate tertiary institutions, five assistant lecturer level critical friends, with both content and educational qualifications, were employed, each handling about ten projects in similar content areas (Kember *et al.* 1997). Interacting with that number of projects meant that their role varied. In some cases personal facilitator was more important, in others expert consultant, but in whatever role, these critical friends played a vital part in bringing about successful outcomes. Specific information on action learning and the role of the critical friend is found in the case studies referenced in the further reading at the end of this chapter.

The department as focus

Let us move a step further into the system. Teaching is normally the responsibility of departments, or it might be faculty, or school. This body, whatever it is, resources teaching, constructs the programmes to which the units you teach contribute, gives its blessing on the curriculum that you are teaching and often requires that your teaching of the unit is exposed to student evaluations. After that, it is up to you. Usually you translate that curriculum into objectives, and the TLAs and specific assessment tasks are yours to decide within resource limitations. The climate you create, once the classroom door is shut, is assuredly yours. My concern here is with helping you deal with those aspects of departmental responsibilities that impinge on your own personal teaching, not with broader or more collective issues such as course design, which is dealt with elsewhere (Ramsden 1998; Toohey 1999).

Nevertheless, changing your own teaching is more likely to be sustained and effective the more the changes are supported by departmental/ institutional policy. Say you decide to go completely criterion-referenced in your assessing. In the first year that you try this, you get unusually high numbers of high distinctions and distinctions, say 37 and 40 per cent respectively, whereas your colleagues usually turn in about 10 and 15 per cent. At the examiners' meeting your results are queried, you explain, your results are passed.

The same happens next semester, but a muttered comment about 'slack standards of assessment' is louder; your unit is becoming known among your colleagues as a 'soft option'. (When the students see what they have to do to get the high distinction, and at what standard, they may not see it as a soft option.) Perhaps the next step is that the student evaluations rate your unit very highly, but refer to the high standards required. You eventually win your colleagues over. Perhaps.

It would have been psychologically (and politically) easier if you and a colleague were critical friends for each other. There would be a replication, as it were, and your remaining colleagues at the examiners' meeting might be more easily convinced. It is a short step from there to establishing a 'buddy system' within the department, whereby all teachers – or as many as are willing – are involved, pairs acting as critical friends for each other. By now, the whole department is becoming involved, not just in improving the skills of individuals, and the offerings and working of the department itself become the subject of collective reflection. Systems being what they are, that greatly increases the effectiveness of what individuals are doing.

If the whole department decided to set up an action learning project on criterion-referenced assessment, it would broaden the scope of the exercise significantly. It would involve departmental discussion and agreement on workloads, standards, deadlines, spreading the nature of the assessment tasks so the students get some experience of 'expensive' assessment tasks, assessing *across* units with a portfolio and so on. Smith *et al.* (1997) reported such a departmental action learning project on assessment, and found that not only did they clear up many assessment related issues, but the staff workshops raised curriculum and teaching issues as well. Smith *et al.* emphasize that collaboration works well only as long as there is a common purpose and philosophy. On the other hand, this could be one way of trying to create that common purpose.

Institutional structures

Teaching as research

If you have borne with me so far, and agree in principle, you might still be wondering how on earth you can find time to reflect even informally on your teaching, let alone do action learning on it. There are other demands on your time, especially that of research.

Research productivity has always been emphasized over teaching for appointments and promotions, but today, additional pressures in that direction arise from the funding of departments, one performance indicator now being the number of research papers published by department members. This makes it departmentally as well as personally worthwhile to focus on research rather than on teaching, even in departments and among teachers who have little tradition of or competence in research.

I think this unbalanced situation will self-correct, given that undergraduates themselves are increasingly becoming a source of funds. Universities, for the right reasons or not, will surely start specializing into research or teaching institutions in a way that was not so clearly the case before. In Australia this is already beginning to happen. Marginson's (1997) analysis of performance indicators in Australian universities shows that they fall into clusters:

- the old 'sandstone' universities;
- the 'middle-aged' universities, such as La Trobe;
- the previous institutes of technology;
- the previous colleges of advanced education that had not amalgamated with a university.

Ramsden (1998b) regrouped the data, looking particularly at the performance indicators on teaching, and found that excellence in teaching and excellence in research clearly parted company. A university could be excellent in one or the other, but not both. The sandstone universities went for international reputation and research productivity, but their performance indicators for teaching were the least favourable of all. Teaching was best in the middle-rank universities, but research lower.

This is to be expected. You can't do two things at once. Some universities will continue to rely on their reputations to ensure a steady flow of high-paying students, but possibly for a while only. In time, other universities, the majority, will focus on teaching, where for them the money is, thereby attracting fee-paying students from the research-oriented universities. The 'teaching' universities will surely then focus on the performance indicators for teaching rather than research, so that the majority of academics would do better to focus on improving their teaching. Such moves seem inevitable. The present situation, where most universities still reward staff for research, thus putting massive pressures on staff to perform competitively in an area where many lack experience and competence, is untenable.

One way of maintaining publication output while encouraging teaching is to publish research projects on teaching innovations. Yet some heads of department in some universities do not even 'count' publications on teaching the content for which the department is responsible. That is changing, and must change even more. For example, thanks largely to the location of PBL in medical faculties, 'medical education' is now an acknowledged avenue of research for medical academics, and there are several very highly respected journals in that area. That is happening too in legal education, and beginning to happen in commerce and business studies. In other areas, teachers who research their own teaching either have to maintain the subject area research in addition, or publish their teaching research and wear the cost, which may well put promotion or even contract renewal at risk.

It should be possible to get the best of both worlds by carrying out action learning, and publishing the results. That way everyone benefits: you and your promotion prospects, the funding to your department, the reputation of the teaching in your university. And, of course, your students.

To staff developers

I should say something specifically to staff developers, who have the officially designated responsibility for enhancing teaching (apart from their many other functions). In fact, everything I have said to date is related to staff development in this sense. This book itself arose out of the manuals I had produced for staff development workshops.

Staff developers are in a position to enhance teaching in many ways:

1 Dealing with individuals, one-to-one, as counsellor or advisor, or as critical friend in an action learning project.

2 Consulting on the teaching of a whole department, again either in a general capacity or as part of an action learning team.
3 Providing specialist advice to department, faculty or institution on mooted changes in policy that affect teaching: for example, optimal ways of reporting assessment results, assessing teaching competence in ways suitable for personnel decisions.

The last point raises a very important matter.

Advice on personnel decisions – how to assess teaching competence, advice on assembling teaching portfolios and how to assess them – should be kept at the purely *general* level. Staff development units should *not* be involved in assessing individuals and reporting the result to human resources, because that compromises their formative role. The argument is exactly the same as that in Chapter 8 on formative and summative assessment. If you are to help individuals teach better, they must feel free to admit to you their uncertainties, weaknesses and failures. If those admissions go into a personnel file for advice to the committee that is renewing contracts . . . well, I needn't labour the point.

It is deplorable that in some universities the directors of staff development units are required to gather such information on individuals for use in personnel decisions. The relationship between staff developer and teacher is exactly the same as that between doctor and patient, psychiatrist and client, and must be respected accordingly.

The focus for staff development

Finally, I return to an issue raised in Chapter 2. Does enduring change in a teacher's approach to teaching come about by *thinking* differently about teaching – that is, moving from levels 1 or 2 to level 3 – or by *acting* differently: for instance, by trying portfolio assessment for the first time?

Kember (1998) puts forward a version of the 3P model that places teachers' conceptions, which he sees as essentially 'teacher-centred' (basically levels 1/2) or 'student-centred' (level 3), as a presage factor determining their approach to teaching. The implication is that staff development should not be carried out in the way it usually is, by teachers attending workshops in order to change their teaching behaviour. Kember argues that if teachers do not really believe in the new way of teaching, they will simply revert to what they were doing before, as the post-workshop enthusiasm wears off.

The first step in his view, therefore, is to change teachers' views of teaching; *then* they will be receptive to adopting techniques that will be attuned to the new view. Changing the way people think is not easy, but Kember cites evidence that such 'perspective transformation' takes place as a result of the plan–reflect–change–reflect cycles of action learning.

Guskey (1986), on the other hand, sees improving teaching as like getting people to quit smoking. Education campaigns, which are aimed at what people think, are not as effective as 'No smoking' signs or making cigarettes much more expensive. Then, when their behaviour is forced to change, people begin to think it might be a good idea to stop smoking anyway. Accordingly, Guskey suggests that staff developers should change teachers' practices first, and their beliefs will follow later, and that will maintain the change.

It almost certainly works both ways. Action learning is likely to bring about perspective change, but action learning involves changed behaviour too. So both thinking and doing are involved, and reinforce each other. I may not really be convinced that portfolio assessment, say, is a good idea, but I am willing to give it a try, just once. I find it works; I am not so sceptical now. I ask why does it work? I begin to see that students really were learning things I couldn't anticipate . . . And so a chain reaction takes place, and which came first, the action or the thinking, becomes rather difficult to disentangle.

Prosser and Trigwell (1998) also emphasize teacher thinking in their principles of academic development, but emphasize that ways of teaching are interlinked with conceptions or views of teaching. Teachers, they write, need:

1 To become aware of the way they conceive of learning and teaching within the subjects they are teaching.
2 To examine carefully the context in which they are teaching and to become aware of how that context relates to or affects the way they teach.
3 To become aware of and to seek to understand the way their students perceive the learning and teaching situation.
4 To be continually revising, adjusting and developing their teaching in the light of this developing awareness.

To help teachers achieve this self-awareness, Prosser and Trigwell have developed the Approaches to Teaching Inventory (ATI), which has both intention and strategy components. They combine levels 1 and 2 in an information transmission/teacher-focused approach, which they contrast with a conceptual change/student-focused approach (level 3). This is a very useful instrument in staff development, making teachers clearly aware of what they really think about the nature of teaching and learning.

The strategy in staff development, then, is to address both teacher thinking and teacher behaviour. Teachers always have some sort of theory of teaching, but it is usually implicit and as such is unexamined (Marland 1997). The possibility that there are different ways of looking at teaching does not occur to many teachers. Entwistle (1997: 129) points out that the systemic (level 3) view 'offers a powerful insight to many staff in higher education who have not thought about teaching and learning in this way before . . . Indeed, that insight can bring about a totally new conception of teaching.' And with that insight will follow the recognition that practice will need to change.

Concluding comment

If the teaching system itself supports the innovation, even better still. Both believing and practising a level 3 approach to teaching is easier where colleagues also believe and teach in that way, and if the university environment supports level 3 teaching, and rewards good teachers for being innovative and reflective. Everyone is in this together.

Whereas my focus in this book has been on the individual teacher, we all must realize that good teaching is a collective responsibility, for which the institution as a whole is ultimately responsible, and which it must support through proper resourcing, staff development and its reward systems. Good teaching awards are not enough. Indeed, they could even be counter-productive in that they imply that good teaching is a natural gift bestowed on the chosen few. That makes it too easy for the rest of us lesser beings to justify struggling on as best we may with large lectures and multiple choice tests. And it lets university administrations off the hook.

The institution is itself part of a wider system. Institutions too should be rewarded for enhancing and maintaining improved teaching and learning, which at the moment they are not. When institutions are funded on the basis that their students actually do learn well as a result of the teaching they receive, then we may indeed get somewhere.

Further reading

On action learning

The material suggested below addresses general principles of implementing action research, with over 60 examples of successful implementation, some of which may well address similar problems to your own. For readings on specific stages or aspects of teaching, refer to the further reading for previous chapters: defining objectives (Chapter 3), 'motivation' and diminishing surface approaches (Chapter 4), choosing effective TLAs (Chapter 6), assessment (Chapter 9).

Elliott, J. (1991) *Action Research for Educational Change*, Milton Keynes: Open University Press.

Gibbs, G. (1992) *Improving the Quality of Student Learning*, Bristol: Technical and Educational Services.

Kember, D. and Kelly, M. (1993) *Improving Teaching through Action Research*, Green Guide No. 14, Campbelltown, NSW: Higher Education Research and Development Society of Australasia.

Kember, D., Lam, B.-h., Yan, L., Yum, J. C. K. and Liu, S. B. (eds) (1997) *Case Studies of Improving Teaching and Learning from the Action Learning Project*, Hong Kong: The Polytechnic University of Hong Kong, Action Learning Project.

Kember, D. and McKay, J. (1966) Action research into the quality of student learning: a paradigm for faculty development, *Journal of Higher Education*, 67, 528–54.

Kemmis, S. (1994) Action research, in T. Husen and N. Postlethwaite (eds) *International Encyclopedia of Education: Research and Studies*, Oxford: Pergamon Press

Schön, D. A. (1983) *The Reflective Practitioner: How Professionals Think in Action*, London: Temple Smith.

Elliott addresses action learning in schools, as one of the important developers of action research; his book is worth reading as background. Kemmis deals with principles of different kinds of action research.

Action learning has been applied more to the school than to the university sector, but apart from Elliott, all readings refer to the tertiary sector. Gibbs's book describes several strategies for deep learning, and ten action research case studies in British tertiary institutions in which one or more of these strategies were used; outcomes were assessed *inter alia* using the Approaches to Study inventory. Kember and Kelly, and Kember and McKay, describe how action research may be implemented, and Kember *et al.* describe 50 action learning projects conducted in Hong Kong tertiary institutions. Schön's book deals with the whole question of improving professional practice by reflection, using examples from several professions.

On reflective practice in general

Brockbank, A. and McGill, I. (1998) *Facilitating Reflective Learning in Higher Education*, Buckingham: Society for Research into Higher Education/Open University Press.

Cowan, J. (1999) *On Becoming an Innovative Teacher*, Buckingham: Open University Press.

After lengthy preambles, Brockbank and McGill provide detailed help in setting up situations (based mainly on the Schön model) to promote reflection with colleagues, and on one's own teaching, with respect to promoting student learning (including higher degree supervision) and formal action learning projects.

Cowan's book is the extended abstract to Brockbank and McGill's relational. It is a delightful and unusual reflective journey by an engineering teacher, now staff developer, who wanted to 'write something practical on the topic of adult learning' for his fellow teachers, and who 'yearned to avoid the use of jargon and of specialized vocabulary' (p. 18). It is a book about *reflection*: what Cowan means by it (which is more powerful than what Schön means). He distinguishes several kinds of reflection, how teachers can best use reflection, how teachers can encourage their students to reflect and how to structure groups and reflective learning journals (as opposed to learning diaries) in ways that best promote the appropriate kind of reflection. The whole book is driven by a cycle of questions, examples, strategies and generalizations from the examples. In all, it is the clearest example of practise-what-you-preach that I have seen.

References

Abercrombie, M. L. J. (1969) *The Anatomy of Judgment*, Harmondsworth: Penguin Books.

Abercrombie, M. L. J. (1980) *Aims and Techniques of Group Teaching*, London: Society for Research into Higher Education.

Albanese, M. and Mitchell, S. (1993) Problem-based learning: a review of literature on its outcomes and implementation issues, *Academic Medicine*, 68, 52–81.

Anderson, C. (1997) Enabling and shaping understanding through tutorials, in F. Marton, D. Hounsell and N. Entwistle (eds) *The Experience of Learning*, Edinburgh: Scottish Universities Press.

Andreson, L. W. (1994) *Lecturing to Large Groups: a Guide to Doing It Less . . . but Better*, Birmingham: Staff and Educational Development Association.

Ashworth, P., Bannister, P. and Thorne, P. (1997) Guilty in whose eyes? University students' perceptions of cheating and plagiarism, *Studies in Higher Education*, 22, 187–203.

Astin, A. W. (1985) *Achieving Educational Excellence: a Critical Assessment of Priorities and Practices in Higher Education*, San Francisco: Jossey-Bass.

Ausubel, D. P. (1968) *Educational Psychology: a Cognitive View*, New York: Holt, Rinehart and Winston.

Ballard, B. and Clanchy, J. (1997) *Teaching International Students*, Deakin, ACT: IDP Education Australia.

Barrows, H. S. (1986) A taxonomy of problem-based learning methods, *Medical Education*, 20, 481–6.

Baumgart, N. and Halse, C. (in press) Globalisation v. cultural diversity, *Assessment in Education*.

Beattie, K. and James, R. (1997) Flexible coursework delivery to Australian postgraduates: how effective is the teaching and learning?, *Higher Education*, 33, 177–94.

Bereiter, C. and Scardamalia, M. (1987) *The Psychology of Written Composition*, Hillsdale, NJ: Erlbaum.

Berliner, D. (1986) In pursuit of the expert pedagogue, *Educational Researcher*, 15(7), 5–13.

Biggs, J. B. (1973) Study behaviour and performance in objective and essay formats, *Australian Journal of Education*, 17, 157–67.

Biggs, J. B. (1979) Individual differences in study processes and the quality of learning outcomes, *Higher Education*, 8, 381–94.

Biggs, J. B. (1987a) *Student Approaches to Learning and Studying*, Hawthorn, Vic.: Australian Council for Educational Research.

Biggs, J. B. (1987b) Process and outcome in essay writing, *Research and Development in Higher Education*, 9, 114–25.

Biggs, J. B. (1989a) Approaches to the enhancement of tertiary teaching, *Higher Education Research and Development*, 8, 7–25.

Biggs, J. B. (1989b) Some reflections on teaching at HKU, *Hong Kong University Staff Newsletter*.

Biggs, J. (1991) Approaches to learning in secondary and tertiary students in Hong Kong: some comparative studies, *Educational Research Journal*, 6, 27–39.

Biggs, J. B. (1992a) A qualitative approach to grading students, *HERDSA News*, 14(3), 3–6.

Biggs, J. B. (1992b) *Why and How Do Hong Kong Students Learn? Using the Learning and Study Process Questionnaires*, Education Paper 14, Hong Kong: University of Hong Kong.

Biggs, J. B. (1993a) What do inventories of students' learning processes really measure? A theoretical review and clarification, *British Journal of Educational Psychology*, 63, 1–17.

Biggs, J. B. (1993b) From theory to practice: a cognitive systems approach, *Higher Education Research and Development*, 12, 73–86.

Biggs, J. B. (1994) What are effective schools? Lessons from East and West, *The Australian Educational Researcher*, 12, 9–39.

Biggs, J. B. (1996a) Enhancing teaching through constructive alignment, *Higher Education*, 32, 1–18.

Biggs, J. B. (1996b) Assessing learning quality: reconciling institutional, staff, and educational demands, *Assessment and Evaluation in Higher Education*, 21, 5–15.

Biggs, J. B. (1996c) Stages of expatriate involvement in educational development: colonialism, irrelevance, or what?, *Education Research Journal*, 12, 157–64.

Biggs, J. B. and Collis, K. F. (1982) *Evaluating the Quality of Learning: the SOLO Taxonomy*, New York: Academic Press.

Biggs, J. B. and Collis, K. F. (1989) Towards a model of school-based curriculum development and assessment: using the SOLO Taxonomy, *Australian Journal of Education*, 33, 149–61.

Biggs, J. B. and Moore, P. J. (1993) *The Process of Learning*, Sydney: Prentice Hall of Australia.

Bligh, D. A. (1971) *What's the Use of Lectures?*, Harmondsworth: Penguin Books.

Bloom, B. S., Hastings, J. T. and Madaus, G. F. (1971) *Handbook of Formative and Summative Education of Student Learning*, New York: McGraw-Hill.

Boud, D. (1985) *Problem-based Learning in Education for the Professions*, Sydney: Higher Education Research and Development Society of Australasia.

Boud, D. (1986) *Implementing Student Self-assessment*, Green Guide No. 5, Sydney: Higher Education Research and Development Society of Australasia.

Boud, D. (1995) *Enhancing Learning through Self-assessment*, London: Kogan Page.

Boud, D. and Feletti, G. (eds) (1997) *The Challenge of Problem Based Learning*, London: Kogan Page.

Boulton-Lewis, G. M. (1998) Applying the SOLO taxonomy to learning in higher education, in B. Dart and G. Boulton-Lewis (eds) *Teaching and Learning in Higher Education*, Camberwell, Vic.: Australian Council for Educational Research.

Bourner, T. and Flowers, S. (1997) Teaching and learning methods in higher education: a glimpse of the future, *Reflections on Higher Education*, 9, 77–102.

Brockbank, A. and McGill, I. (1998) *Facilitating Reflective Learning in Higher Education*, Buckingham: Society for Research into Higher Education/Open University Press.

Brown, G. and Atkins, M. (1988) *Effective Teaching in Higher Education*, London: Methuen.

Brown, S. and Knight, P. (1994) *Assessing Learners in Higher Education*, London: Kogan Page.

Bums, R. B. (1991) Study, stress, and culture shock among first year overseas students in an Australian university, *Higher Education Research and Development*, 10, 61–78.

Candy, P. C. (1991) *Self-direction for Lifelong Learning: a Comprehensive Guide to Theory and Practice*, San Francisco: Jossey-Bass.

Chalmers, D. and Fuller, R. (1996) *Teaching for Learning at University*, London: Kogan Page.

Chalmers, D. and Kelly, B. (1997) Peer assisted study sessions (PASS), University of Queensland, Teaching and Educational Development Institute.

Chalmers, D. and Volet, S. (1997) Common misconceptions about students from South-East Asia studying in Australia, *Higher Education Research and Development*, 16, 87–100.

Chi, M., Glaser, R. and Parr, M. (1988) *The Nature of Expertise*, Hillsdale, NJ: Lawrence Erlbaum.

Cohen, S. A. (1987) Instructional alignment: searching for a magic bullet, *Educational Researcher*, 16(8), 16–20.

Cole, N. S. (1990) Conceptions of educational achievement, *Educational Researcher*, 18(3), 2–7.

Collier, K. G. (1983) *The Management of Peer-group Learning: Syndicate Methods in Higher Education*, Guildford: Society for Research in Higher Education.

Collier, K. G. (1985) Teaching methods in higher education: the changing scene, with special reference to small-group work, *Higher Education Research and Development*, 4(1), 3–26.

Collis, K. F. and Biggs, J. B. (1983) Matriculation, degree requirements, and cognitive demands in universities and CAEs, *Australian Journal of Education*, 27, 41–51.

Cowan, J. (1998) *On Becoming an Innovative Teacher*, Buckingham: Open University Press.

Crooks, T. J. (1988a) The impact of classroom evaluation practices on students, *Review of Educational Research*, 58, 438–81.

Crooks, T. J. (1988b) *Assessing Student Performance*, Green Guide No. 8, Sydney: Higher Education Research and Development Society of Australasia.

Dart, B. (1998) Teaching for improved learning in small classes, in B. Dart and G. Boulton-Lewis (eds) *Teaching and Learning in Higher Education*, Camberwell, Vic.: Australian Council for Educational Research.

Dart, B. and Boulton-Lewis, G. (eds) (1998) *Teaching and Learning in Higher Education*, Camberwell: Australian Council for Educational Research.

Davis, B. G. (1993) *Tools for Teaching*, San Francisco: Jossey-Bass.

Davis, G. and McLeod, N. (1996a) Teaching large classes: the silver lining, *HERDSA News*, 18(1), 3–5, 20.

Davis, G. and McLeod, N. (1996b) Teaching large classes: the final challenge – assessment and feedback, *HERDSA News*, 18(2), 5–7, 12.

Department of Employment, Education, Training and Youth Affairs, *Annual Statistics*, Canberra, ACT: Government Printing Office.

Diederich, P. B. (1974) *Measuring Growth in English*, Urbana, IL: National Council of Teachers of English.

Dienes, Z. (1997) Student-led tutorials: a discussion paper, School of Experimental Psychology, University of Sussex.

Dunkin, M. and Biddle, B. (1974) *The Study of Teaching*, New York: Holt, Rinehart and Winston.

Dunkin, M. and Precians, R. (1992) Award-winning university teachers' concepts of teaching, *Higher Education*, 24, 483–502.

Eley, M. G. (1992) Differential adoption of study approaches within individual students, *Higher Education*, 23, 231–54.

Elliott, J. (1991) *Action Research for Educational Change*, Milton Keynes: Open University Press.

Ellsworth, R., Duell, O. K. and Velotta, C. (1991) Length of wait-times used by college students, given unlimited wait-time intervals. *Contemporary Educational Psychology*, 16, 265–71.

Entwistle, N. (1988) Motivational factors in students' approaches to learning, in R. Schmeck (ed.) *Learning Strategies and Learning Styles*, New York: Plenum.

Entwistle, N. (1997) Introduction: phenomenography in higher education, *Higher Education Research and Development*, 16, 127–34.

Entwistle, N. and Entwistle, A. (1997) Revision and the experience of understanding, in N. F. Marton, D. Hounsell and N. Entwistle (eds) *The Experience of Learning*, Edinburgh: Scottish Universities Press.

Entwistle, N., Kozéki, B. and Tait, H. (1989) Pupils' perceptions of school and teachers – II: Relationships with motivation and approaches to learning, *British Journal of Educational Psychology*, 59, 340–50.

Entwistle, N. and Ramsden, P. (1983) *Understanding Student Learning*, London: Croom Helm.

Falchikov, N. and Boud, D. (1989) Student self-assessment in higher education: meta-analysis, *Review of Educational Research*, 59, 395–400.

Feather, N. (ed.) (1982) *Expectations and Actions*, Hillsdale, NJ: Erlbaum.

Feletti, G. (1997) The triple jump exercise: a case study in assessing problem solving, in G. Ryan (ed.) *Learner Assessment and Program Evaluation in Problem Based Learning*, Newcastle: Australian Problem Based Learning Network.

Fleming, N. (1993) What works and what doesn't in staff development, *HERDSA News*, 15(2), 12–13.

Fox, D. (1989) Peer assessment of an essay assignment, *HERDSA News*, 11(2), 6–7.

Frederiksen, J. R. and Collins, A. (1989) A systems approach to educational testing, *Educational Researcher*, 18(9), 27–32.

Fullan, M. (1993) *Change Forces: Probing the Depth of Educational Reform*, London: Falmer Press.

Gabrenya, W. K., Wang, Y. E. and Latane, B. (1985) Cross-cultural differences in social loafing on an optimizing task: Chinese and Americans, *Journal of Cross-Cultural Psychology*, 16, 223–64.

Gardner, H. W. (1989) *To Open Minds: Chinese Clues to the Dilemma of Contemporary Education*, New York: Basic Books.

Gardner, H. W. (1993) Educating for understanding, *The American School Board Journal*, July, 20–4.

Getzels, J. and Jackson, P. (1962) *Creativity and Intelligence*, New York: Wiley.

Gibbs, G. (1981) *Teaching Students to Learn*, Milton Keynes: Open University Press.

Gibbs, G. (1992) *Improving the Quality of Student Learning*, Bristol: Technical and Educational Services.

Gibbs, G. (1998) Using assessment strategically to change the way students learn, in S. Brown and A. Glasner (eds) *Assessment Matters in Higher Education: Choosing and Using Diverse Approaches*, Buckingham: Society for Research into Higher Education/Open University Press.

Gibbs, G., Habeshaw, S. and Habeshaw, T. (1984) *53 Interesting Ways to Teach Large Classes*, Bristol: Technical and Educational Services.

Gibbs, G., Habeshaw, S. and Habeshaw, T. (1989) *53 Interesting Ways to Assess Your Students*, Bristol: Technical and Educational Services.

Gibbs, G. and Jenkins, A. (eds) (1992) *Teaching Large Classes in Higher Education*, London: Kogan Page.

Gibbs, G., Jenkins, A. and Wisker, G. (1992) *Assessing More Students*, Oxford: PCIFC/Rewley Press.

Ginsburg, H. and Opper, S. (1987) *Piaget's Theory of Intellectual Development*, Englewood Cliffs, NJ: Prentice Hall.

Goodlad, S. and Hirst, B. (eds) (1990) *Explorations in Peer Tutoring*, Oxford: Basil Blackwell.

Goodnow, J. J. (1991) Cognitive values and educational practice, in J. Biggs (ed.) *Teaching for Learning: the View from Cognitive Psychology*, Hawthorn, Vic.: Australian Council for Educational Research.

Gow, L. and Kember, D. (1990) Does higher education promote independent learning?, *Higher Education*, 19, 307–22.

Gow, L. and Kember, D. (1993) Conceptions of teaching and their relation to student learning, *British Journal of Educational Psychology*, 63, 20–33.

Guilford, J. P. (1967) *The Nature of Human Intelligence*, New York: McGraw-Hill.

Gunstone, R. and White, R. (1981) Understanding of gravity, *Science Education*, 65, 291–9.

Guskey, T. (1986) Staff development and the process of teacher change, *Educational Researcher*, 15(5), 5–12.

Guttman, L. (1941) The quantification of a class of attributes: a theory and a method of scale construction, in P. Horst (ed.) *The Prediction of Personal Adjustment*, New York: Social Science Research Council.

Hales, L. W. and Tokar, E. (1975) The effects of quality of preceding responses on the grades assigned to subsequent responses to an essay question, *Journal of Educational Measurement*, 12, 115–17.

Harris, D. and Bell, C. (1986) *Evaluating and Assessing for Learning*, London: Kogan Page.

Harris, R. (1997) Overseas students in the United Kingdom university system, *Higher Education*, 29, 77–92.

Hattie, J., Biggs, J. and Purdie, N. (1996) Effects of learning skills interventions on student learning: a meta-analysis, *Review of Educational Research*, 66, 99–136.

Hattie, J. and Purdie, N. (1998) The SOLO model: addressing fundamental measurement issues, in B. Dart and G. Boulton-Lewis (eds) *Teaching and Learning in Higher Education*, Camberwell, Vic.: Australian Council for Educational Research.

Hattie, J. and Watkins, D. (1988) Preferred classroom environment and approach to learning, *British Journal of Educational Psychology*, 58, 345–9.

Hendry, G. D. and Murphy, L. B. (1995) Constructivism and problem-based learning, in P. Little, M. Ostwald and G. Ryan (eds) *Research and Development in Problem Based Learning. Volume 3: Assessment and Evaluation*, Newcastle: Australian Problem Based Learning Network.

Hess, R. D. and Azuma, M. (1991) Cultural support for schooling: contrasts between Japan and the United States, *Educational Researcher*, 20(9), 2–8.

Hmelo, C. E., Gotterer, G. S. and Bransford, J. D. (1997) A theory driven approach to assessing the cognitive effects of PBL, *Instructional Science*, 25, 387–408.

Hore, T. (1971) Assessment of teaching practice: an 'attractive' hypothesis, *British Journal of Educational Psychology*, 41, 327–8.

Hudson, L. (1966) *Contrary Imaginations*, London: Methuen.

International Association for the Evaluation of Educational Achievement (LEA) (1996) *The Third International Maths and Science Study*, Paris: OECD.

Jackson, M. (1997) But learners learn more, *Higher Education Research and Development*, 16, 101–10.

Johnson, D. W. and Johnson, R. T. (1990) *Learning Together and Alone: Co-operation, Competition and Individualization*, Englewood Cliffs, NJ: Prentice Hall.

Jones, J., Jones, A. and Ker, P. (1994) Peer tutoring for academic credit, *HERDSA News*, 16(3), 3–5.

Jones, R. M. (1968) *Fantasy and Feeling in Education*, New York: New York University Press.

Keller, F. (1968) 'Goodbye teacher . . .', *Journal of Applied Behavior Analysis*, 1, 79–89.

Kember, D. (1998) Teaching beliefs and their impact on students' approach to learning, in B. Dart and G. Boulton-Lewis (eds) *Teaching and Learning in Higher Education*, Camberwell: Australian Council for Educational Research.

Kember, D., Charlesworth, M., Davies, H., McKay, J. and Stott, V. (1998) Evaluating the effectiveness of educational innovations: using the Study Process Questionnaire to show that meaningful learning occurs, *Studies in Educational Evaluation*, 23, 141–57.

Kember, D. and Gow, L. (1991) A challenge to the anecdotal stereotype of the Asian student, *Studies in Higher Education*, 16, 117–28.

Kember, D. and Kelly, M. (1993) *Improving Teaching through Action Research*, Green Guide No. 14, Campbelltown, NSW: Higher Education Research and Development Society of Australasia.

Kember, D., Lam, B.-h., Yan, L., Yum, J. C. K. and Liu, S. B. (eds) (1997) *Case Studies of Improving Teaching and Learning from the Action Learning Project,* Hong Kong: The Hong Kong Polytechnic University Action Learning Project.

Kember, D. and McKay, J. (1966) Action research into the quality of student learning: a paradigm for faculty development, *Journal of Higher Education,* 67, 528–54.

King, A. (1990) Enhancing peer interaction and learning in the classroom through reciprocal questioning, *American Educational Research Journal,* 27, 664–87.

Kingsland, A. (1995) Integrated assessment: the rhetoric and the students' view, in P. Little, M. Ostwald and G. Ryan (eds) *Research and Development in Problem Based Learning. Volume 3: Assessment and Evaluation,* Newcastle: Australian Problem Based Learning Network.

Lai, P. and Biggs, J. B. (1994) Who benefits from mastery learning?, *Contemporary Educational Psychology,* 19, 13–23.

Lai, P., Tang, C. and Taylor, G. (1997) Traditional assessment approaches: saints or devils to learning fostered by PBL?, in J. Conway, R. Fisher, L. Sheridan-Burns and G. Ryan (eds) *Research and Development in Problem Based Learning. Volume 4: Integrity, Innovation, Integration,* Newcastle: Australian Problem Based Learning Network.

Laurillard, D. and Margetson, D. (1997) *Introducing a Flexible Learning Methodology: Discussion Paper,* Occasional Papers No. 7, Griffith Institute for Higher Education, Griffith University, Nathan, Queensland.

Lee, W. O. (1996) The cultural context for Chinese learners: conceptions of learning in the Confucian tradition, in D. Watkins and J. Biggs (eds) *The Chinese Learner: Cultural, Psychological and Contextual Influences,* Hong Kong: Centre for Comparative Research in Education/Camberwell, Vic.: Australian Council for Educational Research.

Leinhardt, G., McCarthy Young, K. and Merriman, J. (1995) Integrating professional knowledge: the theory of practice and the practice of theory, *Learning and Instruction,* 5, 401–8.

Lohman, D. F. (1993) Teaching and testing to develop fluid abilities, *Educational Researcher,* 22(7), 12–23.

MacDonald-Ross, R. M. (1973) Behavioural objectives: a critical review, *Instructional Science,* 2, 1–51.

McGregor, D. (1960) *The Human Side of Enterprise,* New York: McGraw-Hill.

McKay, J. and Kember, D. (1997) Spoon feeding leads to regurgitation: a better diet can result in more digestible learning outcomes, *Higher Education Research and Development,* 16, 55–68.

MacKenzie, A. and White, R. (1982) Fieldwork in geography and long-term memory structures, *American Educational Research Journal,* 19(4), 623–32.

McKeachie, W., Pintrich, P., Lin, Y.-G. and Smith, D. (1986) *Teaching and Learning in the College Classroom,* University of Michigan, Office of Educational Research and Improvement.

McLeish, J. (1976) The lecture method, in N. Gage (ed.) *The Psychology of Teaching Methods,* 75th Yearbook of the National Society for the Study of Education, Chicago: University of Chicago Press.

Margunson, S. (1997) Competition and contestability in Australian higher education, *Australian Universities Review,* 40(1), 5–14.

Marland, P. (1997) *Towards More Effective Open and Distance Teaching*, London: Kogan Page.

Marton, F. (1981) Phenomenography – describing conceptions of the world around us, *Instructional Science*, 10, 177–200.

Marton, F. and Booth, S. A. (1997) *Learning and Awareness*, Hillsdale, NJ: Lawrence Erlbaum.

Marton, F., Dall'Alba, G. and Beaty, E. (1993) Conceptions of learning, *International Journal of Educational Research*, 19, 277–300.

Marton, F., Dall'Alba, G., and Tse, L. K. (1996) Solving the paradox of the Asian learner?, in D. Watkins and J. Biggs (eds) *The Chinese Learner: Cultural, Psychological and Contextual Influences*, Hong Kong: Centre for Comparative Research in Education/Camberwell, Vic.: Australian Council for Educational Research.

Marton, F. and Säljö, R. (1976a) On qualitative differences in learning – I: Outcome and process, *British Journal of Educational Psychology*, 46, 4–11.

Marton, F. and Säljö, R. (1976b) On qualitative differences in learning – II: Outcome as a function of the learner's conception of the task, *British Journal of Educational Psychology*, 46, 115–27.

Masters, G. (1987) New views of student learning: implications for educational measurement, Research working paper 87.11, University of Melbourne, Centre for the Study of Higher Education.

Masters, G. N. (1988) Partial credit model, in J. P. Keeves (ed.) *Handbook of Educational Research Methodology, Measurement and Evaluation*, London: Pergamon Press.

Messick, S. J. (1989) Meaning and values in test validation: the science and ethics of assessment, *Educational Researcher*, 18(2), 5–11.

Meyer, J. H. F. (1991) Study orchestration: the manifestation, interpretation and consequences of contextualised approaches to learning, *Higher Education*, 22, 297–316.

Moss, P. A. (1992) Shifting conceptions of validity in educational measurement: implications for performance assessment, *Review of Educational Research*, 62, 229–58.

Moss, P. A. (1994) Can there be validity without reliability?, *Educational Researcher*, 23(2), 5–12.

Mullins, G., Quintrell, N. and Hancock, L. (1995) The experiences of international and local students at three Australian universities, *Higher Education Research and Development*, 14, 201–32.

National Center for Supplemental Instruction (1994) *Review of Research Concerning the Effectiveness of SI*, Kansas City, MO: NCSI, University of Missouri at Kansas City.

Newble, D. and Clarke, R. (1986) The approaches to learning of students in a traditional and in an innovative problem-based medical school, *Medical Education*, 20, 267–73.

Nicholls, P. D. (1994) A framework for developing cognitively diagnostic assessments, *Review of Educational Research*, 64, 575–603.

Nightingale, P., Te Wiata, I., Toohey, S., Ryan, G., Hughes, C. and Magin, D. (eds) (1996) *Assessing Learning in Universities*, Kensington, NSW: Committee for the Advancement of University Teaching/Professional Development Centre, UNSW.

Novak, J. D. (1979) Applying psychology and philosophy to the improvement of laboratory teaching, *The American Biology Teacher*, 41, 466–70.

Pearson, C. and Beasley, C. (1996) Reducing learning barriers amongst international students: a longitudinal development study, *The Australian Educational Researcher*, 23, 79–96.

Perraton, H. (1997) The virtual wandering scholar: policy issues for international higher education, in R. Murray-Harvey and H. C. Sims (eds) *Learning and Teaching in Higher Education: Advancing International Perspectives*, Adelaide: Flinders Press.

Perkins, D. (1991) Technology meets constructivism: do they make a marriage?, *Educational Technology*, May, 18–23.

Poliquin, L. and Maufette, Y. (1997) PBL vs. integrity of discipline content: the experience of integrated PBL in a BSc in Biology, in J. Conway, R. Fisher, L. Sheridan-Burns and G. Ryan (eds) *Research and Development in Problem Based Learning. Volume 4: Integrity, Innovation, Integration*, Newcastle: Australian Problem Based Learning Network.

Popham, W. J. and Husek, T. R. (1969) Implications of criterion-referenced measurement, *Journal of Educational Measurement*, 6, 1–9.

Prosser, M. and Trigwell, K. (1998) *Understanding Teaching and Learning: the Experience in Higher Education*, Buckingham: Open University Press.

Purdie, N. and Hattie, J. (1996) Cultural differences in the use of strategies for self-regulated learning, *American Educational Research Journal*, 33, 845–74.

Race, P. and Brown, S. (1993) *500 tips for Tutors*, London: Kogan Page.

Ramsden, P. (1984) The context of learning, in F. Marton, D. Hounsell and N. Entwistle, N. (eds) *The Experience of Learning*, Edinburgh: Scottish Academic Press.

Ramsden, P. (1992) *Learning to Teach in Higher Education*, London: Routledge.

Ramsden, P. (1998a) *Learning to Lead in Higher Education*, London: Routledge.

Ramsden, P. (1998b) For good measure, *The Australian Higher Education*, 28 January.

Ramsden, P., Beswick, D. and Bowden, J. (1986) Effects of learning skills interventions on first year university students' learning, *Human Learning*, 5, 151–64.

Romizowski, A. J. (1981) *Designing Instructional Systems*, London: Kogan Page.

Ryan, G. (1997) Promoting educational integrity in PBL programs – choosing carefully and implementing wisely, in J. Conway, R. Fisher, L. Sheridan-Burns and G. Ryan (eds) *Research and Development in Problem Based Learning. Volume 4: Integrity, Innovation, Integration*, Newcastle: Australian Problem Based Learning Network.

Saberton, S. (1985) Learning partnerships, *HERDSA News*, 7(1), 3–5.

Samuelowicz, K. (1987) Learning problems of overseas students: two sides of a story, *Higher Education Research and Development*, 6, 121–34.

Samuelowicz, K. and Bain, J. (1992) Conceptions of teaching held by teachers, *Higher Education*, 24, 93–112.

Santhanam, B., Leach, C. and Dawson, C. (1998) Concept mapping: how should it be introduced, and is there a long term benefit?, *Higher Education*, 35, 317–28.

Schmeck, R. (ed.) (1988) *Learning Strategies and Learning Styles*, New York: Plenum.

Schmidt, W. with 14 others (1996) *A Summary of Characterizing Pedagogical Flow. An Investigation of Mathematics and Science Teaching in Six Countries*, London: Kluwer Academic Publishers.

Schön, D. A. (1983) *The Reflective Practitioner: How Professionals Think in Action,* London: Temple Smith.

Scollon, R. and Wong Scollon, S. (1994) *The Post-Confucian Confusion,* Hong Kong: Hong Kong City Polytechnic University, Department of English Research Report No. 37.

Scouller, K. M. (1996) Influence of assessment methods on students' learning approaches, perceptions, and preferences: assignment essay versus short answer questions, *Research and Development in Higher Education,* 19(3), 776–81.

Scouller, K. (1997) Students' perceptions of three assessment methods: assignment essay, multiple choice question examination, short answer examination, Paper presented to Higher Education Research and Development Society of Australasia, Adelaide, 9–12 July.

Scouller, K. (1998) The influence of assessment method on students' learning approaches: multiple choice question examination vs. essay assignment, *Higher Education,* 35, 453–72.

Shepard, L. A. (1993) Evaluating test validity, *Review of Research in Education,* 19, 405–50.

Shuell, T. J. (1986) Cognitive conceptions of learning, *Review of Educational Research,* 56, 411–36.

Shulman, L. S. (1987) Knowledge and teaching: Foundations of the new reform. *Harvard Educational Review,* 57, 1–22.

Smith, B., Scholten, I., Russell, A. and McCormack, P. (1997) Integrating student assessment practices: the significance of collaborative partnerships for curriculum and professional development in a university department, *Higher Education Research and Development,* 16, 69–85.

Starch, D. (1913a) Reliability of grading work in mathematics, *School Review,* 21, 254–9.

Starch, D. (1913b) Reliability of grading work in history, *School Review,* 21, 676–81.

Starch, D. and Elliott, E. C. (1912) Reliability of the grading of high school work in English, *School Review,* 20, 442–57.

Stedman, L. C. (1997) International achievement differences: an assessment of a new perspective, *Educational Researcher,* 26(3), 4–15.

Steffe, L. and Gale, J. (eds) (1995) *Constructivism in Education,* Hillsdale, NJ: Erlbaum.

Stenhouse, L. (1975) *Introduction to Curriculum Research and Development,* London: Heinemann Educational.

Stephenson, J. and Laycock, M. (1993) *Using Contracts in Higher Education,* London: Kogan Page.

Stevenson, H. W. and Stigler, J. (1992) *The Learning Gap: Why Our Schools Are Failing and What We Can Learn from Japanese and Chinese Education,* New York: Summit Books.

Swanson, D., Case, S. and van der Vlieten, C. (1991) Strategies for student assessment, in D. Boud and G. Felletti (eds) *The Challenge of Problem-based Learning,* London: Kogan Page.

Tang, C. (1991) Effects of two different assessment procedures on tertiary students' approaches to learning, Unpublished doctoral dissertation, University of Hong Kong.

Tang, C. (1993) Spontaneous collaborative learning: a new dimension in student learning experience?, *Higher Education Research and Development*, 12, 115–30.

Tang, C. (1996) Collaborative learning: The latent dimension in Chinese students' learning, in D. Watkins and J. Biggs (eds), *The Chinese Learner: Cultural, Psychological and Contextual Influences*, Hong Kong: Centre for Comparative Research in Education/Camberwell: Australian Council for Educational Research.

Tang, C. (1998) Effects of collaborative learning on the quality of assessments, in B. Dart and G. Boulton-Lewis (eds) *Teaching and Learning in Higher Education*, Camberwell: Australian Council for Educational Research.

Tang, C. and 12 others (1997) Developing a context based PBL model, in J. Conway, R. Fisher, L. Sheridan-Burns and G. Ryan (eds) *Research and Development in Problem Based Learning. Volume 4: Integrity, Innovation, Integration*, Newcastle: Australian Problem Based Learning Network.

Taylor, C. (1994) Assessment for measurement or standards: the peril and promise of large scale assessment reform, *American Educational Research Journal*, 31, 231–62.

Taylor, J. C. (1995) Distance education technologies: the fourth generation, *Australian Journal of Educational Technology*, 11(2), 1–7.

Thomas, E. L. and Robinson, H. A. (1982) *Improving Reading in Every Class: a Source Book for Teachers*, Boston: Allyn and Bacon.

Tobin, K. (1987) The role of wait time, *Review of Educational Research*, 57, 69–95.

Tomporowski, P. D. and Ellis, N. R. (1986) Effects of exercise on cognitive processes: a review, *Psychological Bulletin*, 99, 338–46.

Toohey, S. (1999) *Designing Courses for Further Education*, Buckingham: Open University Press.

Topping, K. J. (1996) The effectiveness of peer tutoring in further and higher education: a typology and review of the literature. *Higher Education*, 32, 321–45.

Torrance, H. (ed.) (1994) *Evaluating Authentic Assessment: Problems and Possibilities in New Approaches to Assessment*, Buckingham: Open University Press.

Trigwell, K. and Prosser, M. (1990) Using student learning outcome measures in the evaluation of teaching, *Research and Development in Higher Education*, 13, 390–7.

Trigwell, K. and Prosser, M. (1991) Changing approaches to teaching: a relational perspective, *Studies in Higher Education*, 22, 251–66.

Trigwell, K. and Prosser, M. (1996) Congruence between intention and strategy in science teachers' approach to teaching, *Higher Education*, 32, 77–87.

Trigwell, K. and Prosser, M. (1997) Towards an understanding of individual acts of teaching and learning, *Higher Education Research and Development*, 16, 241–52.

Trueman, M. and Hartley, J. (1996) A comparison between the time-management skills and academic performance of mature and traditional-entry university students, *Higher Education*, 32, 199–215.

Tulving, E. (1985) How many memory systems are there?, *American Psychologist*, 40, 385–98.

Tynjala, P. (1998) Writing as a tool for constructive learning – students' learning experiences during an experiment, *Higher Education*, 36, 209–30.

Volet, S. and Ang, G. (1998) Culturally mixed groups on international campuses: an opportunity for inter-cultural learning, *Higher Education Research and Development*, 17, 5–24.

Volet, S. and Kee, J. P. P. (1993) Studying in Singapore – studying in Australia: a student perspective. Occasional Paper No. 1. Murdoch University Teaching Excellence Committee.

Volet, S. and Renshaw, P. (1996) Chinese students at an Australian university: continuity and adaptability, in D. Watkins and J. Biggs (eds) *The Chinese Learner: Cultural, Psychological and Contextual Influences*, Hong Kong: Centre for Comparative Research in Education/Camberwell, Vic.: Australian Council for Educational Research.

Walker, J. (1998) Student plagiarism in universities: what are we doing about it?, *Higher Education Research and Development*, 17, 89–106.

Ware, J. and Williams, R. G. (1975) The Dr Fox Effect: a study of lecturer effectiveness and ratings of instruction, *Journal of Medical Education*, 50, 149–56.

Watkins, D. and Biggs, J. (eds) (1996) *The Chinese Learner: Cultural, Psychological and Contextual Influences*, Hong Kong: Centre for Comparative Research in Education/Camberwell, Vic.: Australian Council for Educational Research.

Watkins, D. and Hattie, J. (1985) A longitudinal study of the approach to learning of Australian tertiary students, *Human Learning*, 4, 127–42.

Watkins, D., Regmi, M. and Astilla, E. (1991) The-Asian-as-rote-learner stereotype: myth or reality?, *Educational Psychology*, 17, 89–100.

Watson, J. (1996) Peer assisted learning in economics at the University of NSW, Paper given to Fourth Annual Teaching Economics Conference, Northern Territory University, Darwin, 28 June.

Watson, J. (1997) A peer support scheme in quantitative methods, Paper given to Biennial Conference, Professional Development Centre, University of NSW, 20 November.

Webb, G. (1997) Deconstructing deep and surface: towards a critique of phenomenography, *Higher Education*, 33, 195–212.

Wetherell, J. and Mullins, G. (1997) Self-assessment in dentistry, in G. Ryan (ed.) *Learner Assessment and Program Evaluation in Problem Based Learning*, Newcastle: Australian Problem Based Learning Network.

White, R. T. (1988) *Learning Science*, Oxford: Basil Blackwell.

Whitehill, T., Stokes, S. F. and MacKinnon, M. (1997) Problem based learning and the Chinese learner, in R. Murray-Harvey and H. C. Sims (eds) *Learning and Teaching in Higher Education: Advancing International Perspectives*, Adelaide: Flinders Press.

Wiggins, G. (1989) Teaching to the (authentic) test, *Educational Leadership*, 46, 41–7.

Wilson, K. (1997) Wording it up: plagiarism and the interdiscourse of international students, Paper given to Annual Conference, Higher Education Research and Development Society of Australasia, Adelaide, 8–11 July.

Wiske, M. S. (ed.) (1998) *Teaching for Understanding. Linking Research and Practice*, San Francisco: Jossey-Bass.

Wittrock, M. C. (1977) The generative processes of memory, in M. C. Wittrock (ed.) *The Human Brain*, Englewood Cliffs, NJ: Prentice Hall.

Wong, C. S. (1994) Using a cognitive approach to assess achievement in secondary school mathematics, Unpublished MEd dissertation, University of Hong Kong.

Index

The Society for Research into Higher Education

The Society for Research into Higher Education exists to stimulate and coordinate research into all aspects of higher education. It aims to improve the quality of higher education through the encouragement of debate and publication on issues of policy, on the organization and management of higher education institutions, and on the curriculum and teaching methods.

The Society's income is derived from subscriptions, sales of its books and journals, conference fees and grants. It receives no subsidies, and is wholly independent. Its individual members include teachers, researchers, managers and students. Its corporate members are institutions of higher education, research institutes, professional, industrial and governmental bodies. Members are not only from the UK, but from elsewhere in Europe, from America, Canada and Australasia, and it regards its international work as among its most important activities.

Under the imprint *SRHE & Open University Press*, the Society is a specialist publisher of research, having over 70 titles in print. The Editorial Board of the Society's Imprint seeks authoritative research or study in the above fields. It offers competitive royalties, a highly recognizable format in both hardback and paperback and the worldwide reputation of the Open University Press.

The Society also publishes *Studies in Higher Education* (three times a year), which is mainly concerned with academic issues, *Higher Education Quarterly* (formerly *Universities Quarterly*), mainly concerned with policy issues, *Research into Higher Education Abstracts* (three times a year), and *SRHE News* (four times a year).

The society holds a major annual conference in December, jointly with an institution of higher education. In 1996 the topic was 'Working in Higher Education' at University of Wales, Cardiff. In 1997 it was 'Beyond the First Degree' at the University of Warwick. In 1998 it was 'The Globalization of Higher Education' at the University of Lancaster. The 1999 conference will be on the topic of higher education and its communities at UMIST.

The Society's committees, study groups and networks are run by the members. The networks at present include:

Access	Mentoring
Curriculum Development	Postgraduate Issues
Disability	Quality
Eastern European	Quantitative Studies
Funding	Student Development
Legal Education	Vocational Qualifications

Benefits to members

Individual

Individual members receive

- *SRHE News*, the Society's publications list, conference details and other material included in mailings.
- Greatly reduced rates for *Studies in Higher Education* and *Higher Education Quarterly*.
- A 35 per cent discount on all SRHE & Open University Press publications.
- Free copies of the Precedings – commissioned papers on the theme of the Annual Conference.
- Free copies of *Research into Higher Education Abstracts*.
- Reduced rates for the annual conference.
- Extensive contacts and scope for facilitating initiatives.
- Free copies of the *Register of Members' Research Interests*.
- Membership of the Society's networks.

Corporate

Corporate members receive:

- Benefits of individual members, plus.
- Free copies of *Studies in Higher Education*.
- Unlimited copies of the Society's publications at reduced rates.
- Reduced rates for the annual conference.
- The right to submit applications for the Society's research grants.
- The right to use the Society's facility for supplying statistical HESA data for purposes of research.

Membership details: SRHE, 3 Devonshire Street, London W1N 2BA, UK. Tel: 0171 637 2766. Fax: 0171 637 2781. email: srhe@mailbox.ulcc.ac.uk
World Wide Web: http://www.srhe.ac.uk./srhe/
Catalogue: SRHE & Open University Press, Celtic Court, 22 Ballmoor, Buckingham MK18 1XW. Tel: 01280 823388. Fax: 01280 823233. email: enquiries@openup. co.uk

FACILITATING REFLECTIVE LEARNING IN HIGHER EDUCATION

Anne Brockbank and Ian McGill

A book that puts new forms of relationship and dialogue at the core of teaching and learning. It is likely to give courage to those who are daring to reflect differently on their teaching and learning practice, and to those who recognize the limitations of technology as some 'panacea solution' to challenges of mass higher education.

Professor Susan Weil

This book offers hope and the practical means for university and college teachers seeking a new experience of learning for their students and themselves. The book deals with learning which is real, genuine, relevant to learners now and for the future, and which is significant for their lives. Such learning embraces their relationships, work and careers, community, society and their world.

Anne Brockbank and Ian McGill provide direct support for teachers who wish to move from teaching towards facilitating learning, thereby transforming the relationship between teacher and learner and between learners. Information technology, while useful, is not a substitute for the learning advocated here; facilitation enables learners to use technology productively and complementarily as a part of the learning process.

This book enables teachers to acquire an understanding of facilitation and to enhance their ability to facilitate rather than teach in the traditional way. The authors emphasize the centrality of engaging in reflective dialogue with both colleagues and students. They explore the significance of emotion and action as well as cognition in learning. In addition they examine how teachers can best create the conditions for reflective learning.

This is a practical book for university and college teachers which will help them facilitate their students' reflective learning.

Contents
Part 1: Learning and reflection – Introduction to our themes – Learning: philosophies and models – What is learning? – a review of learning theories – The requirements for reflection – Reflection and reflective practice – Part 2: Facilitating learning and reflective practice – Academic practice and learning – Developing reflective practice: the teacher using reflective dialogue with colleagues – Developing reflective practice: the student using reflective dialogue – Becoming a facilitator: facilitation as enabling reflective learning – Facilitation in practice: basic skills – Facilitation in practice: further skills – Part 3: Exemplars – Action learning – Academic supervision – Mentoring – Conclusion – Bibliography – Index.

304pp   0 335 19685 3 (Paperback)   0 335 19686 1 (Hardback)

ON BECOMING AN INNOVATIVE UNIVERSITY TEACHER
REFLECTION IN ACTION

John Cowan

This is one of the most interesting texts I have read for many years . . . It is authoritative and clearly written. It provides a rich set of examples of teaching, and a reflective discourse.

Professor George Brown

. . . succeeds in inspiring the reader by making the process of reflective learning interesting and thought provoking . . . has a narrative drive which makes it a book too good to put down.

Dr Mary Thorpe

What comes through very strongly and is an admirable feature is so much of the author's own personal experience, what it felt like to take risks, exploring uncharted territory . . . The book has the potential to become the reflective practitioner's 'bible'.

Dr Lorraine Stefani

This unusual, accessible and significant book begins each chapter by posing a question with which college and university teachers can be expected to identify; and then goes on to answer the question by presenting a series of examples; finally, each chapter closes with 'second thoughts', presenting a viewpoint somewhat distinct from that taken by John Cowan. This book will assist university teachers to plan and run innovative activities to enable their students to engage in effective reflective learning; it will help them adapt other teachers' work for use with their own students; and will give them a rationale for the place of reflective teaching and learning in higher education.

Contents
Introduction – What is meant in education by 'reflecting'? – What does reflection have to offer in education – Is there a methodology you can and should follow – What can you do to encourage students to reflect? – What is involved for students in analytical reflection? – What is involved in evaluative reflection? – How can you adapt ideas from my teaching, for yours? – How should you get started? – How can such innovations be evaluated? – Where should you read about other work in this field? – A Postscript: final reflections – References – Index – The Society for Research into Higher Education.

192pp   0 335 19993 3 (Paperback)   0 335 19994 1 (Hardback)

UNDERSTANDING LEARNING AND TEACHING
THE EXPERIENCE IN HIGHER EDUCATION

Michael Prosser and Keith Trigwell

How can university teachers improve the quality of student learning? Prosser and Trigwell argue that the answer lies in determining how students perceive their unique learning situations. In doing so they draw upon the considerable body of educational research into student learning in higher education which has been developed and published over the past three decades; *and* they enable university teachers to research and improve their own teaching.

This book outlines the key principles underlying successful teaching and learning in higher education, and is a key resource for all university teachers.

Contents
Learning and teaching in higher education – A model for understanding learning and teaching in higher education – Students' prior experiences of learning – Students' perceptions of their learning situation – Students' approaches to learning – Students' learning outcomes – Experiences of teaching in higher education – Understanding learning and teaching – Appendix: Approaches to teaching inventory – References – Index – The Society for Research into Higher Education.

208pp   0 335 19831 7 (Paperback)   0 335 19832 5 (Hardback)